Surviving the Great War

AUSTRALIAN PRISONERS OF WAR ON THE WESTERN FRONT, 1916–18

Between 1916 and 1918, more than 3800 men of the Australian Imperial Force were taken prisoner by German forces fighting on the Western Front. Until now, their experiences have been largely overlooked.

Australians captured in France and Belgium did not easily integrate into public narratives of Australia in the First World War and its emerging commemorative rituals. Captivity was a story of surrender and inaction, at odds with the Anzac legend and a triumphant national memory of fighting in France that tended to emphasise the Australian Imperial Force's victories rather than its defeats. Those who had the misfortune of being captured on the Western Front endured a broad range of experiences in German captivity, yet all regarded survival as a personal triumph.

Surviving the Great War is the first detailed analysis of the little-known story of Australians in German captivity in the First World War. By placing the hardships of prisoners of war in a broader social and military context, this book adds a new dimension to the national wartime experience and challenges popular representations of Australia's involvement in the First World War.

Aaron Pegram is a senior historian in the Military History Section at the Australian War Memorial, Canberra.

OTHER TITLES IN THE AUSTRALIAN ARMY HISTORY SERIES

Series editor: Peter Stanley

Phillip Bradley *The Battle for Wau: New Guinea's Frontline 1942–1943*

Mark Johnston *The Proud 6th: An Illustrated History of the 6th Australian Division 1939–1946*

Garth Pratten *Australian Battalion Commanders in the Second World War*

Jean Bou *Light Horse: A History of Australia's Mounted Arm*

Phillip Bradley *To Salamaua*

Peter Dean *The Architect of Victory: The Military Career of Lieutenant-General Sir Frank Horton Berryman*

Allan Converse *Armies of Empire: The 9th Australian and 50th British Divisions in Battle 1939–1945*

John Connor *Anzac and Empire: George Foster Pearce and the Foundations of Australian Defence*

Peter Williams *The Kokoda Campaign 1942: Myth and Reality*

Karl James *The Hard Slog: Australians in the Bougainville Campaign, 1944–45*

Robert Stevenson *To Win the Battle: The 1st Australian Division in the Great War, 1914–1918*

Jeffrey Grey *A Soldier's Soldier: A Biography of Lieutenant-General Sir Thomas Daly*

Mark Johnston *Anzacs in the Middle East: Australian Soldiers, Their Allies and the Local People in World War II*

Mark Johnston *Stretcher-bearers: Saving Australians from Gallipoli to Kokoda*

Christopher Wray *Pozières: Echoes of a Distant Battle*

Craig Stockings *Britannia's Shield: Lieutenant-General Sir Edward Hutton and Late Victorian Imperial Defence*

Andrew Ross, Robert Hall and Amy Griffin *The Search for Tactical Success in Vietnam: An Analysis of Australian Task Force Combat Operations*

William Westerman *Soldiers and Gentlemen: Australian Battalion Commanders in the Great War, 1914–1918*

Thomas Richardson *Destroy and Build: Pacification in Phuoc Tuy, 1966–72*

Tristan Moss *Guarding the Periphery: The Australian Army in Papua New Guinea, 1951–75*

Kate Ariotti *Captive Anzacs: Australian POWs of the Ottomans during the First World War*

Margaret Hutchison *Painting War: A History of Australia's First World War Art Scheme*

Romain Fathi *Our Corner of the Somme: Australia at Villers-Bretonneux*

SURVIVING THE GREAT WAR

AUSTRALIAN PRISONERS OF WAR ON THE WESTERN FRONT, 1916–18

AARON PEGRAM

CAMBRIDGE
UNIVERSITY PRESS

CAMBRIDGE
UNIVERSITY PRESS

University Printing House, Cambridge CB2 8BS, United Kingdom

One Liberty Plaza, 20th Floor, New York, NY 10006, USA

477 Williamstown Road, Port Melbourne, VIC 3207, Australia

314–321, 3rd Floor, Plot 3, Splendor Forum, Jasola District Centre, New Delhi – 110025, India

79 Anson Road, #06–04/06, Singapore 079906

Cambridge University Press is part of the University of Cambridge.

It furthers the University's mission by disseminating knowledge in the pursuit of education, learning and research at the highest international levels of excellence.

www.cambridge.org
Information on this title: www.cambridge.org/9781108486194

First published 2020

Cover designed by Anne-Marie Reeves
Typeset by SPi Global
Printed in Singapore by Markono Print Media Pte Ltd, October 2019

A catalogue record for this publication is available from the British Library

A catalogue record for this book is available from the National Library of Australia

ISBN 978-1-108-48619-4 Hardback

CONTENTS

FIGURES, MAPS AND TABLES

PREFACE

The Australian Army has a long and admirable record in fostering serious research and publication about its history. For more than a century the Army has seen the value of history to its future. From its outset 'Military History' was part of the formal education of officers at RMC Duntroon, and for a time officers' advancement depended upon candidates being able to give a coherent analysis of Stonewall Jackson's Shenandoah Valley campaigns in promotion exams. An understanding of the Army's history and traditions remains central to its *esprit de corps* in its most literal meaning.

From the 1970s (as a consequence of educating officers at university level), the Army has produced several generations of educated soldiers, several of whom became historians of note, including John Coates, Robert O'Neill, David Horner, Peter Pedersen, John Mordike, Bob Hall, Jean Bou, Chris Roberts, Bob Stevenson and Craig Stockings. The creation of an Army History Unit in the late 1990s demonstrated the Army's commitment to encouraging and facilitating serious history. AHU has had a profound impact in managing the Army's museums, supporting research on Army history and publishing its history.

One of the most impressive demonstrations of the Army's commitment to history has been its long association with several major publishers, and notably with Cambridge University Press. This has been a productive relationship between AHU and the former long-standing General Editor of the Army History Series, Professor David Horner.

The Cambridge Army History Series brings to an academic and popular readership historical work of importance across the range of the Army's interests and across the span of its history. The series, which I have the honour to edit, seeks to publish research and writing of the highest quality relating to the Army's operational experience and to its existence as an organisation and as a part of its contribution to the national narrative.

The Army History Unit has created a community of writers and readers (including soldiers in both roles), the product of whose questions, research, debate and writing informs the Army's understanding of itself and its part in Australia's history. It is a history to be proud of in every sense.

Aaron Pegram's *Surviving the Great War* continues and deepens research produced during the war's centenary. Dr Pegram shows that Australian soldiers' trials in war did not end with capture. By using a productive combination of the rich official and private records for which Australia is notable and overseas sources, including from Germany, he has given us a detailed and candid analysis. *Surviving the Great War* does not merely fill one of the most enduring 'gaps' in the history of Australia in the Great War; it also allows us to understand, for the first time, how Australian soldiers experienced, endured and survived captivity.

Professor Peter Stanley
General Editor, Australian Army History Series
UNSW Canberra

Acknowledgements

This book would not be completed without the assistance of a good many people. First, I would like to thank Professor Bill Gammage at ANU and Professor Peter Stanley of UNSW Canberra, who supervised the PhD thesis on which this book is based. Both did their best to remove the verbosity from my writing and were exceptionally patient while I juggled part-time study with full-time employment. I am eternally grateful to Bill, Peter and Professor Paul Pickering at ANU for their overall efforts in crafting the historian I am today. Thank you again to Peter for his preface and for fostering the work of military historians through the Australian Army History Series, and to Dr Roger Lee, Tim Gellel and Nick Anderson at the Australian Army History Unit who supported this publication, gave me a research a grant in 2010 and awarded my PhD thesis the C.E.W. Bean Prize for military history in 2018. Michael Spurr, Siobhan Privitera, Alison Dean and Maxwell Junge at Cambridge University Press helped finalise the manuscript, and Cathryn Game's assiduous editing made silk purses from my sows' ears.

I have drawn on many years of encouragement from friends and colleagues at the Australian War Memorial. I am indebted to Ashley Ekins and Ruth and Steve Lambert for their support in mentoring early career historians and their enthusiasm for my research. Dr Karl James and Dr Lachlan Grant read drafts and made suggestions over many steins of *Schöfferhofer*, and in Lachlan's case, hotly contested games of *Escape from Colditz*. Thank you to Dr Meleah Hampton, Michael Bell, Dr Thomas Rogers, Dr David Sutton, Emma Campbell, Christina Zissis, Gary Oakley, Mick Kelly, Andrew McDonald, Dr Duncan Beard and Garth O'Connell for tolerating me whenever I free-associated about my research over morning and afternoon brews. Staff in the Memorial's Research Centre have been an enormous help, fulfilling seemingly endless retrieval requests and sometimes letting me loose in the stacks. Mark Campbell and Kat Southwell helped with images, while Brigadier Chris Roberts (Rtd) worked hard to get me to think like an infantryman. Moira Drew at the Australian Red Cross Archives in Melbourne, Brian Scales at the National Archives of Australia and

Mark Neal from the Department of Veterans' Affairs were all extremely generous with their time, advice and expertise, while the reference staff and archivists at the Bayerisches Kriegsarchiv in Munich and the Baden-Württemberg Haupstaatsarchiv in Stuttgart ensured my visits were rewarding ones.

My friends Dr Michael Molkentin, Dr Rhys Crawley, Dr Kate Ariotti, James Logan and Colin Garnett shared the PhD journey with me and made the task at hand seem less daunting. Brett Butterworth allowed me to draw on his remarkable collection of German photographs of life and death on the Western Front, and Dr Laura Cook never thought twice about lending a hand during a visit to the National Archives in Kew. To Dr Immanuel Voigt, Peter Barton, Jack Sheldon, Barbara Schäfer, Amelia Hartney, Annerose Scholz and Adrian Henham, *vielen Dank*, for they helped me uncover a view of the Australian experience captivity from the other side of the barbed wire. Thank you to Martial Delebarre, John Bromage, Annette Linthout, Thierry Wiart, Dr Jacques Desbarbieux and Association Eugénies for their warm hospitality and friendship over many years of field research in the towns and villages of northern France and Belgium. John and Michelle Waller of Boronia Travel in Beaconsfield made those visits possible. Christine Webb, Murray Harris, Ian Chalk, Alan Hind, Glen Newing, David Feez, Allison Rackett, Maxine Taylor and Neville and Jan Badcock were all exceptionally kind in sharing letters, diaries, photographs and manuscripts of ancestors captured on the Western Front. Victor Bartley saw it his personal duty to track down the descendants of one former prisoner of war, and Wendy Wakelam and Ella Herbert were kind enough to share precious memories of their father.

I would not have been able to research and write this book without the love and support of my family. Thank you to my father Ray for instilling in me his passion for the past, and to my stepmother Ingrid, who helped me to get away so I could focus on writing. My grandmother Mary did more to help craft my approach to this study than she knows, and despite our competing AFL loyalties, Steve and Janine Scott provide help in ways too numerous to mention. My beautiful wife Erin continues to give infinite amounts of love and support in all that I do, and remains incredibly forgiving whenever my mind is out 'on commando' or in the trenches of the Western Front rather than at home where it should be. My young son Darcy will always bring me back to the present and is a daily reminder of all that is important.

Finally, I dedicate this work to my mother Carol, who one day before she died, asked me what her Poppy had endured as a prisoner of war.

A NOTE ON CASUALTY STATISTICS

Statistics of wartime casualties are notoriously variable, and differ between sources, the period under examination and research methodologies. Figures on the total number of Australians lost as prisoners of war have been largely drawn from A.G. Butler, *Special Problems and Services*, vol. 3, *Official History of the Australian Army Medical Services*, Australian War Memorial, Canberra, 1943. Any discrepancies with the author's findings are presented in endnotes.

GLOSSARY

Abt. IV/ BayHStA	Bayerisches Hauptstaatsarchiv (Abteilung IV, Kriegsarchiv)
ADB	*Australian Dictionary of Biography*
AFC	Australian Flying Corps
AIF	Australian Imperial Force
ARCS	Australian Red Cross Society
ARCS NO	Australian Red Cross Society National Office
AWM	Australian War Memorial
Bde	Brigade
BEF	British Expeditionary Force
Bn	Battalion
B-WürHStA	Baden-Württemberg Hauptstaatsarchiv
Capt	Captain
Div	Division
IWM	Imperial War Museum
Kriegsgefangene	German for 'prisoners of war'
LCpl	Lance Corporal
Lieut	Lieutenant
NAA	National Archives of Australia
NA UK	The National Archives, United Kingdom
NCO	Non-Commissioned Officer
OHL	Oberste Heeresleitung (German Supreme Army Command)
Pnr Bn	Pioneer Battalion
POW	Prisoner of war
Pte	Private

RFC	Royal Flying Corps
RSSAILA	Returned Sailors', Soldiers' and Airmen's Imperial League
SBO	Senior British Officer
Sgt	Sergeant
SLNSW	State Library of New South Wales
SLSA	State Library of South Australia
SLVIC	State Library of Victoria
SROWA	State Records Office Western Australia
WMB	Wounded and Missing Enquiry Bureau

GREAT BRITAIN

North Sea

NETHERLANDS

BELGIUM

GERMANY

LUXEMBOURG

FRANCE

Zeebrugge
Ostend
Nieuport
Bruges
Antwerp
Lys River
Meuse River

Calais
Ypres
Passchendaele
Boulogne
St Omer
Messines
Lille
Armentières
Aachen
Hazebrouck
Neuve
Chapelle
Fromelles
Mons
Charleroi
BEF HQ
Loos
Douai
Montreuil
Vimy
Valenciennes
Dinant
Arras
Bullecourt
Ham-sur-Heure
Flers
Cambrai
Pozières
Abbeville
Albert
Péronne
Amiens
Le Hamel
St Quentin
Villers-Bretonneux

Somme R.

Aisne River
Reims
Compiègne
Oise River
Verdun
Seine River
St Mihiel

Paris

Seine River

Meuse River

Belfort

N

Trench warfare, 1915–17

Furthest German advance, September 1914

Furthest German advance, Spring 1918

0   50 km

Map 1 The Western Front, 1914–18

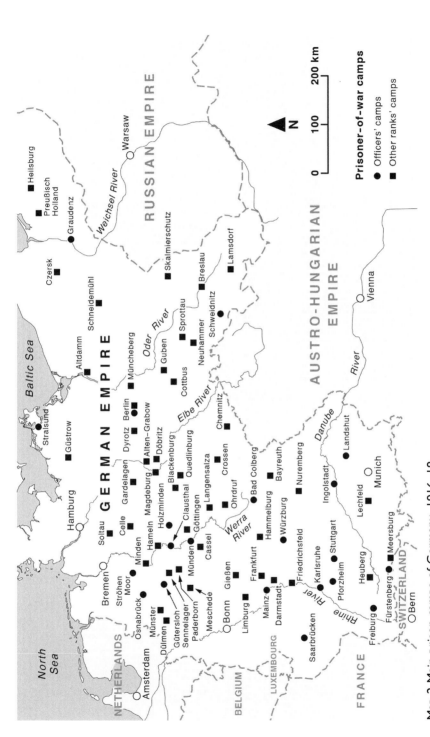

Map 2 Main prison camps of Germany, 1916–18

INTRODUCTION

Towards the end of *Somme Mud*, Edward Lynch's fictionalised memoir of fighting on the Western Front, the book's protagonist, Nulla, encounters a group of British and French soldiers who had spent the previous three years as prisoners of war. Among them is a 'tall, gaunt figure' who sways up to Nulla and introduces himself as an Australian who 'got knocked' and was taken prisoner at Fleurbaix in July 1916. 'Can you spare a couple of tins of bully beef?' he asks. Nulla looks pitifully on the 'poor, half-starved wretches. All dirty yellow skin, hollow cheeks and sunken, hopeless eyes.' He gives food and cigarettes to these 'scarecrows on legs' that clutch with 'long, claw-like, grasping fingers that shake'. Nulla was appalled. 'How we pity these poor beggars! How we thank our lucky stars we escaped the ordeal of being prisoners of war. We look upon [these] fellow men reduced to skin-clad skeletons and are sickened.'[1]

The First World War casts a long shadow over Australian history. In four years, the Australian Imperial Force (AIF) suffered more than 215 000 casualties, of whom around 60 000 died, and countless others and their families lived with the war's physical and psychological consequences for decades after. Among them were 4044 Australians who became prisoners of war. Some 200 were taken prisoner by the Ottomans in Mesopotamia, Gallipoli and the Middle East, while 3848 were lost to German forces in the fighting on the Western Front in France and Belgium.[2] Not long after arriving in France from Egypt in March 1916, three Australian infantry divisions were committed to the Franco-British offensive on the Somme, where the violence was so extreme that many

1

Australian soldiers came to believe that it would be near impossible to survive the war without injury. The Australian war correspondent Charles Bean realised this after witnessing the fighting at Pozières and Mouquet Farm, where the Australians lost more than 23 000 casualties in just six weeks of fighting. He recorded in his diary, '[T]here is only one way out of this war for an infantryman, and that is on his back. Either sick, wounded or dead. They will be put at it to fight and fight and fight again – until if not in this battle then in the next, each man gets his bullet. There is no way out.'[3]

Figure 0.1 Frank Hurley's staged photograph of Château Wood near Ypres, Belgium, October 1917. It depicts conditions on the Western Front, where trench warfare and the dominance of artillery made capture an unlikely prospect. (AWM E04599)

Their staggering losses made Australian troops increasingly fatalistic the longer the war continued, with many accepting the likelihood that they would probably be wounded or die.[4] But such a bleak outlook overlooked what would happen if they fell into the hands of the enemy. Reflecting the static nature of trench warfare, which limited face-to-face contact with the enemy to trench raids, patrols and a relatively few major engagements, prisoners of war represented less than 2 per cent of Australian battle casualties on the Western Front. Capture was therefore an unlikely prospect soldiers considered before going into battle:

We reckoned on three things that could happen. We could either get through unscathed or perhaps get what they called a 'blighty' – that was a light wound to get us out of it – or perhaps get skittled for all time and that would be the finish of it ... About the only thing we didn't reckon on was being wounded and being taken prisoner. And that's what happened to me.[5]

Australian troops also accepted the grim realities of combat knowing that demoralised soldiers who begged their enemies for mercy in the white heat of battle were sometimes killed. This was informed, in part, by their own battlefield practices and attitudes towards surrendering German soldiers.[6] At Pozières in July 1916, troops of the 1st Australian Division killed demoralised and surrendering Germans while 'ratting' for souvenirs.[7] Negotiating the politics of surrender at the moment of capture was therefore both difficult and dangerous for combatants of the First World War. Despite this, the German Army suceeded in capturing more than 182 000 troops of the British Empire, who then endured up to four years in captivity.[8] While all prisoners of war experienced hardship and anguish of varying degrees in German captivity, the mortality rate among British and dominion prisoners of war varied between 3.1 per cent based on German figures and 7.1 per cent based on British figures.[9] These suggest overall treatment neither usually deliberately violent nor extreme, but when broken down into national and dominion forces, the mortality rate among Australian prisoners of war was slightly higher. Australians in German captivity died at a higher rate than British and South African prisoners of war, but fared better than Indians, Newfoundlanders, New Zealanders and Canadians (see table 0.1).

Table 0.1 Mortality of British and dominion prisoners of war in German captivity, 1914–18

Regiment	Mortality (%)
Indian	30.93
Newfoundland	16.75
New Zealand	10.1
Canadian	8.07
Australian	8.04
British	6.91
South African	3.25
Total	**7.1**

Source: War Office, *Statistics of the Military Effort of the British Empire During the Great War, 1914–20*, HMSO, London, 1922, p. 237

Yet basic statistical analysis suggests that in some respects, a German prison camp was a much safer place to be than in the trenches of the Western Front. For British and dominion forces, the chances of being captured during the First World War were approximately five times less than being killed or wounded in combat. If an Australian soldier was taken prisoner by the Germans, his odds of seeing through the war were significantly better. According to figures in A.G. Butler's *Official History of the Australian Army Medical Services*, 295 000 Australians troops served in France and Belgium, of whom 46 000 died, equating to a loss of 15.6 per cent.[10] Butler's figures show that in captivity, 337 of the 3848 Australians taken prisoner died in the hands of the Germans, but most of these (267) died from gunshot and fragmentation wounds received in battle, putting the number of Australians who died as a direct consequence of German captivity at 70, or 1.8 per cent.[11] Considering that Australians engaged in combat on the Western Front had approximately a 1 in 6 chance of dying, those who spent the remainder of the war in the hands of the Germans had somewhere between a 1 in 11 to a 1 in 50 chance of dying, depending on whether they were nursing wounds when they fell into the hands of the enemy. Surrender and imprisonment did not guarantee survival, but the distinction between combat in the trenches and life in German prison camps is striking. If conditions in German captivity were so awful, why, then, did so many Australian prisoners of war survive and return home?

Despite popular and scholarly interest in the First World War, captivity remains what Heather Jones has called a 'missing paradigm' of that conflict.[12] This is true of the Australian experience, where prisoners of war have been confined to the margins of the national story. This is primarily because the experiences of a relative few who had the misfortune of falling into enemy hands were overshadowed by Australia's 60 000 war dead, who became the focus of private and public mourning in the interwar period. With 397 Australians dying in Ottoman and German captivity (representing 0.6 per cent of Australian wartime deaths), the experiences of prisoners of war did not integrate easily into public narratives and emerging commemorative rituals of the First World War.[13]

Defeat and surrender also sat uneasily within the dominant narrative of Australians at war, the Anzac legend, which celebrated the qualities of Australian soldiers as citizens in arms. Australians saw themselves as courageous and resourceful in battle, contemptuous of authority, loyal to their mates and natural-born soldiers who, above all, made significant contributions to the Allied victory over Germany and Ottoman Turkey. Surrender also challenged the Victorian military tradition of celebrating last-stand actions of British soldiers who died holding ground in the presence of the enemy. Battles such as Balaclava in the Crimean War (1854), Isandlwana in the Anglo-Zulu War (1879) and Gordon's last stand at Khartoum (1885) were all seen as heroic deeds of the British Empire in the decades before the First World War.[14] By contrast, captivity was a story of surrender and inaction at odds with a triumphant national memory of the Western Front fighting that gave prominence to the AIF's victories rather than its defeats.[15] Some Australians taken prisoner in the First World War felt they had 'surrendered manhood' the moment they were captured.[16] An Australian officer described his capture at Bullecourt as one of the 'sorest and bitterest feelings of my life'.[17] Another, captured near Bapaume, was so ashamed 'I cared little whether I lived or died'.[18]

In contrast, Second World War prisoners hold central place in the Australian memory of war because of their significant numbers.[19] This was not always the case, but the rediscovery of the Australian prisoner-of-war experience from this conflict coincided with complex global trends in the mid-1980s that made it easier to engage with traumatic aspects of the past.[20] Australia's reassessment of captivity in the Second World War occurred, in part, because of a number of wartime memoirs depicted some prisoner groups as worthy inheritors of the Anzac legend.[21] Coinciding with this, a mode of war memory had emerged by the 1990s that privileged victims of trauma, which validated those who had suffered as prisoners of war, particularly the 22 300 Australian prisoners of the Japanese, of whom around 8000 had died in captivity.[22] This trend gathered momentum over the intervening decades and culminated in the linking of experiences of Australian prisoners of the Japanese with Australian national identity. As the Australian Defence Minister said at the Anzac Day ceremony at Kanchanaburi War Cemetery in Thailand in 2013, 'The Australian sacrifices we honour today helped forge our national identity, helped forge our national characteristics and helped set out national values and virtues ... The traditions forged at Gallipoli, and later by the POWs who suffered and sacrificed on the Thai–Burma Railway, have become an indelible part of our history.'[23]

In February 2017, public commentary during commemorations for the seventy-fifth anniversary of the Fall of Singapore highlighted the extent to which Australian prisoners of the Japanese have been integrated into the Anzac legend. In captivity, 'The Australians survived because they were fit young men, most recruited to the AIF from country areas. They had bush skills, which helped them put up rough shelters in the jungles of Thailand and Burma, start a cooking fire in the rain, and – importantly – good old values of Australian mateship.'[24]

Australian prisoners of the Japanese have become so prominent in national memory that there exists a general ambivalence towards prisoners of war from other conflicts and theatres who did not fare as poorly. In some ways, this trend has been global. Historians have been less inclined to address the ambivalence towards the First World War because of a perception that the conflict had little impact on the lives of non-combatants. According to John Keegan, the First World War 'saw no systematic displacement of populations, no deliberate starvation, no expropriation [and] little massacre or atrocity', although there now exists a substantial body of evidence to the contrary.[25] This would seem to apply to the Australian prisoners of war from the First World War, where the overall mortality rate in Ottoman and German captivity (9.7 per cent) was significantly less than in Japanese captivity in the Second World War (35.9 per cent).[26] Disease, malnutrition and wartime atrocities defined the lives of the latter prisoner group, leading to more than thirty years of scholarship on their awful experiences and their place in the memory of Australians at war.[27]

Some Australian scholars have begun to address the missing paradigm of captivity in the First World War. The high mortality rate among Australians captured by Ottoman forces (28.9 per cent) suggests conditions in captivity almost as extreme as those of Changi, Ambon and the Thailand–Burma Railway, but recent studies suggest that the realities were a little more nuanced. In her analysis of the 67 Australians captured on Gallipoli, Jennifer Lawless argues that those who died in Ottoman captivity predominantly did so from wounds received in action and epidemics sweeping the country. Survivors were not always beaten or starved, but many were paid for work and often had access to alcohol and brothels.[28] Kate Ariotti explains that perceptions of Ottoman captivity were shaped by nineteenth-century Western attitudes towards race and the 'unspeakable' Muslim Turk, which, for captured Australians, made imprisonment appear worse than it actually was.[29]

These works fill a void in the literature of Australia in the First World War, but are not representative of the broader prisoner-of-war story. Overwhelmingly most Australians taken prisoner during the First World War were captured by German forces on the Western Front. David Coombes' research on the men of the 4th Australian Division who fell into German hands at Bullecourt in April 1917 is a step in the right direction, but their horrible experiences during the reprisals in occupied territory affirms rather than challenges the dominating influence of captivity in the Asia Pacific and the associated narrative of victimhood and trauma.[30] Other than Coombes' work, the Australian experience of captivity on the Western Front has not attracted scholarly attention beyond a handful of articles and unpublished works by predominantly undergraduate and postgraduate students.[31] These show that interest has not been entirely absent, but do not adequately explain the high survival rate of Australian prisoners of war. Did surviving captivity depend on 'mateship', that 'key ingredient' said to have helped Australian prisoners survive the Thailand–Burma Railway in the Second World War, or something else?[32]

Figure 0.2 G. Goddard Jackson, *Schwarmstedt Camp*, oil on board, 12 cm x 30 cm, c. 1918 (IWM ART 1857)

German captivity is more commonly associated with tales of escape and evasion, which offered the possibility of transforming a story of surrender, inaction, confinement and oppression into an exciting battle of wits between captives and captors.[33] As Stephen Garton writes, prisoners of war who tried escaping were transformed into 'heroic men of action in a lineage stretching back to the siege of Troy'.[34] Escapes are today more commonly associated with the Second World War, but they were deeply ingrained in the British cultural imagination in the decades before. One of the earliest stories was Winston Churchill's memoir *London to Ladysmith via Pretoria* (1902), which detailed his escape in the Boer War in South Africa and helped to elevate his political career in the years before the First World War.[35] After the First World War, British escape stories included *The Tunnellers of Holzminden* (1920), *The Road to En-Dor* (1920), *Escapers All* (1932), *An Airman's Escape* (1933) and *Cage Birds* (1940), which all portrayed captivity as something of an adventure where prisoners (predominantly officers) spent their days digging tunnels and making maps and counterfeit uniforms. Ian Isherwood explains that commercial publishing encouraged heroic narratives such as these, since they portrayed an image of martial Britishness and helped former prisoners to assuage feelings of humiliation brought on by surrender and an ignominious war in captivity.[36]

Films such as *Barbed Wire* (1927), *Two Arabian Knights* (1927), *Captured!* (1933) and Jean Renoir's classic, *La Grande Illusion* (1937), reinforced the popularity of the interwar escape genre and perhaps played a role in inspiring escapes among British and Commonwealth prisoners of war in Germany during the Second World War.[37]

These, in turn, generated a fresh wave of popular books, films and games that continue to shape perceptions of captivity in today's popular imagination.[38] While the subject still lives in the shadow of captivity during the Second World War, the few modern representations of captivity in the First World War revolve around the theme of escape, as depicted in the television movie *Young Indiana Jones and the Great Escape* (1992). Following his capture on the Western Front while serving with the Belgian Army, the protagonist, Indy, makes a dash for freedom after just three on-screen minutes in German hands. He attempts two more escapes over the program's thirty minutes before finally succeeding as the end credits roll.

The heroic portrayal of prisoners as escapees has become so quintessential that popular author Jacqueline Cook claims that all British prisoners of the First World War turned their minds to escape as soon as 'the key turned in the lock'.[39] But, writing about British and Commonwealth prisoners in Europe in the Second World War, historian S.P. MacKenzie makes the point that escape stories drastically oversimplify and distort the realities of captivity where 'privation, boredom, uncertainty, occasional danger and much else made POW life for most men resemble an endurance test rather than a light-hearted game'.[40] Writing about Australians in German captivity in the Second World War, Peter Monteath adds that escape stories favoured the political circumstances of the post-war order, particularly the integration of West Germany into the Western alliance and the emergence of Soviet Russia as the new enemy.[41] If this can be said of captivity in the Second World War, how representative was escape in the lives of prisoners in the First World War?

The general ambivalence towards captivity during this period is evident in the twelve-volume *Official History of Australia in the War of 1914–1918* edited by C.E.W. (Charles) Bean and published in various editions between 1921 and 1943. Although Bean cannot be credited with creating the Anzac legend, he was sympathetic to it, and enshrined it for a receptive public audience.[42] Alistair Thomson argues that Bean's history was a sanitised version of the Australian war experience that diminished aspects of the AIF that challenged the heroic Anzac archetype. Bean wrote carefully about instances of cowardice, desertion, self-inflicted wounds and poor discipline, and was similarly cautious about the capture of Australian troops. The way in which he wrote about surrender supports Thomson's conclusion that Bean was a brilliant mythmaker, not because he denied or ignored evidence that contradicted his ideal, 'but because he admitted and then reworked that evidence in terms of his own preconceptions so that it was less challenging'.[43]

Few pages of the official history covered captivity in detail. The most attention prisoners received is two and a half pages in Frederic Cutlack's volume on the Australian Flying Corps, which recounts the experience of the nine Australian Half-Flight mechanics captured at Kut in Mesopotamia in April 1916: their gruelling thousand-kilometre forced march across the Syrian Desert involved battling exposure, disease and fatigue as prisoners of the Ottomans. Seven of the nine mechanics were among 1800 white British prisoners of war who died, along with a staggering 70 per cent of the British Indian rank and file captured at Kut who are believed to have died in the hands of the Ottomans.[44]

In the four volumes Bean wrote on the Western Front, the experiences of Australians captured in France and Belgium were consigned to a series of footnotes parenthetic to the main battle narrative.[45] By comparison, prisoners of the Second World War received substantial attention from the Australian official historians. It has been claimed that captivity 'barely rates a mention' in these volumes, but chapters and appendices of captivity in Europe and the Asia Pacific amount to more than 400 pages – enough to constitute a separate volume on the experiences of Australian prisoners of war.[46] Bean never set out to write a history that included the experiences of prisoners of war, but even if he did, he might not have had the sources to do so. As part of the repatriation process, the Australian War Records Section collected statements from prisoners returning to Britain from Germany 'for historical record purposes', but these were not transferred to the Australian War Memorial until 1959.[47]

Nevertheless, the way Bean wrote about the capture of Australian soldiers left the heroic archetype of the Australian fighting soldier unchallenged. We see this in the language and phrases he used in the official history to imply that capture was a fate beyond the personal control of individuals. At Fromelles, wounded men 'found themselves' prisoners as German troops overran their positions, while those who remained fighting were captured possessing 'no opportunity for resistance'.[48] There was similar treatment of Australians at Bullecourt who 'received no order to withdraw' and were 'entirely cut off' as German troops counter-attacked, while those at Dernancourt who put up 'a very hard fight' surrendered 'to avoid any further useless loss of life'.[49] Germans appeared to surrender quite differently. They were usually portrayed as 'scared, mud-bespattered' 'young boys' who pleaded for their lives, 'terrified and shrieking'.[50] Bean even drew the distinction between 'weaker spirits' who surrendered easily whereas those who died at their posts 'fought with bravery that always drew on them the admiration of Australians'.[51]

These very different descriptions of surrender on the Western Front suggest that Bean found it difficult to write critically about the capture of Australian troops without contradicting the emerging Anzac archetype. It resulted in a sanitised version of combat that emphasised the courageous efforts of Australians fighting bravely to the bitter end instead of surrendering in terror when faced with the certain prospect of death. Bean also chose not to include the identities of officers who had not performed well in battle, but emphasised the deeds of those who had fought courageously. This included Lieutenant Albert Jacka of the 14th Battalion, Australia's first Victoria Cross recipient of the First World War, whose Military Cross action at Pozières on 7 August 1916 excluded mention of an officer whose less than heroic decision was just as important to the story. Bean describes how Jacka led his platoon in an assault on forty German soldiers escorting a party of captured Australians to the rear in the midst of a German attack. Jacka and his men surprised the Germans, causing the prisoners of war to turn on their escorts. Jacka was wounded in the resulting melee, but had reversed the situation and personally killed several Germans.[52]

Bean praised Jacka's actions as 'the most dramatic and effective act of individual audacity in the history of the AIF' and considered it worthy of a bar to his existing Victoria Cross.[53] Yet he made no mention of the captured men who set the scene for Jacka's gallant charge. Among Bean's papers is a letter from Lieutenant Lionel Carter of the 48th Battalion, who sent an apology to his battalion commander from hospital the following day:

> I wish to make it quite clear the fact that I was responsible for the
> surrender. Now that I think of it calmly I am ashamed and feel
> I deserve every censure which you and our Brigadier can give me ...
> I feel very sorry for having brought this disgrace to the finest Battalion
> in the AIF and to its best Company.[54]

Carter had not shown qualities that fitted the heroic archetype of the Australian fighting soldier. He was relieved of command and given a base job, and, although he was awarded the Military Cross later in the war, made no further cameos in Bean's official history.[55] There might have been a reason for this. After the war, Carter joined the Nationalist Party of Australia and held the seat of Leederville in the West Australian Legislative Assembly from 1921 to 1924, which was around the time Bean was preparing work for the official history volume dealing with the fighting in France in 1916. Bean went to great lengths to write a history of unrivalled detail but, writing in footnotes, using carefully worded phrases and omitting details on the capture of Australian troops, helped to manage a version of the official war record the nation could be proud of. He protected the identities of men like Carter who had not performed heroically because, as Bill Gammage writes, it pained Bean to write ill of any man.[56]

This book seeks to address these oversights while challenging the familiar narrative of victimhood and trauma that defines most studies of the Australian prisoner-of-war experience. By considering some of the factors that helped Australian prisoners captured on the Western Front to overcome the challenges of their imprisonment, it adds a distinctly Australian dimension to a growing body of scholarly work in Britain and Europe in which transnational studies have focused on the ways captors and prisoners responded to the challenges of captivity during the conflict.[57] Richard Speed and Uta Hinz argue that Germany observed international law and treated Allied prisoners humanely amid rapidly deteriorating conditions and a faltering wartime economy.[58] Despite widespread food shortages and the enormous suffering of Russian prisoners, Germany adhered to the pre-war agreements that largely protected prisoners of war from the violence of their captors. Hinz concludes that the German treatment of Allied prisoners shows that the First World War was 'not a total war that negated each international law or humanitarian norm'.[59] This differs from the findings of Heather Jones, whose study of violence in captive labour units in forward areas on the Western Front shows that Britain, France and Germany deliberately undermined laws that protected prisoners and mistreated them. These sanctioned reprisals against prisoners set new precedents for future conflicts.[60]

This is the first major study of the Australian experience of captivity on the Western Front using archival records. It builds upon the existing scholarly literature by showing that Australians fared as well as any other group of British prisoners of war in German captivity. It takes the middle ground in the broader discussion on captivity in the First World War by arguing that the German treatment of Australian prisoners of war was neither brutal nor benign, but somewhere in between. In the First World War, captivity was a dynamic and complex historical event that failed to produce a single, dominant narrative that encapsulated the broad range of Australian experiences. This study shows that the German treatment of Allied prisoners was not based on a policy of violence, neglect or deliberate mistreatment, but an informal bilateral principle of reciprocity informed by international laws established to ensure the well-being of German prisoners of war in British and French captivity.

Although these agreements were sometimes ignored and abused, the hardships experienced by Australians occurred within a broader social, economic and military context that also affected Germany's ability to care properly for the vast number of prisoners of war in its camps throughout the war. Australian prisoners regularly endured hardship, both behind the lines in France and in the prison camps in Germany, but Germany treated prisoners mostly as well as it could. When treated well, Australian prisoners could be valuable sources of military intelligence, could be motivated to work productively to help the German war effort, and could be used to ensure fair treatment of Germans in British and French hands. This aspect of the Western Front modifies the heroic archetype of the Australian fighting soldier and the dominant prisoner-of-war narrative of victimhood, adding depth and dimension to scholarly and popular understanding of the nation's First World War experience.

Whereas most prisoner-of-war studies rely on oral histories and published memoirs, this study draws on archival records created during the war and immediately after it for a more balanced assessment of life in German captivity. Among these are approximately 2500 written statements made by repatriated prisoners upon returning to England, which are now held in the Australian War Memorial, and fifty diaries and unpublished manuscripts either kept illegally in captivity or written in the interwar period. These have been used selectively and in corroboration with other sources to ward against the influence of the Second World War experience.

A collection of oral history interviews held in the Australian War Memorial were not used in this study, mainly because of Alistair Thomson's warning that private wartime memories in Australia were shaped by the Anzac legend and often changed over time.[61] Recorded in the mid- to late 1980s by Tasmanian researcher David Chalk, these thirty-nine interviews with 'old Gefangeners' from captivity on the Western

Front were recorded immediately after the highly popular *POW: Australians Under Nippon* (1984) radio series had broadcast repeatedly on ABC Radio National throughout the late 1980s and early 1990s. The sixteen-part radio program by Hank Nelson and Tim Bowden brought the private sufferings of Australian prisoners of the Japanese during the Second World War to a receptive public audience and helped to enshrine their awful experiences in the national memory.[62] It is possible that memories of captivity in the First World War (then seventy years distant) were influenced by the more recent public memories of Changi, Ambon and the Thailand–Burma Railway.[63] Primary sources created before the Second World War have been used to offer more immediate (but not necessarily more complete) comment on the Australian experience of captivity during the First World War.

This study also attempts to quantify aspects of the Australian prisoner-of-war experience. Prosopography is commonly used by social scientists and ancient historians to study the changing roles in society of social groups, but this study uses Lawrence Stone's broad definition of an 'investigation of the common background characteristics of a group of actors in history by means of a collective study of their lives'.[64] A database listing all men identified by the Australian Red Cross Prisoner of War Department as having been captured on the Western Front formed the framework for this study. Regimental details for each individual were matched with service dossiers at the National Archives of Australia and cross-referenced with battalion war diaries from the Australian War Memorial to determine the date and place of capture for each individual. This then allowed for the total sample to be sorted chronologically on the basis of their date of capture, making it possible to find statements by repatriated prisoners of war describing how, when, where and under what conditions they became prisoners. This also made it possible to identify a sample of 264 men of the 13th Battalion, whose post-war lives were researched using Ancestry.com, digitised newspapers at the National Library of Australia, Department of Veterans' Affairs nominal rolls and Repatriation Department case files.

Death and escape are other aspects of the prisoner-of-war experience included in this study. Cross-referencing the regimental details of all individuals captured on the Western Front against the Australian War Memorial's Roll of Honour helped to establish the identities of 327 men who died in or as a result of their time in German captivity, spanning the first Australian engagement in France on 5 May 1916 and the disbandment of the AIF on 31 March 1921.[65] Extending the end date beyond the Armistice of November 1918 gives some indication of how many former prisoners of war died as a consequence of their wounds, disease and other causes after their repatriation to England and Australia. German death notifications and reports sent to the Australian Red Cross office in London via the International Red Cross office in Switzerland determined whether an individual died from wounds received in battle, disease or misfortune at the hands of his captors. Burial returns from the Imperial (later Commonwealth) War Graves Commission established whether prisoners died behind the lines in France or Belgium or in a prison camp or hospital in Germany. Graves could not be located for twenty-one men known to have died as prisoners of war, mainly from wounds received in combat in France.[66] This analysis produced statistics that put Australian deaths in captivity in a broader context and gives some indication of the prevalence of violence in its most extreme form in the lives of Australian prisoners of war.[67]

The mortality study also guided research on the repatriated prisoner statements and written material by Australians who reported being well treated by their captors and whose stories did not fit the traditional prisoner-of-war narrative. Attention was given to factors affecting prisoners' lives in captivity: the paucity of food and medical supplies, and ways prisoners used the minor freedoms available to them to improve their chances of survival. British prisoners who made successful escapes were almost always decorated for their efforts, so all but four Australians who succeeded in their escapes were identified by finding their names and regimental details in the *London Gazette* and citations in the archives at the Australian War Memorial. The repatriation statements do not give consistent detail to determine how many attempted to escape but failed and remained in German hands.

This study also uses German intelligence records based on the interrogation of Australian prisoners of war. First World War scholars have been hindered by a lack of German sources since a single bombing raid by the Royal Air Force on Potsdam near Berlin in April 1945 destroyed 90 per cent of the Imperial German Army's operational records. The significance of this loss cannot be overstated, but copies of Prussian material, including some reports based on the interrogation of prisoners, survive in archives at Dresden, Munich, Stuttgart, Karlsruhe and Freiburg im Breisgau.[68] Some operational records relating to German formations from Bavaria, Saxony, Baden and Württemberg survived the Second World War, including files from a number of German divisions that captured and interrogated Australian troops on the Western Front. Repatriated prisoners often gave anecdotes about interrogation in their statements and unpublished memoirs, but on their own do not establish what information the German Army learned from their capture. German intelligence reports were used in conjunction with the database, making it possible to associate regimental and biographical details of individual prisoners referred to in the German records only by rank, unit, and date and place of capture. This made it possible to locate corresponding statements by the men referred to in the German reports for an account of the interrogation process from both sides. In some cases, it was possible to piece together the details of the same conversation shared between prisoners of war and German intelligence officers more than a century ago.

This study spans the AIF's service on the Western Front, beginning with its first engagement in France on 5 May 1916 and concludes with the repatriation of some 2700 Australian prisoners to Britain by 31 December 1918.[69] While mortality rates indicate the long-term effects of captivity following repatriation, some attempt has been made to consider how Australian prisoners of war fared in the post-war years through a study of 264 men of the 13th Battalion who survived captivity and returned home. Not included in this study are Australians captured in theatres other than the Western Front. This includes around a hundred men of military age either living in or visiting Germany at the outbreak of hostilities who spent the war in the civilian camp at Ruhleben near Berlin, and around 35 soldiers and sailors of the Australian Naval and Military Expeditionary Force and merchant navy captured in southern waters when their vessels were boarded and scuttled by the crew of the German commerce raider SMS *Wolf*.[70] 'Australians' defined by this study refers specifically to soldiers of the AIF and airmen of the Australian Flying Corps (AFC) captured by German forces in France and Belgium.[71]

The book is structured thematically around the different phases of captivity as experienced by Australian prisoners of war. Chapter 1 sets the scene by discussing the capture of Australian troops on the Western Front. It looks at German infantry tactics and defensive doctrine between 1916 and 1918, and maintains that battlefield conditions and the hopelessness of their immediate situation resulted in the capture of Australian troops. Those who had the misfortune of falling into enemy hands generally represented units that succeeded in taking their objectives when neighbouring units failed to do so, leaving them exposed to counterattacks and German troops equipped with weapons that favoured taking prisoners over killing. As well as discussing a number of actions that resulted in the loss of large numbers of Australians as prisoners of war, this chapter considers the impact of training and tactical development within the broader British Expeditionary Force (BEF) and its improved ability to hold captured ground in the final 18 months of the war.

The following two chapters consider the benefits of prisoners of war to their captors. Chapter 2 evaluates how captured Australians were treated and mistreated behind the lines by German troops who did not always have the niceties of pre-war agreements foremost in their minds. Following a discussion of the ways Australians negotiated the politics of surrender, this chapter establishes that German formations did not always possess the resources to care for vast and unexpected numbers of prisoners in their charge. The belligerents found the principle of reciprocity an alternative and more effective way of policing pre-war agreements and protecting prisoners from mistreatment behind the lines. The Australian experience with this informal understanding supports Heather Jones' insights into violence in prisoner labour companies, and shows that the German Army was willing to tolerate a certain level of violence towards captured men. This chapter also considers the experiences of the wounded and shows how some of the most vulnerable prisoner groups benefited from the principle of reciprocity.

Chapter 3 illustrates how Australian prisoners could sometimes be valuable assets in the German Army's intelligence network. Expecting to be poorly treated, many were surprised to be treated well by German troops who had previously tried to kill them in combat. While relatively good treatment adhered to the pre-war agreements, it was also part of the intelligence-gathering game, whereby violence and verbal insults were largely ineffective in eliciting information from prisoners. German intelligence officers found good treatment and polite conversations over cigars and cognac more effective in lulling prisoners into a false sense of security. This chapter also looks at the consequences of talking openly to the enemy through the stories of two Australian soldiers who willingly deserted to the Germans. Taking important information with them, they gravely affected the well-being of their comrades who remained fighting in the trenches.

The remaining chapters look at factors that helped Australians overcome the privations of daily life behind German barbed wire. Chapter 4 examines the insurmountable humanitarian effort for prisoners of war by patriotic volunteers of the Australian Red Cross Society. It considers two branches of the Australian Red Cross Society operating in London: Vera Deakin's Wounded and Missing Enquiry Bureau, and Mary Chomley's Prisoner of War Department.

Chapter 5 questions the centrality of popular escape narratives through a critical study of their prominence in the Australian wartime experience. It shows that the War Office gave no direction on what was expected if soldiers of the British Empire fell into enemy hands, so the decision to escape in this war rested with individuals. The dynamics affecting individual decisions to escape are then weighed against the inherent difficulties for prisoners making a bid for freedom from behind the lines in France or from Germany. With just 43 Australian prisoners of the Germans succeeding in their bids for freedom, this chapter maintains that escape was not representative of the Australian experience of captivity in Germany during the First World War. There is no evidence suggesting that prisoners were aware they had the option of returning to Australia if they were successful, but the thought that escaping would mean a return to the trenches was probably the greatest of all incentives to remain where they were.

Chapter 6 looks at ways Australian prisoners coped with the daily stresses of confinement in Germany. It recognises the often harsh German treatment of prisoners, but argues that conditions varied so much that no two prison camps, hospitals or work parties were alike. What distinguished the otherwise disparate array of experiences among Australian prisoners was the way most regarded survival as a personal triumph. Once they were receiving Red Cross parcels and mail from home, prisoners generally overcame the stigma of capture and began exerting themselves as autonomous, masculine and disciplined soldiers who maintained a sense of pride by avoiding work, sabotaging the German war effort and resisting their captors. They also spent time tending the needs of other prisoners and carrying out camp duties.

Finally, chapter 7 looks at what happened to Australian prisoners of war after the Armistice and how one group of former prisoners of war fared in the decades afterwards. Challenging the notion that captivity was an emasculating experience, this study offers a more representative look at what life was like for Australian soldiers who endured and survived captivity in the First World War.

RAISING THE WHITE FLAG

THE CAPTURE OF AUSTRALIAN TROOPS
ON THE WESTERN FRONT

No sooner had the barrage lifted from the Australian trenches on the night of 5 May 1916 than two German raiding parties entered the shattered remnants of the Bridoux Salient and began searching through the smoke and debris for underground mining galleries. They picked their way through the tangle of sandbags and smashed timber, lobbing grenades into makeshift shelters where the surviving Australian garrison sought refuge. Three grenades were lobbed into a dugout and exploded, after which five stunned and terrified figures emerged with hands raised above their heads. After eight minutes, three sharp whistle blasts signalled the raiders to return across No Man's Land. With them went two 3-inch Stokes mortars and eleven men of the 20th Battalion, who had the misfortune of being the first Australian soldiers taken prisoner by German forces on the Western Front.[1]

Capture defined the beginning of the Australian prisoner-of-war experience, but it is not an aspect of the wartime experience that features prominently in studies of the First World War.[2] Roger Noble recognised that Australian soldiers were not immune to fear and panic, and at times became demoralised, lost the will to continue fighting and surrendered to the enemy. In examining the causes of surrender, he ruled out the possibility that the number of casualties sustained during an engagement were in some way proportionate to the number lost as prisoners, nor was surrender found to be a product of the number of troops involved or a particular phase of the war. Instead, Noble found that a prescribed set of battlefield conditions was more likely to result in demoralisation and the surrender of Australian troops. Fire, terrain, reduced visibility, noise, and the disintegration of command and control systems were all factors that impaired soldiers' willingness to fight. For Noble, Australian troops surrendered because of low morale and low resilience.[3] This was an unwelcome aspect of Australia's wartime experience because, as Niall Ferguson observed, surrender was vital in determining the outcome of the First World War, where 'victory is won not by killing the enemy: as important is getting him to desert, mutiny or surrender'.[4]

Figure 1.1 A German aerial photograph of the Bridoux Salient near Armentières in April 1916, where, just several days later, the first of 3848 Australians were taken prisoner on the Western Front. (AWM G01534GBA)

Much evidence supports Noble's argument, but there are problems with the notion that morale on its own caused men to become prisoners of war.[5] The idea that surrender was an issue of morale does not adequately explain why so comparatively few Australian prisoners were captured on the Western Front. Statistics from the War Office show that capture was less common among British Empire troops (3.3 per cent of battle casualties) than among the French (11.6 per cent),

Belgians (11 per cent) and Portuguese (37.2 per cent).[6] Given the squalor of trench life, the heavy casualties and the industrial scale of the fighting and dying, it is remarkable just how resilient combatants were. Owing to the static nature of trench warfare, which significantly reduced the prospect of close-quarter contact with German forces, Australian troops engaged in the fighting in France and Belgium were more likely to die in combat or in dressing stations behind the lines, suffer from gas and be hospitalised with an illness than be captured by the Germans.[7]

If surrender reflected combat ineffectiveness, we would expect the German Army to have captured large numbers of Australians when the AIF suffered bouts of low morale. This includes the Somme winter of 1916–17, which Charles Bean considered 'the bottom of the curve' in troop morale on the Western Front.[8] Winter was not usually the fighting season owing to the inclement weather, but the conditions in the sector the Australians occupied near the villages of Flers and Gueudecourt after the Battle of the Somme made them miserable. Rain turned ground churned by months of shellfire into a morass, and the winter was the coldest in forty years. The strain was too much for some, who did whatever they could to avoid returning to the trenches. Desertion was common; men shot or injured themselves; and some welcomed venereal diseases from *estaminets* behind the lines as they would be removed from the battlefield for treatment.[9]

Yet it is surprising just how few Australians were captured during the Somme winter. Between November 1916 and February 1917, the AIF lost just a hundred men as prisoners of war. Most were lost in a series of costly attacks throughout late November and early December, which failed owing to the squalid conditions. Australian soldiers were not averse to breaking military law to avoid returning to the trenches during this time, but the one offence they abstained from committing was deserting to the enemy – a crime Bean considered 'the most certain symptom of demoralisation'.[10] This study uncovered just two Australian soldiers who willingly deserted to the Germans (discussed in chapter 3), which implies that demoralisation alone did not make soldiers surrender in battle. Under section 98 of the Australian Defence Act, Australian soldiers found guilty of deserting to the enemy faced the prospect of the death penalty if the sentence was approved by the Governor General, but not one of the 3400 Australians charged with desertion during the war was found guilty of desertion to the enemy.[11]

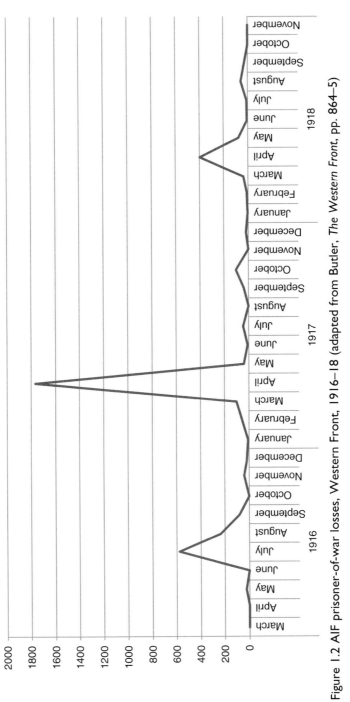

Figure I.2 AIF prisoner-of-war losses, Western Front, 1916–18 (adapted from Butler, *The Western Front*, pp. 864–5)

Since surrender could not always be attributed to low morale, how can we adequately explain the capture of Australians in the fighting on the Western Front? Perhaps the greatest weakness in the existing thinking is a lack of distinction between the conscious act of surrender and being captured without the ability to offer any further means of resistance. The database on which this study is based shows an intermediary state that was neither coexistent nor autonomous but drew upon elements of both. This means that Australian troops might have considered flight only when the seemingly futile gesture of fight meant certain death. An Australian sergeant captured at Bullecourt was conscious of this distinction, describing many years after the war how 'our giving up was not a surrender in the accepted sense ... it was an unavoidable surrender of the body, but not of the spirit, or of the mind.'[12]

Seeing capture in terms of morale and resilience also overlooks the role the enemy plays in taking prisoners of war. Since more than 70 per cent of Australian prisoners were lost to the German Army within the first year of the AIF on the Western Front, there is an operational dimension to the Australian prisoner-of-war experience worth considering.[13] Recognising that morale played a role in the surrender of soldiers, this chapter proposes that capture was also a function of the dynamics of the battlefield and the ability of one military force to achieve tactical superiority over the other. This is shown by a survey of the AIF's battle experience on the Western Front between 1916 and 1918.

The Western Front was in its second year of stalemate when the first AIF troops arrived in France in March 1916. By then, the trenches were elaborate defensive networks. German positions varied depending on the terrain, but ultimately comprised belts of barbed wire, underground dugouts and concrete fortifications with belt-fed machine-guns. Salients allowed German troops to fire in enfilade down the length of No Man's Land and into the flanks of an attacking formation. Heavy mortars and batteries of field guns pre-registered areas where attacks were likely to develop, and detachments of German infantry waited in forward, support and rest positions ready to defend against Allied attacks. German units also came to know their sectors intimately, extending their defences beyond their wire entanglements and into No Man's Land through active patrolling and trench-raiding. This included the relatively quiet Armentières sector on the Franco-Belgian border where the Australians entered the Western Front trenches for the first time in April 1916. The area's high water table made it unsuitable for a major attack, so the British used it to condition new and inexperienced troops to the rigours and routine of trench warfare. Owing to an informal state of 'live-and-let-live' that appeared to characterise the fighting in the area, the German Army used the Armentières sector to rest its more veteran formations.[14]

Eager though the Australians were to begin operations in France, it was the more experienced German troops who dealt the first blow with the raid on the Bridoux Salient on the night of 5 May 1916. The raiders found the Australians holding the position sheltering in dugouts and offering little resistance. One Australian described how 'we were caught like rabbits in a trap ... They very soon over-ran the salient and had us bottled up in the dugout.'[15] More raids followed, with the Germans raiding the Cordonnerie Salient near the village of Fleurbaix on 30–31 May. Under the cover of a heavy fog and smoke from the supporting German bombardment, the raiding party located underground mining galleries and set explosive charges in them, capturing eleven men from the 11th Battalion and 1st Pioneer Battalion who were underground at the time. 'A German unter-officer who could speak a little English came to the sap-head and called on us to come out. There were five of us left unwounded, and we did so.'[16]

These opening clashes demonstrated that the German Army domin-ated No Man's Land in the Armentières sector and showed that Austra-lian troops were sometimes caught in situations where the only alternative to certain death was an ignominious surrender. Australian commanders were embarrassed by the way the AIF had begun operations in the main theatre of war, although the series of German raids served as an incentive for the Australian divisions then in the line to improve defences and begin their own program of trench-raiding and aggressive patrolling.[17] For the Australians – and indeed the rest of the British and dominion forces in France at that time – raiding involved small assault groups armed with weapons suited to close-quarter fighting in the German trenches, where they spent several minutes killing and ransacking before withdrawing. Attacks were generally considered successful if ground was captured and held against enemy counter-attacks, but raids were intended to be short, sharp and extremely violent enterprises in which success was measured by the ability of the raiding party to get in and out of the German trenches with fewer casualties than it inflicted. Raiding also gave inexperienced troops combat experience and boosted their confidence before participat-ing in a major offensive action where the stakes were much higher.[18]

Raiding party members faced the possibility of being wounded and left behind in the German trenches. One objective was to take prisoners for intelligence, but losing men as prisoners during raids was obviously counter-productive. The Germans elicited information from an Australian prisoner following the 9th Battalion's raid on a position known as the Sugar Loaf near Fromelles on the night of 1 July 1916.[19] Of the two

mortally wounded Australian soldiers left behind in the German positions, Private Louis Braganza was taken to a German hospital where he
openly spoke about the Australian defences, the location of 1st Australian
Division headquarters and the battalion's movements since arriving in
France. The German officer who cross-examined Braganza before he died
reported that 'the prisoner was visibly in great pain and was very weak. It
was therefore necessary to discontinue the interrogation several times and
confine it to the most important parts.'[20]

Figure 1.3 German infantry were masters of the art of counter-attack. Those seen
here are equipped with *Grabenkeulen* (trench-raiding clubs) and *Stielhandgranates*
(stick grenades) for close-quarter fighting. (Photo courtesy of Brett Butterworth)

The Australian raids demonstrated that the AIF had no problems
getting into the German positions. In major attacks, the real problem
was holding their modest gains against counter-attacks by German infantry. Sharp and efficient counter-attacks were an essential part of the
German system of defence and were mastered by infantry divisions all
along the Western Front. During Allied attacks, German troops in the
forward areas would draw in an attacking force and encircle them,
preventing them from withdrawing, thereby allowing counter-attack
squads to 'roll up' (*Aufrollen*) their positions from the flanks with grenades.[21] Grenades could be thrown considerable distances or lobbed
around the traverse of a trench, and required less maintenance than rifles
and machine-guns. But a notable characteristic of the ubiquitous German

Stiehlhandgranate (stick grenade) was its limited fragmentation and considerably small blast radius, which tended to stun and incapacitate intended victims instead of killing them.[22] Consequently, grenades feature prominently in Australian accounts of capture:

> I was suddenly surprised to hear a gruff voice demand 'Come on
> Australia'. On looking up I beheld several Jerry bombers with bombs –
> of the 'potato masher' type – each pointing a revolver. I was compelled
> to submit to the worst humiliating experience of a lifetime, surrender!
> As the alternative meant death, and I was in a helpless situation, one
> must naturally excuse my choice.[23]

Australian patrolling and raiding in the Armentières sector ended in July 1916 when I Anzac Corps moved south to take part in the Battle of the Somme. They were replaced by the recently formed 5th Australian Division, which was loaned to the British XI Corps in the Armentières area for use in a feint attack near the village of Fromelles. The idea was to attack the Germans and pin them in the Lille area to prevent their reserves from being moved south to the Somme, where British formations were making their main offensive effort. Whereas the 1st, 2nd and 4th Australian Divisions benefited from raiding and patrolling in the Armentières area, the 5th Division prepared to attack the German positions outside Fromelles after two weeks in France, and no raids. Zero hour was fixed for 6pm on 19 July 1916, and attacking alongside them was the equally inexperienced British 61st Division.

The attack was a disaster. After a seven-hour bombardment, the 5th Australian Division made its assault hoping the German machine-guns had been destroyed. Instead, they were met by a fusillade of rifle and machine-gun fire, especially from the Sugar Loaf, which poured enfilade fire into the flanks of the 15th Brigade and virtually annihilated it as it attempted to cross No Man's Land. Spared such devastating fire, troops from the 14th and 8th Brigades succeeded in crossing No Man's Land at its narrowest point further away from the Sugar Loaf. They entered the German trenches, where they suffered heavy casualties repelling counter-attacks during the night. The survivors were forced to withdraw the following morning, but isolated groups were ultimately surrounded and captured. By morning, the 5th Division had lost more than 5500 casualties, which included 470 men lost as prisoners of war.[24]

The situation the Australians encountered at Fromelles was precisely what German troops hoped for. German infantrymen were able to use the cover of darkness, a thick fog and their intimate knowledge of the battlefield to work their way around the exposed flanks of the beleaguered attackers and cut off their withdrawal. After regaining their front-line positions, German troops then rolled up isolated groups of Australians with rifles and grenades. A 54th Battalion soldier holding out in the enemy trenches described how 'German bombers came along our trench. As they advanced they were throwing bombs in front of them.'[25] After dawn, German attacks killed or captured the remaining Australians in the German trenches. A private from the 53rd Battalion recalled seeing an Australian officer 'with a white flag raised and other men of the company throwing down their arms and surrendering. I was with another man, and we decided we better do likewise.'[26] A 30th Battalion private, wounded in the knee, lay helpless as German troops reoccupied their positions. 'The Germans came over at daylight. As soon as they sighted me one of them attempted to throw one of their "potato-masher" hand grenades at me, but a German sergeant stopped him.'[27] Fromelles demonstrated that units that lost the greatest number of men as prisoners of war were often the most successful: they had taken their objectives when neighbouring units failed to do so. Of the Australians captured at Fromelles, nearly all represented battalions of the 8th and 14th Brigades who had succeeded in crossing No Man's Land and were captured the first two lines of German trenches.

Figure 1.4 The bodies of Australian soldiers in the German trenches at Fromelles. In many instances, Australian troops were compelled to surrender when the futile gesture of resistance meant certain death. (Photo courtesy of Brett Butterworth)

After Fromelles, the 5th Australian Division spent months recovering its losses, while further south I Anzac Corps was drawn into the Battle of the Somme – the BEF's first major offensive effort on the Western Front in 1916. Beginning on 1 July 1916, the purpose of the offensive was to relieve the French fighting at Verdun by drawing the Germans into a separate offensive in the north while trying to achieve a breakthrough towards Bapaume. Progress was slow, with the assaulting British divisions nowhere near the objectives set for the first day fighting at the cost of more than 57 000 casualties. I Anzac Corps entered the fighting three weeks later and was given the task of capturing the fortified village of Pozières and the ground leading towards the heights of Thiepval. Just 400 of the 26 000 Australian casualties suffered on the Somme were lost as prisoners of war.[28] This relatively small number reflected the inherent difficulties of taking prisoners in trench warfare, where the dominance of artillery reduced the prospect of close-quarter fighting.

The 1st Australian Division captured Pozières on 23 July 1916 following a concentrated bombardment that either overwhelmed or destroyed key German defences. This pushed a significant bulge into the German positions, which the guns of an entire German army corps then shelled from three sides. While it inflicted a heavy toll on the Australians holding their positions in Pozières, the devastating fire made it near impossible to lose men as prisoners. The 1st Australian Division lost 5200 casualties in three days, of which just ten men fell into German hands.[29] One was a 5th Battalion sergeant who reported being knocked unconscious by the concussion of a high-explosive shell during a patrol on the night of 23 July: 'While in this condition I was made a prisoner, awaking to find myself in a German dugout.'[30] Another was severely wounded in the side: 'I lay where I fell for about three hours, and then tried to get back, but was picked up by a German patrol just before daybreak.'[31]

The AIF lost more men as prisoners over the followings weeks as I Anzac Corps started pressing attacks against a series of defences known as the Old German (OG) Lines east of Pozières village. Five attacks were made against these formidable German positions, the most significant being the 2nd Australian Division's unsuccessful assault on the Windmill on the night of 28–29 July. The attacking waves of the 6th and 7th Brigades spent up to fifteen minutes forming up in open ground in full view of German machine-gun crews ready to meet the coming attack. The supporting artillery failed to destroy the wire entanglements in front of the German positions, making the assaulting waves of Australian infantry easy targets. By dawn, the 2nd Australian Division had suffered more than 2000 casualties and had nothing to show for its efforts.[32]

Australian troops at Fromelles had fallen victim to a series of strong and determined counter-attacks, yet most captured in this attack at Pozières were wounded men collected by German patrols. At dawn, patrols moved through a thick fog that descended across the battlefield to search for survivors, some using ruses to lure unwounded Australians out from nearby shell holes to avoid an otherwise deadly encounter. A 26th Battalion soldier reported hearing a voice call out through the fog: 'You can't get through that way. Come over here.' The man walked towards the voice, whereupon he was covered by German rifles and captured.[33] Dozens of wounded lay close to the uncut wire where they were found by German medical orderlies who administered first aid before carrying them to a nearby dressing station. One man mindful of the difficulties in negotiating the politics of surrender was relieved to find his captors willing to assist. 'I could not understand them, but by their gestures and their general being I was reassured they meant me no harm.'[34]

After further fighting, men of the 2nd Division captured the OG Lines on 4 August, making Mouquet Farm, a kilometre north, the next operational priority. Over the next four weeks, the 1st, 2nd and 4th Australian Divisions made nine separate attacks in the approaches towards Mouquet Farm. Situated on a slight rise overlooking Pozières, Mouquet Farm and its network of underground cellars and tunnels was a veritable stronghold that barred the southern approach to Thiepval. When the autumn rain came and turned an area churned by weeks of shellfire into a morass, Mouquet Farm represented some of the worst fighting on the Somme.

The AIF lost 200 men as prisoners of war in the fighting for Mouquet Farm, most falling victim to the confusing nature of the terrain and the line constantly changing between Australian and German hands. Since most of the fighting occurred at night amid a maze of trenches in a shell-torn landscape devoid of any discernible geographic feature, it was not uncommon for Australian and German troops to stumble mistakenly into positions held by the other. On 9 August, a 15th Battalion corporal escorting German prisoners through the Australian trenches was challenged by a sentry in an area thought to be occupied by his brigade: 'I complied and entered the trench with the prisoners. To my disgust I found the trench was occupied by Germans and thus I in turn became a prisoner.'[35] Attacking troops hit by shrapnel or machine-gun fire sought refuge in shell holes only to discover that the trenches around them had changed hands during the night.[36] Sometimes, attacking units that succeeded in pressing deep into German lines became lost and discovered at dawn that they had no way of returning. In an attack near Mouquet Farm on 21 August, a 10th Battalion Lewis gunner spent the night 30 metres from a company of German troops without the ammunition to engage them: 'We had Sgt White with us and he advised us that all we could do under the circumstances was surrender. We were cut off and surrounded by the enemy ... of the 16 of us, five were wounded.'[37]

Australian troops reached Mouquet Farm on 29 August when a depleted company of the 16th Battalion fought their way into the underground cellars and engaged the Germans in a grenade duel before being driven out. Most were captured when German troops overran their positions and were nursing grenade fragmentation wounds.[38] The result was much the same for men of the 13th Brigade who succeeded in reaching Mouquet Farm on 3 September in what was I Anzac Corps' last major attack before being withdrawn from the Somme. Like the 16th Battalion, men of the 51st Battalion fought their way into the underground cellars and killed or captured its German occupants. The 52nd Battalion alongside them failed to hold their position, leaving the 51st Battalion's flank exposed. This was precisely the situation faced by Australians at Fromelles several weeks earlier. Waiting for the Australians to spend their ammunition in defence of their gains, German troops rolled up their flanks and forced them to surrender. 'We could not see the enemy though he was pasting us with bombs. We had no bombs with which to reply ... I managed to wriggle into one of the shell holes, and then someone hoisted a white flag. At that point, we all became prisoners of war.'[39]

The Canadians relieved I Anzac Corps on 3 September, bringing an end for the AIF to what had been a costly and bloody contribution to the Battle of the Somme. Bitter fighting at Fromelles, Pozières and Mouquet Farm had cost the AIF 28 000 dead, wounded and missing, of which 950 had fallen into German hands.[40] As a result of the Battle of the Somme, the German Army built a new defensive system behind the Somme battlefront. Known to the British as the Hindenburg Line (and the Germans as *Die Siegfriedstellung*), this elaborate fortification strengthened existing German positions in France while solving a critical manpower shortage following the 1916 battles. The Hindenburg Line ran between Arras and Soissons via St Quentin and intersected a salient the Allies had driven into German-occupied territory during the Somme fighting. Relinquishing this territory shortened the front by about 50 kilometres and released up to thirteen divisions to be used elsewhere. German commanders expected the British and French to resume their offensives early in the New Year and withdrew troops to their new positions in February 1917.

Australian operations on the Western Front resumed in February 1917 when German troops on the Somme withdrew to the Hindenburg Line. From their winter positions near the villages of Flers and Gueudecourt, Australian troops from I and II Anzac Corps advanced through Bapaume and were within sight of the northern portion of the Hindenburg Line by April. The AIF lost around 200 men as prisoners during this brief phase of mobile warfare, clashing with German rear-guards in fortified villages that remained behind to delay a rapid advance.[41] Eighty-five Australians were captured on 2 April 1917 when men of the 50th Battalion passed through the village of Noreuil without clearing German troops behind them.[42] One of the battalion's assaulting companies busily engaging Germans to their front was surprised to take fire from its rear. The South Australians were caught in the cross-fire, and went to ground until their positions were overrun. As two officers later described, 'We ran out of ammunition … we could not repel the enemy counter-attack. They had practically surrounded our position and our communication with the rear was cut off. We were considerably split up and divided into small parties and eventually taken prisoner.'[43]

German troops withdrew from Noreuil the following morning, allowing I Anzac Corps to advance to positions within sight of the Hindenburg Line between the villages of Bullecourt and Riencourt. Significant gains had been made elsewhere as part of a wider British offensive at Arras, most notably the Canadian capture of Vimy Ridge on 9 April. It was thought that an attack on the Hindenburg Line at Bullecourt would achieve a further breakthrough in an area where the Germans least expected it. Two divisions, the British 62nd Division and 4th Australian Division, were to attack between Bullecourt and Riencourt and eject the Germans from their positions. Instead of the artillery bombarding the Hindenburg Line – a sure sign to the Germans that an attack was coming – the infantry would assault behind twelve tanks. Still considered a new weapon, the tanks were to crush the barbed wire and deal with nearby strongpoints. Those employed at Bullecourt, however, were poorly armed and armoured and were plagued with mechanical problems. They failed to reach the rendezvous and delayed the attack for twenty-four hours. This news did not reach the British 62nd Division whose men assaulted Bullecourt as planned, completely unsupported. This so-called 'dummy stunt' cost the British around 160 casualties and alerted the Germans that a major attack was coming.[44]

The 'dinkum stunt' occurred the following day, 11 April, with Australians from the 4th and 12th Brigades attacking the Hindenburg Line in the snow before dawn. Just two of the twelve tanks reached the German wire before they were destroyed. The rest were knocked out of action, suffered mechanical failure or encountered obstacles in No Man's Land they could not overcome. Left unsupported, the infantry advanced through a torrent of artillery and machine-gun fire sweeping the kilometre of open ground and fought their way into the German trenches. German troops withdrew and prepared their counter-attack. After sunrise, any attempt to resupply the Australians fighting in the Hindenburg Line would take place in full view of German machine-gun crews and artillery observers directing fire on No Man's Land. As Charles Bean wrote, it was as if 'the German machine-gunners had with impunity closed a gate behind the Australian infantry, and forced it to withstand attack until its supplies ran out'.[45]

Figure 1.5 Prisoners from the 4th Australian Division being led through the rear-area village of Villers-lès-Cagnicourt, several hours after their capture at Bullecourt on 11 April 1917. (Photo courtesy of Peter Barton)

While the 4th and 12th Brigades held their positions, German troops worked their way around their flanks and rolled up their positions with grenades. A 14th Battalion sergeant described 'a hail of stick bombs' showering his company's isolated position before 'hundreds upon hundreds of the enemy ... popped up on all sides, like rabbits from burrows'.[46] Many Australians who tried to withdraw fell victim to machine-gun and artillery fire, but a large number remained in the German trenches where they were captured. Surprised to have survived a close-quarters encounter with German troops, a 14th Battalion sergeant had a 'hazy recollection' of the moment he became a prisoner of war. 'A fair young German ... advanced menacingly towards me, swinging a stick bomb by the handle, shouting *Los! Los! Los!* by which I understood that I'd better watch my step and go quietly.'[47] Bullecourt cost the AIF more than 3000 casualties, of which 1170 were taken prisoner – the largest number of Australians captured in a single engagement during the First World War.[48] These losses affected Australian confidence in British command and their willingness to rely on the help of tanks in future operations. But Bullecourt also reflected the strength of the German Army's defensive network and its effectiveness in recapturing lost ground.

Four days later, on 15 April 1917, the Germans attacked Australian positions at Lagnicourt. Four German divisions assailed the 1st Australian Division's thin defensive screen between Lagnicourt and the Canal du Nord, which sought to disrupt British operations in the Bullecourt area. German pioneers, *Sturmtruppen* ('storm troops'), flamethrower teams and mobile field guns led assaulting waves of regular line infantry who penetrated deep into Australian lines and took 320 men prisoner.[49] They overran Australian outposts, killing and capturing the occupants and penetrating far enough to overrun battery positions of the 2nd Field Artillery Brigade. An 11th Battalion officer defended his isolated position for four hours until his men ran out of ammunition. 'We could not offer any resistance to the enemy whose number I estimated at 300 men. I therefore decided my only course was to surrender.'[50] Others had no such choice. A wounded artilleryman described a 'stupid feeling' of doubt and uncertainty after regaining consciousness in German hands: 'At first there was a feeling of numbness, of stupor, then [a] feeling that everything is over and all ambitions and hopes were snapped to pieces in a moment. A soldier sometimes thinks of being killed or wounded, but never of being captured ... which he had always looked upon as being worse than death.'[51]

Those in Lagnicourt village were caught completely by surprise. One man was told that the figures on the skyline were Australian troops attacking the German positions. It was not until they were upon him that he realised they were Germans. 'The nearest Fritz noticed me, and instantly smiled, seeing that I was unarmed – an easy capture ... Neither of us spoke. I stepped out [from a cellar] and they were all around me like bees.'[52]

Lagnicourt marked a turning point in the capture of Australians on the Western Front because relatively few became prisoners in the remaining eighteen months of the war. By April 1917, more than 75 per cent of all Australians who would eventually be captured were already in captivity (see figure 1.2).[53] Australian troops continued to be raided by the Germans, to stumble into the German trenches by mistake, to be picked up wounded by German stretcher-bearers or to be caught where they had no alternative but to surrender, but never after Lagnicourt in such numbers. After continued fighting in the Bullecourt sector throughout May (where the AIF lost a further forty-three men as prisoners), the focus of British operations shifted north into Belgium, beginning with the fighting at Messines between 6 and 14 June (losing fourteen men as prisoners).[54] At Nieuport on the Belgian coast, forty-two men of the 2nd Australian Tunnelling Company were forced underground when German troops launched a spoiling attack on the British positions on 10 July 1917.

> The enemy threw bombs into the sap head and forced us below into the tunnel. We barricaded the tunnel up with sand bags and held out until 4.30 next morning . . . Some of the men fainted from lack of pure air. The men came to me and asked if something could not be done. I pointed out that our only alternative was to surrender. They replied: 'Anything is better than this.' I left the men and went to the sap head mouth. The Germans were there waiting.[55]

The Australians participated in a series of actions that collectively formed part of the third Battle of Ypres. In eight weeks between September and October 1917, the AIF lost just 150 men as prisoners amid 38 000 other battle casualties.[56] It incurred its heaviest losses of the war in October 1917 when 6800 Australian soldiers were killed or died of wounds.[57] The few Australians lost as prisoners during the third Ypres campaign were captured when they advanced too far forward without the means to hold their tenuous positions against counter-attacks. Just twenty-five men of the 5th Division were captured at Polygon Wood on 26 September when troops of the 8th and 15th Brigades took their objectives without support from the British alongside them, allowing German troops to surround the positions of the most advanced platoons and overrun them.[58]

Two weeks later, on 12 October, a hundred men of the 12th Brigade were captured in the costly and unsuccessful assault on Passchendaele village. The only formation in the attack to take its objectives, the 12th

Brigade held ground until the following morning when they were sub-jected to German counter-attack. One man from the 47th Battalion described how 'the enemy launched his attack on our right front ... [and] covered his attack with an intense barrage of machine-gun fire and eventually swarmed over our position, outnumbering us in the proportion of about 15 to 1'.[59] Four regimental stretcher-bearers made their way up the line after the position had been overrun.

> As we approached the trench a voice called to us in English, 'Come over here; we want you here.' We naturally thought it was one of our own officers, and got into the trench as directed. We then found that we were being covered by a German officer with his revolver, and two or three German soldiers were approaching us with fixed bayonets, and our party had to surrender.[60]

While these actions represented instances when Australian troops could not hold their gains, the battles the AIF fought throughout September and October 1917 were largely successful in breaching the German defences. By this stage of the war, the infantry had more firepower at its disposal and were sufficiently trained and experienced to use it effectively against counter-attacks. Every brigade had batteries of Stokes mortars and companies of Vickers machine-guns that could be brought forward when needed; platoons comprised specialist sections of Lewis gunners, bombers and rifle grenadiers that could overcome and capture German strongpoints and fend off developing counter-attacks.[61]

The fighting at Third Ypres was characterised by massive amounts of artillery firepower employed in concentration on a limited front to 'bite' a section of the German line and allow the infantry to capture it before another bite was taken. The dominance of artillery supporting Australian troops in their bite-and-hold advance towards Passchendaele village diminished the likelihood of German troops being able to outflank and overrun positions occupied by isolated infantrymen. As Charles Bean wrote of the attack at Menin Road on 20 September 1917: 'The advancing barrage won the ground; the infantry merely occupied it, pouncing on any points where resistance survived. Whereas the artillery was generally spoken of as supporting the infantry, in this battle the infantry were little more than a necessary adjunct to the artillery effort.'[62]

Increasing air support was characteristic of the fighting around this time. With the AFC having started operations on the Western Front in September 1917, Australian pilots from the scout squadrons, No. 2 and No. 4 Squadrons AFC, flew patrols deep into German territory, where they faced the daily reality of being shot down on the wrong side of No Man's Land. Parachutes had been invented before the war, but the Air Board and Royal Flying Corps felt pilots would fight less aggressively if they were tempted to abandon their aircraft at the first sign of trouble.[63] Casualties across all front-line RFC squadrons were exceptionally high when airmen possessed no means of escaping a burning aircraft. Within a year of arriving on the Western Front, forty-four AFC scout pilots had been killed.[64] But not all aircraft hit by German fire burst into flames or disintegrated in the air. Fighting the air war without parachutes, an additional twenty-one Australian airmen were forced from the sky and crash-landed their stricken machines in German-occupied territory, where they were captured.

The first two AFC battle casualties in France were typical of the way most Australian airmen became prisoners of war, although others were brought down by German ground fire during ground-attack sorties, and one Australian airman became lost and landed at a German airfield by mistake.[65] A number of Australian pilots were sent to RFC squadrons for experience and flew operations in the lead-up to the third Battle of Ypres. Lieutenant Victor Norvill, attached to No. 29 Squadron RFC, was shot through the shoulder when German scouts jumped his patrol of Nieuport 23s over Douai on 29 June 1917. With Norvill unconscious, his aircraft plummeted from 11 000 feet after a bullet severed his fuel line. He regained consciousness in time to crash-land upside down, over a shell hole, four miles behind German lines: 'On releasing the safety belt I fell to the bottom of the shell hole ... About 30 seconds later 10 Germans with an NCO came and carried me back into a trench.'[66] Also attached to No. 29 Squadron RFC, Lieutenant Arthur Wearne's SPAD VII was 'shot through the controls and engines' by German scouts during a patrol near Ypres on 26 July 1917. 'I was forced to land, or rather I crashed to earth.' Wounded in the engagement, Wearne lost consciousness and could not report how he landed or was captured.[67]

The AIF was relieved from the fighting near Passchendaele in November 1917, and its five divisions spent the following winter rotating through the relatively quiet Hollebeke–Messines sector south of Ypres. I and II Anzac Corps were restructured and combined under the newly formed Australian Corps. The AIF did not suffer the same morale problem here as it had at Flers and Gueudecourt the previous year, although some Australians were captured when German troops raided isolated listening posts in No Man's Land, or when salvage patrols strayed too close to enemy trenches.[68] But by January 1918, the AIF was facing a critical manpower shortage primarily caused by casualties the previous year. This coincided with the failure of the second conscription plebiscite and fewer volunteers enlisting in Australia. Adding to this, five hundred Australians were captured in the final year of the war. If surrendering soldiers were symptomatic of an army suffering fatigue and low morale, we would perhaps expect this figure to be higher – particularly when desertion rates in the AIF were at their highest.[69]

Most Australians captured in 1918 were lost as a consequence of the fighting when, in March 1918, German troops launched a major offensive that succeeded in achieving a long sought-after breakthrough. On 21 March 1918, German guns unleashed the most concentrated artillery bombardment employed on the Western Front. German assault troops broke through the British Fourth and Fifth Army fronts on the Somme, recaptured Bapaume, Péronne and the 1916 Somme battlefields, and threatened the important logistical and communications hub of Amiens. British troops were forced to withdraw, suffering 178 000 casualties in the fighting throughout March and April 1918, which included 75 000 lost as prisoners.[70]

The Australian Corps was still in the Hollebeke–Messines sector when the German onslaught began. Brigades from the 3rd and 4th Divisions were rushed south with other British formations to defend Amiens and shore up the British Third Army's southern flank. The depleted 12th and 13th Brigades were sent to Dernancourt, where they formed a thin defensive screen along a railway embankment overlooking the village. Before dawn on 5 April 1918, German assault troops used the cover of a thick fog to exploit a gap between the two brigades and captured a tactically important machine-gun post in a chalk quarry on the hill without firing a shot. Two Australian machine-gunners described how German troops 'surrounded the chalk pit and had full command of the only entrance to it. We surrendered. There was no alternative.'[71] Having disabled the key to the Australian defences at Dernancourt, the weight of three German infantry divisions assailed the railway embankment in the heaviest attack the AIF encountered on the Western Front. A 45th Battalion private reported, 'We were completely surrounded by the enemy. Further fruitless endeavours were then made to fight our way out, but owing to being hopelessly outnumbered we were obliged to surrender.'[72] In addition to the men captured in the quarry, 400 men of the 12th and 13th Brigades were captured by the time this short and violent engagement ended. Later that day, further to the south at Hangard Wood near

Villers-Bretonneux, a further fifty Australians were led away to the German rear as prisoners of war.[73]

The German offensive ended the stalemate of trench warfare on the Western Front, but the breakthrough was not decisive. Despite initial gains, the Germans suffered enormous casualties against British troops who proved much more resilient than most popular accounts suggest. Inadequate logistical support, a lack of mobility and an insistence of senior German commanders to splinter attacking forces and shift objectives denied the German offensive any chance of success. As Charles Bean wrote in the official history, '[T]he great German offensive was nowhere literally brought to a stop by Australian troops. On practically the whole front taken up by them the stoppage had already occurred.'[74]

Australian troops fought a highly successful action at Villers-Bretonneux on 24–25 April 1918, about 20 kilometres from Amiens, with smaller attacks and raids occurring at Morlancourt in an effort to exploit gaps that developed in the German front lines. In one such attack, on 8 May 1918, two platoons of the 33rd Battalion became lost and inadvertently strayed beyond the German front-line positions and into the supply and communications area. 'We took shelter in a wood close to several German batteries of artillery. When daylight came, Capt McMinn said it was impossible to get back to our own lines. He walked over to a German battery and reported to the German Officer in charge. 44 Australians were captured. We were unwounded.'[75]

In the weeks that followed, the Australian Corps stabilised the front line south of the Somme River and used new offensive tactics at le Hamel on 4 July 1918, involving close coordination between infantry, artillery, tanks and aircraft that further limited the prospect of soldiers becoming prisoners of war. This stood the Allied armies in good stead for their own counter-offensive, which began with the Battle of Amiens on 8 August 1918 and continued throughout September and October. With Australian troops succeeding in breaking through German lines near Villers-Bretonneux, the assaulting waves of Australian and Canadian infantry captured more than 12 kilometres of ground on the offensive's first day. Over the following weeks, the AIF took key German positions at Mont St Quentin, Péronne and Bellenglise and pushed them to their last line of defence on the Western Front, in what was a sure sign that the Germans were on the verge of defeat.

A hundred Australians were lost as prisoners in this final stage of fighting, largely owing to a rapid advance over a vast area and soldiers inadvertently stumbling into German positions which they believed had been captured. At Bellicourt on 29 September 1918, a private from the 58th Battalion volunteered to guide British tanks to their rendezvous point: 'The tank caught on fire ... The crew made off in different directions. I, with the tank officer and an English private, got into a shell hole where we remained until dark. Then I tried to make my way back to our own lines but strayed into a German post where I was captured.'[76] Hours later, a Lewis gun section went to ground in a shell hole in front of a German strongpoint. 'When daylight came we discovered that we were surrounded by enemy troops ... There were about six of us left in the post and all wounded except one, when we surrendered by order of Lieut. Cox.'[77] Some Australian prisoners had the fortune of being rescued as the offensive swept over positions where their captors were themselves taken prisoner, but most were moved to the German rear where they remained until the Armistice.[78]

Australians continued to be lost as prisoners of war right up to their last engagements in France. After breaking through the Hindenburg Line, the 6th Brigade's attack at Montbrehain on 5 October 1918 represented an attempt to breach the final elaborate system of German defences known as the Beaurevoir Line. Resistance was fierce, and the Australians suffered heavy casualties in what turned out to be their last infantry action before the Armistice. Within three hours, troops from the 21st and 24th Battalions and the 2nd Pioneer Battalion took their objectives, but were heavily shelled and forced to repel counter-attacks from several directions. Second Lieutenant John Peacock of the 2nd Pioneer Battalion was wounded in the thigh and unable to move, and was the only man among 430 casualties to be taken prisoner.[79] 'Lieut. Robinson said he would send the stretcher-bearers for me but before he could do so the Boche came over and picked me up', he reported.[80] On 29 October 1918, Lieutenant Melville Kilsby of No. 4 Squadron AFC crash-landed his damaged Sopwith Snipe near a German aerodrome at Roubaix and had the distinction of being the last Australian to be captured in the fighting on the Western Front.[81]

The experience of the AIF in France and Belgium showed that soldiers were sometimes captured when their enemy proved tactically superior. Their ability to remain fighting also depended on the dynamics of combat, which played a far greater role on the Western Front than has previously been ascribed. The German defensive doctrine of drawing in an attacking force and rolling up their flanks with grenades was effective in capturing thousands of Australian soldiers, who possessed little means to resist after expending their ammunition. Many were captured in costly and unsuccessful actions like Fromelles, Bullecourt and Dernancourt, where infantry tactics employed by the German Army forced them to consider surrender when the seemingly futile gesture of fighting meant certain death. Hundreds had no such choice, and were shocked to have survived a close-quarters encounter with German soldiers who had previously tried to kill them.

Whether they surrendered or were captured in compromising circumstances, Australian troops taken prisoner on the Western Front had otherwise survived the ordeal of trench warfare. They were ignominiously stripped of their weapons and equipment at rifle point; they were shepherded to the German rear as prisoners of war, and began a battle radically different from the one from which they had just emerged.

CHAPTER 2

THE RECIPROCITY
PRINCIPLE

RESPECTING AND ABROGATING
WARTIME AGREEMENTS

Not all captured Australians survived the tumult of battle. After the 7th Brigade's failed attack on the Windmill at Pozières on 28 July 1916, a German officer approached an Australian Lewis gunner nursing a bullet wound to his leg. 'You are the Machine Gunner?' asked the officer. 'Yes, sir,' the man replied. Without hesitation, the officer drew his automatic pistol and shot the man through the heart and the head, killing him instantly. 'That's the way to deal with English swine.'[1]

Capture did not always guarantee survival. By laying down their weapons and raising their hands, surrendering soldiers were forced into a state of vulnerability that implored mercy from the enemy who had previously tried to kill them. All prisoners encountered this awkward and sometimes violent transition from combatant to captive, and some were killed out of spite, for revenge or in the heat of the moment.[2] It is statistically impossible to establish how often German soldiers killed surrendering Allied soldiers, but knowing that 182 000 British and dominion soldiers survived the extremely dangerous and often violent encounter suggests that the German Army generally honoured the surrender of Australian soldiers.[3] Deliberately killing prisoners was counter-productive to the prosecution of the war, since soldiers who believed they were going to be killed after falling into the hands of the enemy were generally less likely to surrender.[4]

Killing prisoners prolonged the fighting and increased the likelihood of reciprocal killings. Just as men of the 1st Australian Division gave no quarter at Pozières on 23 July 1916, German troops killed surrendering

Australians in the fighting for the OG Lines several days later.[5] The morning after the 2nd Australian Division's costly and unsuccessful attack on the Windmill on 28 July, survivors from the 6th Brigade emerged from shell holes and were captured. 'We saw [German troops] beckon Fox and his mate to come over to them. They stood up to surrender ... then they were shot down by rifle fire. Fox stood up again & was shot down a second time.'[6] At Mouquet Farm, a German officer emptied the magazine of his automatic pistol into a group of unarmed Australian prisoners from the 14th Battalion. Four were killed, while a fifth stopped a bullet with his pocket Bible. Left for dead, the man lay among the bodies of his platoon mates until nightfall, whereupon he made his way back to Australian lines.[7]

The reciprocal killing of prisoners reflected the violence of the Western Front but, as Alan Kramer writes, there is no effective way of measuring how widespread it was. On the basis of available evidence, which is largely anecdotal, Kramer maintains that the killing of prisoners was opportunistic, sporadic and usually perpetrated by impulsive individuals rather than units fulfilling orders from a higher authority.[8] While this study is concerned with Australian troops who survived capture, the killing of prisoners establishes that there was no guarantee that those who fell into enemy hands would survive or always be treated humanely. Captivity might have spared Australian troops the horror of trench warfare, but prisoners were still exposed to violence from their captors.

Captured Australians were beaten, starved and deliberately mistreated, and while this had a profound impact on their mental and physical state, their hardships were exacerbated by Germany's inability to adhere properly to pre-war agreements that sought to guarantee the humane treatment of captured men. That said, there were many instances when German soldiers showed compassion and reassurance to captured Australians by offering prisoners food and cigarettes. A wounded private of the 5th Battalion captured in a German raid near Bapaume in March 1917 was surprised by his captor, who 'went to a lot of trouble in bandaging my wounds, and ... succeeded in making me feel quite comfortable' before carrying him to a dressing station.[9] One man captured at Lagnicourt told of a German soldier who offered him his own overcoat, thinking he was cold.[10]

The foundation for a code of conduct on the fair treatment of prisoners was established in the 1899 and 1907 Hague conventions and the 1906 Geneva Convention. The signatories included Britain, France and Germany, who all agreed to treat prisoners humanely and keep them in areas away from combat areas. Prisoners were to be granted the freedom of religious worship and were to be respected according to their age and rank. Once they were moved to a prison camp, officers were not obliged to work, NCOs could work only in a supervisory capacity and other ranks could work only if the task required was not directly related to the captor's war effort. The agreements also guaranteed that prisoners would be paid a wage at the same rate as their equivalent rank in the captor's military forces, and those who could be legally used as a labour force had to work the same hours. The Hague Convention of 1907 ensured that prisoners received the same rations as their captors, and could write home, receive mail and have access to welfare assistance from international aid agencies. Britain, France and Germany also signed the 1906 Geneva Convention, which ensured that sick and wounded prisoners of war would receive proper medical treatment.

Figure 2.1 A long file of Australian prisoners of war in the streets of Harbourdin near Lille, just hours after their capture at Fromelles on 20 July 1916. (Photo courtesy of Brett Butterworth)

These agreements were infinitely better than previous laws, but they contained many loopholes, omissions and clauses open to different interpretations. The most significant issue was how to police the wartime agreements in areas immediately behind the front line. Neutral representatives from the United States, Spain, Switzerland and Holland took on the role of 'protecting power' and carried out a regulated system of bilateral prison camp inspections to monitor the treatment of prisoners held in camps across Britain and Germany.[11] Inspection teams published reports to exert moral pressure on opposing governments to improve conditions in poorly run and administered camps. But neutral representatives were not permitted to inspect transit camps and other places where prisoners of war were held within the forward area. This included the front-line areas on both sides of the Western Front, which one inspector described as 'an impenetrable screen' behind which prisoners could be held for an indeterminate length of time before being transported to a prison camp that could be inspected.[12]

The limitations to the existing agreements allowed captors on both sides to exploit the labour of prisoners to help sustain their respective war efforts. Since the humane treatment of prisoners could not always be guaranteed, a principle of reciprocity was found to be an effective alternative and more efficient way for the belligerents to police the Hague and Geneva conventions. If British and French prisoners were treated humanely, German prisoners would be well treated in return. But if German prisoners were treated poorly, British and French prisoners could be – and were – subjected to violent reprisals until conditions for German prisoners improved, and vice versa. Surviving capture was therefore based on a principle of reciprocity and the knowledge that it was better to accept the surrender of Australian troops than risk the lives of German soldiers who would be forced to surrender to British troops in future engagements. It was therefore in Britain's and Germany's best interests to treat prisoners humanely or risk reprisals. By the time the first Australians were captured in France, there were 13 800 Germans in British captivity and 28 500 British in German camps.[13]

How Australian prisoners fared in German captivity was also dependent on Germany's ability to adhere to the pre-war international agreements. As Gerard Davies observed, taking prisoners came with long-term economic consequences that often had a profound impact on a captor's wartime resources.[14] It is clear that Germany was struggling to maintain the pre-war agreements by the time the first Australian soldiers were captured in France in May 1916. Having prepared for a short war of mobility, Germany had given very little consideration to the resources for accommodating, feeding and caring for large numbers of captured men from a war being fought on multiple fronts. In the opening engagements of the war, the German Army's successes resulted in the capture of more than 285 000 Allied prisoners who had been transported to the camps by October 1914. That winter, French, Russian and British prisoners were detained in a small number of overcrowded camps with insufficient food and medical supplies. One early German policy was to treat all prisoner nationalities equally, so that no claim could be made that one group received better treatment than another.[15] This proved disastrous at Wittenberg on the Elbe River, where 19 000 Russian, French and British prisoners were imprisoned in an overcrowded camp that suffered from typhus and claimed the lives of more than 130 prisoners. Fearing infection, the German authorities abandoned the camp and left its administration to six British doctors who struggled to fight the epidemic for a further eight months.[16] By March 1915, the number of Allied prisoners in Germany had swelled to 650 000, and already Germany was failing to treat Allied prisoners humanely in accordance with the pre-war agreements.[17]

Events at Wittenberg underlined a number of problems with the German prison system that had largely been resolved before the first Australian prisoners arrived in Germany. Perhaps the most significant was the even distribution of prisoners across twenty-five military districts so that the burden of their care was shared across the country. This improved conditions in such places as Wittenberg, but also ensured that the labour of 1.6 million other ranks prisoners in German captivity by August 1916 could be employed wherever they were needed.[18]

The domestic needs of civilians had also suffered from the economic oversight of a long and protracted war, leading to a critical food shortage as soon as the Royal Navy started blockading German ports. A Raw Materials Department was established in Berlin to relieve this crisis and to monitor the use of prisoner-of-war labour to help support Germany's domestic needs. By 1916, more than a million Allied prisoners were working to support the German economy, with 750 000 employed in the agricultural sector and 330 000 in mining, textiles, iron and steel.[19] Despite efforts to improve conditions, the food crisis in Germany gradually worsened as longer the war continued. Bread rationing was introduced in 1915, and meat was soon as scarce as flour and potatoes. Conditions worsened during the infamous 'turnip winter' of 1916–17 (Der Steckrübenwinter) when potato crops needed to replace essential foodstuffs failed during one of the worst winters on record – exacerbated by the Royal Navy's blockade of imported fertilisers from overseas markets. All social classes in Germany went hungry and experienced low morale that winter as all subsisted on strict food rationing and vegetables usually reserved to feed cattle.[20]

Germany was able to evade some of the maintenance costs of feeding Allied prisoners by allowing British, French and Belgian humanitarian aid agencies to send consignments of food and clothing parcels, although this depended on willing support from the prisoners' home governments. As British prisoners of war, Australians fared better than the 1.6 million Italian, Russian and Romanian prisoners in Germany by the end of 1918 (comprising 64 per cent of Allied prisoners in German captivity) who did not benefit from parcels and were forced to live on whatever provisions the Germans could give them.[21] The home governments of these prisoners saw deteriorating conditions as a deterrent against desertion within their own armies, and sending parcels to Germany as potentially assisting the enemy's war effort.[22]

Although their mortality rate was slightly higher than other British prisoners, Australians generally fared as well as all other *Engländer* in the German camps as they waited for Red Cross parcels to arrive. The rations for prisoners arriving in Germany in mid-1916 largely consisted of watery soup, coffee made from roasted acorn and barley, and substitute war bread that included sawdust and other ersatz foodstuffs. Other ranks at the processing and distribution camp at Dülmen in Westphalia ate turnip soup 'and a sort of broth made out of bone dust which the men called "Sandstorm Soup"'.[23] Convalescent officers at Parchim in Mecklenburg subsisted on a diet that largely comprised bread made from sawdust, artificial honey, cabbage stew, turnips and potatoes. All being well, they received an uncooked herring once a week.[24]

It was against this backdrop of severe economic hardship that Australian prisoners were treated and mistreated by their German captors. Prisoners were not always treated kindly and were often seen as objects of curiosity. They were 'ratted' for souvenirs and sometimes photographed as a visual reminder of a victory over the enemy. There was nothing explicit in the wartime agreements that prohibited 'ratting', but surrendering a watch or wallet to an armed German soldier was often a small price to pay for trying to appear recognisably human.[25] Captain William Cull of the 22nd Battalion lay wounded and bleeding at the bottom of a shell hole near Bapaume in February 1917 and was captured by a German stretcher-bearer who was more preoccupied with the whereabouts of his watch than his wounds. 'It was on my wrist, and, with the contents of my pockets, soon disappeared. My Sam Browne belt, which he next examined, had little interest for him, and he tossed it out onto No Man's Land.'[26] German soldiers filched wallets, watches, colour patches and regimental titles from prisoners of war. A man captured at Mouquet Farm was stripped of his Queen's and King's South Africa ribbons for service in the Boer War, while at Bullecourt an Australian prisoner of war was robbed of photos, letters, fountain pen – even his false teeth.[27]

The experiences of wounded prisoners offer an insight into how some of the most vulnerable prisoners of war on the Western Front fared in the hours after their capture. Their treatment is of considerable interest to this study, because 200 of the 327 Australians who died in or as a result of German captivity succumbed to wounds received in action.[28] The effectiveness of German medical facilities is significant because an analysis of causes of death among Australian prisoners of war shows that 145 died immediately behind the German front line from wounds received in action. Medical treatment from the Germans did not guarantee survival, and might explain the higher mortality rate among Australians relative to all other British prisoners of war groups: German troops at Fromelles and Bullecourt might have been more willing to recover wounded Australians who ultimately died in German dressing stations as prisoners of war. Although the mortality varies among British and dominion prisoners of war in German captivity, the overall mortality of captured Australians would have undoubtedly been higher if German forces deliberately neglected wounded prisoners of war. As such, Fromelles is an excellent case study on how well some groups of wounded Australians fared in the hands of the Germans. Of the 470 Australians captured at Fromelles on 20 July 1916, German records show that 180 of them required urgent medical assistance.[29]

A survey of the nature of wounds shows that more than half of the wounded captured that morning were suffering shrapnel or grenade fragmentation wounds to the upper and lower limbs. The severity of wounds differed among casualties, but Private William Barry's experiences typified the experiences of many wounded Australian prisoners. After crossing No Man's Land, Barry was knocked unconscious by a high-explosive shell and woke sometime later in the presence of German soldiers. A German officer 'with a pair of scissors ... cut the legs of my strides & showed a gaping wound in the right knee & another in the calf of the right leg. He bandaged up [my] injuries using my field dressing & then his own.' Barry asked to see a doctor, but the German officer refused: 'No. We have too many of our own wounded to look after.' Barry was then rendered unconscious with 'three of the worst beltings that . . . was possible to give a man' and was carried further to the rear. He woke three hours later in a dugout with German medical orderlies inspecting his dressing and treating him for shock. He was given

a piece of their black bread (& horrid tasting stuff it is) with a piece of bully beef & a drink of black coffee. [One] German asked if I felt cold ... & brought me a German overcoat wet with blood, but that didn't matter. He also gave me a tin of Bully beef & more bread and left me propped up against a heap of earth.[30]

Figure 2.2 Captured Australians at a collecting station near Fromelles, 20 July 1916. Identified are Pte Andreas Voitkun, 32nd Battalion (sitting, left) and LCpl Arnold Mason, 14th Field Company Engineers (centre). At the time, Mason had a diary hidden in his helmet lining. That day he wrote: 'I managed to get across No Man's Land but . . . had the bad luck to get a piece of shell in the left cheek . . . At the time I thought that half my face had been blown off.' (AWM A01551; diary entry 20.7.16, PR01877)

The main purpose of the German Field Medical Service was to treat German casualties, but in accord with the 1906 Geneva Convention, prisoners of war were given the same medical treatment in a medical system that one wounded Australian described as 'much the same as our own'.[31] Able-bodied men were sometimes made to collect the wounded from No Man's Land, but this task was also carried out by German regimental stretcher-bearers and orderlies of the German field ambulance. These medical personnel applied tourniquets, splints and field dressings and carried wounded prisoners to either a dressing station or a wagon rendezvous point where casualties were triaged and given food and a hot drink to lessen the prospect of wound shock.[32] Casualties were then transported by stretcher and ambulance wagon to a main dressing station, where they were inspected by a German medical officer who dressed open wounds, examined broken bones, stopped haemorrhaging vessels, plugged sucking chest wounds, removed shattered limbs, gave injections against tetanus and administered morphine. Once stable, casualties were moved further rearwards, based on information written on a diagnosis card pinned to the casualty's tunic. The walking wounded were sent to a collecting station where they joined able-bodied prisoners, while the more serious cases went to field hospitals for surgery.[33]

The German casualty evacuation system was not always able to manage the influx of casualties, both German and Allied. Bottlenecking was as much a problem in German aid posts and dressing stations as it was in Australian ones following major actions like Fromelles, with German casualties usually given priority over the needs of prisoners of war.[34] Depending on the intensity of the action and the number of units involved, it could take days before wounded prisoners received proper medical attention. German aid posts at Pozières, for example, became so congested with casualties that Australian stretcher-bearers were allowed to collect wounded prisoners from the German parapet.[35] Not all captured men fared so well, as some of the badly wounded were shot following an unsuccessful attack by the 23rd Battalion on the village of Velu near Bapaume on 20 March 1917.[36] At Bullecourt, there came a point when German troops stopped collecting wounded Australians altogether. A 15th Battalion man reported burying Australian dead in shell holes 'twenty and thirty in each ... After this was done, we had to remove our wounded who had been left in the barbed wire. Those who had leg wounds and could not walk were shot [by German medical orderlies] with a revolver through the head.'[37] Shooting the wounded was a clear violation of international law that reinforced the wartime stereotype of German Hun brutality. But it clearly demonstrates that the unexpected capture of large numbers of prisoners of war placed an enormous strain on armies and both their ability and their willingness to treat them humanely.[38]

It took William Barry three days to make the 60-kilometre journey from Fromelles to Valenciennes, where he was eventually admitted to a field hospital for surgery. Most of this time was spent on a rail platform at Lille, where German medical orderlies were too busy with their own wounded to tend to the needs of prisoners of war. The first night was the worst: 'That night I suffered great pain & thirst & of course had very little sleep. The following day after breakfast I thought of the tin of bully beef I still had & I had just started to open it when the German sentry saw me & at once he took the lot from me.'[39]

Delays in travelling to a field hospital increased the likelihood of wounds becoming infected and developing gas gangrene, sepsis or wound shock, all of which could be fatal if untreated. In the era before antibiotics,

German medical orderlies minimised the risk of infection by painting iodine on open wounds and giving injections against tetanus, if medical supplies permitted.[40] Surgical treatment was vital during this period but not always available. An analysis of Australian mortality statistics shows that of the 145 Australians who died of wounds behind German lines in France and Belgium (see table 2.1), 121 succumbed to their wounds before arriving at a German field hospital.

Table 2.1 Australian prisoner-of-war deaths in German captivity, 1916–21

	France & Belgium	Germany	Switzerland	After Repat (–1921)	Total
Wounds	145	52	0	3	200
Disease	29	55	2	10	96
Other	18	6	0	7	31
Total	192	113	2	20	327

Sources: death certificates, ARCS WMB, 1DRL/0428, AWM; POW statements, AWM30; service dossiers, NAA B2455; 'AIF statistics for deaths of prisoners of war whilst in German Hands, 1914–18 War', AWM27, 424/1. For alternative but less complete figures, see Butler, *Special Problems and Services*, pp. 896–97.

How did wounded Australians captured at Fromelles fare in the German casualty evacuation system compared with those who passed through the aid posts of the Australian Army Medical Service? There is a noticeable difference in this mortality rate – the seemingly 'acceptable' rate of Australians who died in Australian aid posts and dressing stations was 6.5 per cent, whereas 10 per cent of wounded Australians captured at Fromelles died in German ones.[41] The difference is significant, and reflects the bottle-necking problem and medical staff preferring Germans over prisoners. But it cannot be said that wounded Australians captured at Fromelles were neglected entirely, because more than 90 per cent of them survived the ordeal of capture and their subsequent experiences behind German lines. Similar records and statistics are not available for other engagements involving Australians, but it can be said that Fromelles represented how most wounded Australian prisoners of war fared behind German lines. The relatively high survival rate does not mean that the wounded were always treated with compassion. An Australian who had been wounded in the elbow at Dernancourt asked German soldiers for a drink as he made his own way to the rear without an escort. They asked who he was, and when he said 'Australian', they hit him in the mouth and told him not to make a noise or risk being run through with the bayonet.[42]

After negotiating the front-line casualty evacuation system, seriously wounded prisoners passed through one of three major field hospitals in German-occupied France: Douai, Valenciennes or Cambrai. All three were out of British and French artillery range, were at the junction of major railway and communication lines and were important logistical centres. Prisoners with severe wounds faced a very good chance of survival once they were admitted to a field hospital as the hospitals were staffed by medical officers and orderlies and equipped with theatres and the necessary apparatus to perform surgery. Wounded prisoners were often accommodated alongside German soldiers until they were stable enough to be transported to a prison camp. It was necessary for the critically wounded to spend time in a field hospital, but they were never pleasant places to be. Captain William Cull said 'there could be no worse torture chamber than [the hospital] at Cambrai'.[43] A 16th Battalion private admitted to the hospital at Valenciennes wrote, 'I have seen horrible sights … in France and Gallipoli, but they cannot bear comparison with this.'[44] Conditions were hardly any better for wounded German soldiers being admitted to the same hospitals. In his classic war memoir, *In Stahlgewittern* (*Storm of Steel*; 1920), *Leutnant* Ernst Jünger of the 73rd Infantry Regiment describes conditions at Valenciennes after being wounded on the Somme in November 1916:

> Day after day, a procession of corpses left its portals to a leaden thump of drums. Doctors did their bloody best at a row of operating tables. Here, a limb was amputated, there a skull chipped open, or a bandage that the flesh had grown over was peeled away. Whimpers and cries echoed through the harshly lit room, while white-clad sisters bustled efficiently from one table to the next with instruments or bandages.[45]

What made field hospitals such awful places for prisoners and German soldiers alike was the same bottlenecking problem as in the aid posts and dressing stations behind the front lines. After Dernancourt in April 1918, German medical officers and orderlies at Valenciennes were inundated with Australian and British wounded whose needs came after an influx of German casualties. A wounded Australian from the 4th Pioneer Battalion wrote in his diary describing 'hundreds of our poor lads Badly & lightly wounded [are] lying down in any corner they could find … Badly wounded groaning day & night As no attention could be given them, the germans [*sic*] having no dressings [or] anything in the line of giving ease to these poor lads.'[46] Material shortages had a profound impact on the ability of medical staff to care properly for casualties, with many prisoners reporting their wounds being dressed with paper bandages and operations conducted with little or no anaesthetic.[47] While bottlenecking caused delays that increased the likelihood of wounds turning septic, environmental factors added to the overall misery. In warmer months, flies tormented prisoners left without medical treatment, leading to festering wounds and gangrene.[48]

The main tasks for German medical staff were keeping wounds clean and free from infection, preventing wound shock, and stopping blood vessels from haemorrhaging. With limited medical supplies, this sometimes seemed an almost impossible task. Captured at Bullecourt in April 1917, Lance Corporal George Bell spent two days at Valenciennes before receiving clean bandages: 'My knee is still bleeding and the wound in my back is discharging. The paper [bandage] absorbs moisture rapidly, so my comfort is hardly improved ... My leg is black, swollen and painful; my entreaties for a clean dressing, however, are ignored.'[49] High-velocity projectiles from bullets and shell fragments shattered bones, ruptured blood vessels, and introduced dirt and uniform fabric into open wounds, causing infection, tetanus and gas gangrene. German surgeons were sometimes able to overcome the supply shortage by administering excruciating yet effective preventative methods. At Cambrai, Captain William Cull experienced a surgeon with 'about as much humanity as one might expect in a Bengal tiger' who kept his wound fresh and free from infection by drawing 'rough-cloth, see-saw fashion, back and forward through my side ... I ground my teeth in agony and prayed that I might not gratify him with a groan.'[50]

Some wounds inevitably turned septic. The high percentage of wounds to the upper and lower limbs meant amputation was often the most common form of preventative treatment against blood poisoning, although the loss of limbs or parts thereof were just as likely to throw the body into a fatal state of shock.[51] Sometimes it seemed there was little point in treating mortally wounded prisoners when medical attention and resources were needed elsewhere. George Bell saw several men die the night he arrived at Valenciennes:

Sgt Mjr Smith [*sic*] of my own battalion was strapped to his bed where he laid struggling and screaming in delirium. He was badly wounded in the stomach and received no attention. Towards evening several Huns approached his bed and watched him for a few minutes, then tightened the straps. He died a few hours later. Pte Moore ... had a leg amputated and shared Smith's fate.[52]

If the German treatment of wounded prisoners represented instances of the reciprocity principle maintaining pre-war agreements, punishing prisoners with violent reprisals marked occasions when captors used it to force change. In this respect, prisoners who underwent reprisal punishment were treated more like hostages than non-combatants, something that violated the terms of the 1907 Hague Convention. Reprisals were not universally experienced among all Australian prisoners of war: rank protected captured officers from working behind German lines, so they were usually transported to Germany within a week of their capture. The wounded were also spared reprisal punishment, since they were rarely in any physical state to be put to work.[53] For the wounded, time spent recovering in a hospital in Germany seemed punishing enough. From Cambrai, William Cull went to St Elisabeth Hospital at Bochum where he was bedridden without contact with the outside world for three months. 'My conviction was that they had determined to drive me "mental", and but for one little decorative detail of that cell they would probably have succeeded. Near the ceiling the greenish grey wall had its one note of relief in a coloured frieze. Counting the dots of colour in that frieze was my mind's salvation.'[54]

Australian prisoners captured in the fighting in 1916 were transported to Germany without significant delay. Other ranks captured at Fromelles arrived at the processing and distribution centre at Dülmen in Westphalia after just four days in German captivity. 'The camp was surrounded by a double row of barbed wire which was continuously patrolled by sentries ... A "Coo-ee" as we first approached signalled the presence of Australians.'[55] The only Australians significantly affected by violent reprisals were around 1400 unwounded Australian other ranks captured in the fighting for the Hindenburg Line in 1917, of whom more than 900 were captured at Bullecourt on 11 April.[56] While this group represented the largest loss of Australians as prisoners in a single action during the war, their experiences were not representative of how most fared in German captivity. But their unique experiences behind the lines also go some way to explaining the higher mortality rate of Australians relative to other British and dominion prisoner groups.

Heather Jones has traced the origins of their particular cycle of violence to a dispute between the British, French and German governments over the use of captive labour on the Western Front. Germany was the first to use captive labour in such a way, employing Russian prisoners on the Eastern Front in 1915. The British and French armies soon followed, using German prisoners to meet their growing logistical and manpower demands on the Somme and at Verdun respectively. By the end of 1916, the BEF had up to 12 000 Germans felling timber, engaged in quarries and laundries, supplying water and on burial detail. With German prisoners also used to unload timber and stone from ports at Rouen and Le Havre, there were 70 000 German prisoners working behind the British line by 1918.[57] The War Office was mindful that using prisoner labour close to the forward area could lead to reprisals, but the increasing logistical demands towards the end of 1916 left Britain, France and Germany dependent on captive labour. Germany relied on prisoner labour the most, employing 250 000 Russian, French and British prisoners to clear roads, build engineering and ammunition depots, and construct defensive positions of 'incalculable importance' to military operations.[58] This included the formidable Hindenburg Line, which was completed in early 1917 using the labour of more than 26 000 French and Russian prisoners.[59]

Working prisoners in areas prone to bombardment demonstrates that Britain, France and Germany were all willing to tolerate a certain level of violence against prisoners of war. But the German reprisals in the spring of 1917 took what had become an accepted practice to the extreme. Reprisals had started early in the war in the form of petty restrictions on mail and food parcels that evolved into more severe punishments, including the German decision to place British and French prisoners in special 'reprisal camps'.[60] According to Jones, the reprisal that had significant consequences for Australian prisoners began at Verdun in June 1916, when General Robert Nivelle's Second Army retained German prisoners in areas where they were subjected to bombardments. Prisoners were killed and wounded, but they were also given little food and suffered appallingly from dysentery and frostbite. These conditions were primarily due to supply problems and the inability of local French units to house and feed the prisoners they captured, but Jones adds that there existed an attitude within the French Army that saw prisoners as expendable. A belief that German troops had mistreated French prisoners caused middle-ranking officers to ignore instructions on the legitimate use of captive labour in forward areas.[61]

The French Government denied German reports about the deplorable conditions under which German prisoners were working, not knowing that the French Second Army had been employing prisoners as labourers within artillery range for months. The German Government retaliated by sanctioning a reprisal order that denied French prisoners proper accommodation and washing facilities, and forced them to work on restricted rations in areas shelled by French artillery.[62] The German Government threatened to extend the reprisal to British prisoners in February 1917 amid growing concerns that some of the 28 000 German prisoners employed behind British lines at the time were working close to the front.[63] When the British Government denied claims that prisoner labour companies were being mistreated and refused to limit their use beyond 30 kilometres of the forward area, the German Government extended the reprisals to all recently captured British prisoners of war. Jones estimates that the German reprisals affected up to 33 000 British and French prisoners, but these developments had a significant impact on the 1400 Australians captured in April 1917, many of whom spent the following six months behind German lines.[64]

It is clear from the testimony of men captured in April 1917 that their captors were not fully prepared for the responsibility of housing, feeding, guarding and transporting such an unexpected quantity of prisoners. All able-bodied men captured at Bullecourt were separated from their officers immediately after capture. They spent their first night in German hands locked inside the church at Écourt-Saint-Quentin where they had their first meal in captivity – a modest issue of black German war bread and ersatz coffee:

> Coffee they called it! But how insipid! Certainly minus milk is nothing but there was not any sugar, and to me, the drink was ... both bitter to the taste as well as the feelings. However, it was warm, so one had to accept this as an advantage. The bread was sour, but to hungry mouths this was merely a trifle.[65]

After a long and uncomfortable night filled with uncertainty, the prisoners were marched to the railhead at Le Quesnoy, where they were kept for several days in an abandoned farmhouse that had been converted into a makeshift transit camp. Overcrowded, dirty and infested with lice, conditions were made more miserable when 300 men captured at Lagnicourt arrived four days later and stretched the already meagre food ration further.[66] Starving prisoners still reeling from the shock of capture began exhibiting signs of mental breakdown. Corporal Lancelot Davies of the 13th Battalion described the situation:

> A few of the men are very dejected, and appear to be losing all interest in themselves, their habits and practices not being approved by the majority. In some cases, for the most miserable reward, [men] cringe to the Germans for the chance of being some service; others also, despite the fact their bodies could ill-afford the sacrifice, trade their boots and other clothing in exchange for food and smokes, which gives them a

measure of contentment ... Most of us have resolved to maintain some sort of dignity, though it is difficult. [67]

Front-line units usually treated prisoners well after accepting their surrender, but German troops from rear-echelon units had a tendency to harass, torment and abuse prisoners when escorting them between transit camps. On the march between Le Quesnoy and Lille, sentries spat on prisoners in their charge; they verbally abused them and robbed them for souvenirs. One German soldier even lobbed a hand grenade without priming it into a group of exhausted prisoners of war in an effort to hurry them along.[68] Along the isolated roads between rear-area villages, it was not uncommon for sentries to beat prisoners with fists and rifle butts on the slightest provocation.[69] Once at Lille, the long file of prisoners captured at Bullecourt were paraded through the streets in front of thousands of French civilians, with German sentries using violence to keep the two groups separated. One man reported seeing a little girl who approached the column of prisoners offering a packet of cigarettes: 'One of the file of guards rushed forward to meet her. With one jab of his rifle-butt he sent her spinning to the pavement – then bent down and confiscated the packet to the delight of his *Kameraden*.'[70]

Figure 2.3 Edwin Martin, *The Black Hole of Lille (Fort MacDonald)*, oil on canvas, 28 cm x 33 cm, 1918. (IWM ART 3760)

The prisoners were taken to a disused artillery barracks known as Fort MacDonald in one of Lille's outer suburbs, where, over the following days, they were broken to a weak physical and mental state before being sent to work in the forward area.[71] On arrival, the column was divided into groups of 120 and locked in casemates that proved too small to hold them comfortably. There were no beds, blankets or straw to sleep on, and three small windows provided the only light and ventilation. Rations consisted of a daily issue of bread and ersatz coffee, but this did little to satisfy the prisoners' growing hunger. Some men coped by playing cards, singing hymns, reading pocket Bibles and keeping warm by marching around what many deemed to be an overcrowded dungeon. One man focused on writing poetry:

> Curse the long wait that
> Irks my weary soul,
> This lack of food, that makes
> My tummy roll,
> This floor that mocks my weary aching bones
> These men who talk in ceaseless undertones.
>
> Curse these grey guards forever in our sight.
> These three barred windows letting meagre light
> Illuminate these four impressive walls
> And curse the long restraint that
> Surely galls.
>
> A thousand bastards on the hated power
> Which caused this cursed war, and fateful hour
> Which sent me o'er the top that April dawn
> And saw me captured. Had I not been born.[72]

Within time, prisoners began arguing over the issue of food. 'Chaps began to show signs of jealousy, when some more fortunate ones received a slice larger than the others.'[73] The effects of the food situation were mental as well as physical. 'Regularly, some of the frenzied fellows would approach a stone door, thump wildly against it with no result, and fall in a faint. Faintings became quite common – so common that we took no notice of them … We possessed no medicines, not even a drop of water, so we were unable to offer the poor devils any help.'[74] Hygiene was also a problem. Lice were already endemic in those who had fought and lived in the trenches that winter, but in each of the casemates was a small wooden barrel where 'perilously perched on the edge, back to the corner and

Figure 2.4 Australian prisoners of war await processing at Écourt-Saint-Quentin, several hours after their capture at Bullecourt, 11 April 1917. (Staatsarchiv Sigmaringen N 1/68 Nr. 1800)

fronting the crowd, the individual carried out his sorry relief of nature'.[75] German sentries opened the doors once a day to feed the prisoners but refused to empty the latrines, which eventually overflowed, polluting the air and floor on which the prisoners ate and slept.[76]

After a week of neglect in the so-called 'Black Hole of Lille', German commanders issued the following notice explaining why the prisoners were being so poorly treated:

A Declaration to the British Government

Upon the German request to the British Government to withdraw the German prisoners of war from the front line to a distance of not less than 30 kilometres, the British Government has not replied; it has been decided that all prisoners of war who will be taken in future will be kept as Prisoners of Respite[77] and treated as under: Very short of food, bad lodgings, no bed, hard work, also to be worked beside the German guns under British shellfire ... The British Prisoners will be allowed to write to their relatives or friends of influence in England stating how badly they are being treated and that no alteration in the ill treatment will occur until the English Government has consented to the German request ...[78]

Figure 2.5 Inside one of the casemates at Fort MacDonald near Lille that once held Australian prisoners of war during the reprisals in 1917. Now known as le Fort de Mons en Barœul, the site is today used as a cultural and recreation centre. This 'dungeon' is today used as a ballet studio. (Author's photograph)

The German authorities were clearly attempting to force change in the BEF's use of prisoner labour behind the lines. Some Australian prisoners refused to write home, mindful that names, addresses and regimental details accompanying letters would perhaps divulge sensitive information of interest to German intelligence staff. Others refused, knowing that news of their deliberate mistreatment would cause unnecessary distress among loved ones at home, although some who did write letters learnt after the war that their messages never made it past the German mail censors.[79]

One letter written several weeks after this declaration at Fort MacDonald was received by the Australian High Commissioner in London. A private of the 14th Battalion described being in a 'state of exhaustion ... covered in lice and other vermin' at an engineering dump near Lens in May 1917. 'It is a life of torture and hell', he wrote. 'For God's sake, do what you can for us.'[80] A 50th Battalion man wrote to the office of the Agent General for South Australia in London, describing his 'filthy horrible life' under the reprisals.

Personally I have never been so starved in my life and am in a very weak state, not being used to heavy work, and every other man is in a thoroughly run down state, several have collapsed while out at work and 2 have gone to hospital. The food is not sufficient to live on, much less work on. It is a miserable poor existence and we are all getting weaker every day.[81]

Once the reprisal declaration had been issued to the prisoners, they were expelled from Fort MacDonald's casemates and marched back to the forward area, where they were assigned to labour companies composed of British and French prisoners in the Lille, Douai, Lens and Valenciennes areas. For the next six months, they worked fifteen hours a day digging machine-gun pits, trenches and dugouts, clearing roads, and unloading barges and supplies at engineering and ammunition dumps – all work associated with the German war effort that violated the 1907 Hague Convention. They were housed in stables, farmhouses and ruined churches near where they worked. One party in the shell-damaged church at Flers-en-Escrebieux was so close to the forward area that the concussion of exploding artillery shells caused parts of the ceiling to cave in on them as they slept.[82] Australians at a work detail at Marquion slept in the barn of an abandoned farmhouse infested with lice, next to two heavy field howitzers that frequently drew fire from British siege guns.[83] One man on canal work at Ancoisne described his work party being subjected to another deadly threat: 'Our aeroplanes have been over a lot lately. On 6th they came over 8 of them and dropped bombs on the huts where we were working, and wounded one of our Sergeants.'[84]

The German authorities forwarded all names and details of the Australian prisoners subjected to the reprisals to the Red Cross in Switzerland via the national office in Berlin. Around June 1917, confirmation that these missing men were prisoners of war reached the Australian Red Cross in London, who were of the understanding that all other ranks had gone to the prison camp at Limburg in the Rhineland. Believing this to be true, volunteers in the Australian Red Cross Prisoner of War Department went about dispatching thousands of food and clothing parcels to this address to ease the suffering of prisoners. In all reality, the men were being illegally detained in France and had to wait a further five months before they received their first Red Cross food issue. Private Jack Hind of the 4th Battalion had been captured near Boursies on 15 April 1917 and transcribed the German declaration notice that made specific reference to a Limburg postal address. 'Our real address at this particular time is "Iwuy" Nord France', he added.[85] The Limburg address was a ruse, intended to obscure the real location of the Australian prisoners, as Private Ernest Chalk of the 15th Battalion explained:

> The [prisoners] worked behind the lines until it was a physical impossibility for them to do another stroke, and then, in many cases, their number had been reduced by half, caused by sickness, due chiefly to starvation and heavy work combined. When they are reduced to this state, they are sent back to registration camps in Germany. Here they are at last registered, their names and particulars going through to the British government for the first time. This of course means that a very great many have perished as prisoners of war whom the people at home know nothing about, only that they are reported 'missing'.[86]

Chalk was not far off the mark. Until they were in contact with the Red Cross, Australian prisoners under the reprisals were kept on a 'starvation diet' that largely consisted of vegetable soup, bread, ersatz coffee and whatever meat could be locally procured. They were worked hard on meagre rations as the declaration had threatened, but the statements of repatriated prisoners of war make it clear that conditions reflected the material shortages of the German Army at that time, and were little better for the sentries overseeing prisoners of war.[87] A German officer at the village of Iwuy told a work party of Australians that the dietary needs of German troops and French civilians ranked above those of the prisoners. 'If there's any food left, you dog-Australians will get some,' he said.[88]

Private John Murphy of the 50th Battalion was responsible for fixing meals for 200 British and Australian prisoners digging machine-gun pits at Flers-en-Escrebieux. He made do with mangle-wurzel, a few loaves of bread and a small amount of meat every two days. The meat ration was either 150 salted herrings or a 'good-sized lump of horseflesh, very often a whole leg with the shoe still on', from an artillery dray cut down by fire or dead from exhaustion. Murphy used utensils found in ruined buildings and rubbish dumps, and admitted 'it was not nice food but we had to eat it to keep body and soul together'.[89]

The combination of heavy labour and a restricted diet deficient in protein and nutrients resulted in prisoners scavenging whatever they could to satisfy their chronic hunger. A group of men working at the engineering dump at Marquion made 'scrounge bags' to take on their work details to collect stinging nettles, rape, dandelions, frogs and snails. Once the sentries had turned in for the night, everything went into a pot and was stewed. Boiled stinging nettles, according to one Australian prisoner of war, 'tasted much like spinach'.[90] Prisoners working near canals often collected fresh-water mussels, eels and small fish, while those on engineering and ammunition dumps gathered shrubs and the carcasses of rabbits, foxes and small birds killed by the concussion of exploding artillery shells.[91] Starving prisoners ransacked vegetable crops cultivated by German troops, quickly consuming their spoils while sentries were not watching. Eating raw potatoes and turnips would often cause stomach complaints and bouts of diarrhoea, and on one occasion proved fatal. Private Harold Hall of the 16th Battalion died after eating raw potato peelings he had scavenged from the work party at Bronchain near Cambrai.[92] Scrounging could also have fatal consequences if German sentries discovered that prisoners had strayed from their work party or were caught outside their compound at night. Thus, in July 1917, Private Joseph Miller of the 16th Battalion was shot dead ransacking a potato crop at Saint-Saulve by a sentry who thought he was escaping.[93]

Behind the lines in France, prisoners generally respected the mounted Uhlans and infantrymen who had seen front-line service as they had. The guards they detested the most were the older *Landsturm* reservists whom age and fitness excluded from front-line service, and who were more likely to use fists, rifle butts and verbal insults to drive productivity and maintain discipline within work parties.[94] These so-called *Etappenschwein* (rear-area pigs) were seen by the men as being the 'hardest and least humane'.[95] Beatings were frequent, particularly as the physical condition of the prisoners deteriorated. An Australian prisoner at Iwuy was struck over the head with a shovel after collapsing from exhaustion.[96] At Phalempin, an Australian prisoner found with a makeshift knife received several hours field punishment known as *Anbinden*: he was hanged, hands bound behind his back and feet barely touching the ground, and choked for several hours.[97]

Over time, the cumulative effects of a poor diet and unsanitary living conditions led to outbreaks of disease – dysentery, enteritis, pneumonia and malaria – all of which affected the prisoners more than the physical abuse. Men deficient in nutrients suffered from beriberi, a condition more readily associated with prisoners of the Japanese in the Second World War, which caused swelling in the legs, arms and face. As one man captured at Noreuil explained, '[I]f you poked your finger in [the] flesh it would leave a hole.'[98] Prisoners were given the right to attend sick parades at *Appell* (roll call) each morning, but sentries were just as likely to force them to work regardless of their condition – and then beat them when they collapsed.[99] At Jeaumont, Private Herbert Freeman of the 57th

Battalion had already been suffering from dysentery before deteriorating into such a poor physical state that he had to be carried to the latrines. Unable to work, he was struck on the head twice with rifle butts and was refused medical attention on three separate occasions before he was finally taken to see a doctor. Freeman died five minutes before an ambulance arrived to collect him. The prisoners of war with him when he died said that he left 'no messages and [was] only asking for cigarettes at the end'.[100]

Sick men in other camps were permitted to seek medical attention, but in many cases spent several days in hospital at Mons or Valenciennes before returning to the forward area until their health broke down completely. Disease was endemic at some work camps. Within a two-month period, half of the 200 Australians employed at the Marquion engineering dump had been hospitalised because of sickness and exhaustion.[101] Artillery posed less of a threat than disease, mainly because the likelihood of British shells falling on work parties varied depending on their proximity to the fighting and operational activity in the sector they were working. Most prisoner labour companies were located up to 10 kilometres behind the front line, putting them beyond the range of British field artillery but still within range of the heavy siege guns. The latter were used for counter-battery work and bombardments on ammunition and supply dumps, stores, roads and railway depots, which were precisely the areas where prisoners of war were then working.

The area most vulnerable to British artillery during this period was the German-occupied villages along the Scarpe River, several kilometres from where British and Canadian troops had made gains during the Battle of Arras in April 1917. This included the villages of Brebières and Corbehem, about 15 kilometres behind the front line, where a party of 150 Australian prisoners were digging saps for mining bridges, burying German dead and carrying out general fatigue work.[102] On 1 May 1917, British siege guns fired on an ammunition dump as Australian prisoners were unloading shells from a supply train. A 15-inch high-explosive shell landed among the work party, killing seven and wounding five when the dump exploded.[103] British artillery also destroyed a nearby supply depot and blew up an armoury where machine-guns and a supply of small arms ammunition were being stored. One man reported how the prisoners 'were not allowed to stop work while those shells were falling, even though the Germans got well into their dugouts'.[104]

Once it became known how British prisoners of war were faring during the reprisals, the War Office sent reassurances to the German

Government in May 1917 that German labour companies had been moved 30 kilometres beyond the forward area. In return, by mid-June, all British and French prisoners of war working behind German lines were moved to work parties further to the German rear. The new work camps were no longer within range of British siege guns, but the limited rations, verbal and physical abuse and squalid conditions remained pretty much the same for months to come. By November, when the reprisals formally ended, eighty-seven Australians had died of disease and seven had been killed by shellfire. The higher mortality rate of Australians than other British prisoner groups can probably be explained to some extent by the treatment they endured during the reprisals in the spring of 1917, when insufficient food and accommodation and exposure to violence and disease reduced their ability to see through the end of the war.[105]

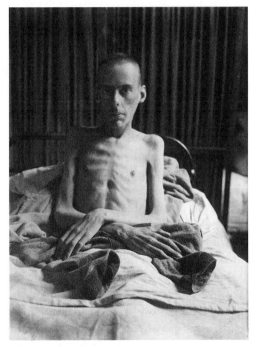

Figure 2.6 A repatriated British soldier who spent six months working behind German lines in 1918. Images like this one are more commonly associated with captivity in the Asia Pacific in the Second World War, but they also reflect the extreme conditions behind German lines on the Western Front.
(IWM Q 31277)

The terrible treatment of prisoners of war in France during the reprisals of 1917 demonstrates how Germany was able to exploit the principle of reciprocity to effect change on the use of German prisoners as labourers in the British forward area. Those most affected by the reprisals would not be treated so poorly once they arrived in Germany, where their treatment could be monitored and they were in contact with the Red Cross. But one of the consequences of their mistreatment was the role it played in standardising violence towards prisoners as the fighting continued into 1918. The German Army's increasing material shortages and growing dependence on prisoner labour was formally recognised when the German High Command issued orders in March 1918 that permitted the use of prisoner labour for all road- and rail-building tasks in the forward area during the German spring offensive.[106] As Heather Jones writes, the deliberate mistreatment of prisoners took on more violent and extreme forms as German commanders sought to achieve decisive victory or risk *Endkampf* (a final battle) that would result in Germany's ultimate destruction.[107]

These developments had significant consequences for 75 000 British and 15 000 French troops captured during the German spring offensive, but had little bearing on the AIF divisions that were still in their relatively quiet winter positions in Belgium when the offensive began. The only Australians affected were the four hundred men of the 3rd and 4th Australian Divisions who fell into German hands during the fighting at Villers-Bretonneux and Dernancourt on 5 April 1918. Officers and the wounded went to Germany as had previous prisoner groups, but remaining batches of other ranks men worked behind German lines clearing roads, moving stores, loading wagons and digging trenches for the remaining months of the war.

Most went to labour companies near Péronne and Saint-Quentin, which was beyond British artillery range until September 1918, but were regularly attacked from the air. Supply dumps and railway junctions were bombed and strafed by aircraft of the Royal Air Force supporting Allied ground troops during the offensive between August and October 1918.[108] These were dangerous locations for prisoners to be working, but surprisingly, no Australian prisoners were killed. Several lost limbs or were blinded, and one man was gassed when an ammunition dump exploded, but these were the only known instances when the dangers of the front line harmed Australians working behind German lines in the final months of the war.[109]

This was a drastically different experience from the vast majority of British prisoners of war, who suffered terribly behind the lines during this period. Mark Spoerer shows that prisoners taken later in the war were at a greater risk of dying in captivity than those captured earlier, as highlighted by the deaths of some 4600 of the 88 700 British prisoners of war captured in the last nine months of the war (unfortunately, the statistics do not reveal what percentage of these had died of wounds received in combat).[110] Nevertheless, this does not mean that overall conditions were any better for captured Australians behind German lines, since the general mistreatment remained much the same as the previous year. The only difference was that it happened to a significantly smaller number of Australian prisoners of war who seemed to have been exposed to less extreme violence from their captors. Captured Australians sent to work parties at Etricourt, Marchelpot and Tincourt still reported being 'brutally treated, the Huns using their rifle-butts and sticks on the prisoners upon the slightest provocation. The work … was so hard that each day several men were brought back in a state of exhaustion.'[111]

The limitations of the pre-war agreements meant there was no formal way of policing the proper treatment of prisoners of war behind the front line. Belligerents relied on a tacit understanding of mutual respect so that their own men would be treated well in enemy hands. While the principle of reciprocity ensured that wounded Australian prisoners received adequate medical assistance in German medical facilities, there were times when captors lacked the resources and facilities to treat prisoners humanely. Once prisoners were transported to Germany, the protecting powers could police the wartime agreements and guarantee humane treatment through regular inspections of camps and work parties. There, the reprisals were less frequent and the abuse and suffering were less extreme. Although Germany's economic, social and military circumstances continued to deteriorate the longer the war continued, Australians arriving at the prison camps in Germany were struck by the vast quantity of food and clothing from international aid agencies that awaited them. Australian prisoners of war would continue to experience fear and uncertainty in German captivity, but once they were transported to Germany, they could live in hope that the rest of their time in the hands of the enemy would be spent far away from the indiscriminate violence behind the lines on the Western Front.

CHAPTER 3

GIVING THE GAME AWAY

THE INTELLIGENCE VALUE OF
AUSTRALIAN PRISONERS OF WAR

Captain Charles Mills was captured at Fromelles on the morning of 20 July 1916. At first light, German soldiers showered his position with grenades before rushing in from the flanks, firing their rifles from the hip. A German NCO stopped his men on the parapet, jumped into the water-logged ditch and seized Mills by his wounded hand. 'Why did you not put up your hands, officer?' he asked. As the fighting came to an end, Mills and the surviving members of the 31st Battalion were escorted along a communication trench to a farmhouse the Germans called Neuhof. In the courtyard there, they joined three officers and 200 other ranks in what was evidently a collecting station for prisoners of war. A German medical officer took care of the walking wounded, and Mills had his hand cleaned and bandaged. What happened next altered German knowledge of British intentions in the Fromelles area.

At the request of a German intelligence officer, Mills turned out the contents of his pockets, producing a photograph and a diary. The photograph was a studio portrait of Mills, which the German officer kept to assist with the visual recognition of Australian troops. The diary was of interest because it gave an account of the 31st Battalion's activities since it arrived in France from Egypt just a few weeks earlier. The diary also contained a copy of the orders by British XI Corps headquarters, which clearly stated that the Fromelles attack was a feint designed to pin the Germans in the Lille area and prevent their reserves from moving south to the Somme. The Germans had confirmed through Mills that the attack was nothing more than a diversion, so, by taking the orders into battle,

Mills had inadvertently revealed sensitive information that undermined the very purpose of the operation. Mills made no mention of the incident after his return from captivity, but to German intelligence officers at the 6th Bavarian Reserve Division headquarters, he confessed it was 'a serious error of judgement' to allow such an important document to fall into their hands.[1]

Figure 3.1 Captain Charles Mills, 31st Battalion (left), in conversation with *Hauptmann* Fritz Lübcke (taking notes) at the Neuhof farmhouse on 20 July 1916. The diary containing the orders for the Fromelles attack can be seen in Mills' tunic pocket. (AWM A01549)

Mills' indiscretion shows why prisoners of war were important for German formations fighting on the Western Front. For centuries, armies that took prisoners denied their enemies the manpower to fight on the battlefield and used them as hostages and forced labourers. While chapter 2 showed that the treatment of prisoners was carried out in accord with the principle of reciprocity, captured men were also a valuable source of information on the morale, strength, disposition and activities of enemy formations. The bloody calculus of fighting was such that demoralised soldiers who begged their enemy for mercy were sometimes killed. While prisoner-killing was counter-productive and potentially prolonged the war by making the enemy less likely to surrender, doing so might also have denied the Germans important military information that Australian soldiers carried with them into battle. British, French and German armies on the Western Front collected intelligence from a range of sources, including aerial photography, signals intelligence and espionage.[2] But according to *Oberst* Walter Nicholai, the German Army's first senior intelligence officer, Allied prisoners of war were the 'most valuable source of news in the western theatre of war'.[3]

Few researchers have looked at the value of prisoners to their captors, although Niall Ferguson writes that prisoners of war were 'especially important' intelligence sources. Even the most recent literature on captivity in the First World War has overlooked this aspect of the prisoner-of-war experience.[4] In spite of this, Charles Bean acknowledged in the official history that Australian soldiers 'were usually under intense strain and suffering from shock' after falling into German hands. They were 'sturdily determined' not to give away intelligence of value, but 'comparatively seldom' did they refuse to answer questions from German intelligence staff.[5] There are examples that show Australian prisoners making 'a good military impression' on their captors by refusing to respond to questions under interrogation beyond citing their name and rank, as they were instructed to do.[6] However, a study of German records shows that the German Army was still able to elicit valuable military information from captured Australians. When used alongside Australian operational records, such as war diaries, after-action reports and the statements of repatriated prisoners of war, the German records provide a different view of captivity that highlights the value of prisoners as intelligence sources.

The benefits of using both Australian and German records can be seen by looking at a 13th Battalion trench raid on the German positions at Piccadilly Farm in the St Eloi sector in Belgium on the night of 27–28 September 1916. According to Australian records, the officer leading the fourteen-man raiding party, Lieutenant Frank Fitzpatrick, had studied the ground by telescope over the preceding days and was confident that he could bring his troops close to the German wire before the artillery bombarded it. When the raid started, Fitzpatrick almost instantly lost his bearings and led his men to a position unfamiliar to the raiders. Artillery fell on the raiding party, Fitzpatrick was killed and four others were wounded.[7] The raiding party returned to Australian lines without Fitzpatrick or Private Donald Muir – an experienced soldier who had been awarded a Military Medal several weeks earlier for his role in a grenade duel with German troops at Pozières.[8]

Rather than retire across No Man's Land with the rest of the raiders, Muir continued to assault the German position on his own. According to German records, 'a soldier from this patrol managed to get through our wire defences and approach our position ... from behind with a sack of hand grenades. By the determined and clever intervention of *Gefreiter* Joseph Kieselbert of the 12th Company, 127th Infantry Regiment, the enemy was forced to throw away his hand grenades and was then taken prisoner.'[9] Muir was wounded and captured by *Gefreiter* Kieselbert, whereupon he was searched for documents and afterwards interrogated. Muir mentioned very little of the exchange in his prisoner-of-war statement after repatriation, but the German intelligence officer who questioned him described Muir as 'very stubborn'.[10]

Muir might not have said anything of real significance during his cross-examination, but his uniform, colour patches and national insignia identified him as a member of the 4th Australian Division, which German Supreme Army Command (*Oberste Heeresleitung* or OHL) thought was still fighting on the Somme. A German intelligence officer at XIII (Royal Württemberg) Army Corps headquarters considered this 'very important information' for the Allied order of battle because 'it has become very likely that an Australian division has replaced the Canadian division which had been there before'. To encourage German troops in the St Eloi sector to keep bringing in British prisoners, *Gefreiter* Kieselbert was rewarded with 300 Marks, while *Grenadiers* Schock, Ebhard, Kübler and Huß from the 123rd Grenadier Regiment received 100 Marks for retrieving the body of Lieutenant Fitzpatrick.[11] Private Muir did not have to divulge information to his captors for them to acquire 'very important information' on AIF formations, but because he could be questioned and elicit a meaningful response, his capture shows that the German Army considered prisoners more important intelligence sources than the bodies of dead Allied soldiers.

The ways in which Australians responded to cross-examination was partly informed by the counter-intelligence training they received before they were captured, although it must be said that Australian troops received no formal training before the first members of the AIF were captured in France in May 1916. Neither *Field Service Regulations* nor *Notes for Infantry Officers in Trench Warfare* gave any indication of what was expected if soldiers had the misfortune of falling into enemy hands.[12] Machine-gun crews were issued with instructions to 'never abandon their position ... if necessary they must allow themselves to be surrounded, and must defend themselves to the last'.[13] The issue reflected the broader BEF as a whole, not just the AIF. In the build-up to the Battle of the Somme, British Second Army stressed the importance of ciphers in all forms of telecommunications and reminded troops of counter-espionage measures, but never mentioned what was expected of soldiers who had the misfortune of being taken prisoner.[14]

This is not to say that the AIF was completely unaware of the possibility that the Germans could obtain information from captured men. In June 1916, as the 7th Brigade prepared for the AIF's first trench raid in the Armentières sector, all members of the raiding party were instructed that 'neither officers or men [should be] carrying anything likely to be of value to the enemy, such as letters, identity discs, badges, pay-books etc'. Rifles, revolvers and other items of field equipment had identifying markings removed, and men were instructed to wear generic British tunics with sandshoes and puttees instead of their distinctive Australian pattern uniform.[15] These counter-measures masked the national identity and units of raiders who might be killed, but these alone were not adequate in detailing what a man should say and do in the event of being captured alive.

It was not until after the Battle of the Somme that it became clear that soldiers taken prisoner could sometimes be an operational liability. In September 1916, GHQ received reports via neutral countries that the Germans obtained British XI Corps orders for the Fromelles attack from a captured Australian officer. Lieutenant Colonel Cyril Wagstaff, chief of staff of 5th Australian Division, issued a memorandum informing all units under his command 'that they are betraying their duty by giving any information other than their name and rank if they shall fall into the hands of the enemy'. The memorandum made three key points:

I. Prisoners taken by the Germans carried on them copies of our battalion orders;

II. A German posing as an American interrogates all prisoners who arrive in Prisoners of War Camps;

III. The colonial troops in particular are found to give information very readily. The attention of this Division is specifically directed to (III).[16]

Wagstaff directed that 'no documents of use to the enemy are to be forward of Battalion Headquarters in an attack' and made platoon commanders sign affidavits attesting that the memorandum had been read to all ranks.[17]

This memorandum marked the beginning of a counter-intelligence training program within the AIF. According to article IX of the 1907 Hague

Convention, 'a prisoner of war is bound to give, if he is questioned on the subject, his true name and rank, and if he infringes this rule, he is liable to have the advantages given to prisoners of his class curtailed'. Lectures on the rules and customs of war on land were given to troops in rear-area billets and rest camps as part of routine training.[18] The most important messages were distilled into simple instructions like 'DON'T refuse to give your name and regiment; it doesn't do any good, and your people won't know what has become of you'.[19] This training program coincided with a broader endeavour across the BEF to instruct troops and remind them of their obligations if they had the misfortune of falling into enemy hands. After the Somme, official memoranda from GHQ instructed all units that a captured man was 'not to give any information beyond his name and rank. The enemy cannot and will not compel him to say more – though he may threaten to do so – on the contrary he will respect a man whose courage and patriotism do not fail even though wounded or a prisoner.'[20]

Since capture was a more likely occurrence in the air war, RFC and AFC airmen were trained and reminded about what was expected of them if they fell into enemy hands. Aircrew were highly skilled, sound in operational matters, had a good sense of geography and navigation and were equipped with some of the most advanced technology of the period. These qualities made them extremely valuable assets in the intelligence-gathering process, and they were therefore better prepared for cross-examination. So that their machines would not be captured, studied, salvaged or pressed into service by the Deutsche Luftstreitkräfte (German Air Service). Australian pilots flew with a Very flare pistol in their cockpits so that a disabled aircraft and any associated maps, letters or operational documents could be set alight and burnt after a crash landing behind German lines.[21] To minimise the likelihood of a 'confidence trick' being used during interrogations, airmen were instructed not to disclose the identity of their squadron. Instead, they were instructed to write a letter addressed to 'Major — C/o Cox & Co.' (the financial military agents in London), who then passed all incoming correspondence to the War Office and confirmed with the Red Cross and the RFC (and by proxy the AFC) that a missing airman was alive and a prisoner of war in German hands.[22]

On the ground, Australian experiences in the hours after capture were largely shaped by the German procedures for handling prisoners with the intention of collecting intelligence from them. After capturing 470 Australians at Fromelles in July 1916, regiments of the 6th Bavarian Reserve Division received new instructions on how to process large numbers of captured men. Units were instructed to report to army headquarters with the number of prisoners taken, their units from division down to company level, the time and place of their capture, and details of how they were captured. This was usually communicated by telephone, whereupon a written report was sent to an OHL intelligence officer based at corps headquarters. This officer was responsible for examining prisoners and evaluating material captured within their allocated sectors, usually at brigade or divisional headquarters when it involved large numbers of prisoners, or at corps headquarters for smaller groups.[23]

Prisoners were stripped of their weapons and equipment before being shepherded to the rear. Officially, they were permitted to retain personal items such as identity discs, pay books, personal photographs, money and uniform insignia (although these were often filched) but had to forfeit military documents, letters, maps, newspapers and diaries. Officers were separated from NCOs and other ranks to disrupt the chain of command and heighten the prisoners' state of uncertainty. Talking among prisoners was forbidden, and German soldiers were not permitted to talk with prisoners until intelligence staff had questioned them.[24] Since looting was common, German troops were told about the importance of colour patches and national insignia on uniforms as they allowed positive identification of Allied units. Interrogations were usually conducted within hours of capture so that information could be assessed and immediately distributed to line regiments for use in the forward area.[25]

German intelligence officers would often begin cross-examinations with prisoners by asking seemingly innocuous questions. This included the identity of the prisoner's battalion, where it fitted in the order of battle, where a man had previously fought and how long he had been in combat. Prisoners captured in raids and major engagements were asked about their objectives, how many casualties they suffered and when their units were last reinforced. Intelligence officers also asked about the prospect of further attacks and the location of troop billets, artillery and mortar batteries so that they could be shelled.[26] The awkward conversation between Private Ernest Gaunt of the 13th Field Ambulance and a German intelligence officer was typical of the exchange between captive and captor during the interrogation process:

> 'Have you been very busy, had many wounded?'
> 'No.'
> 'How many patients have you carried today?'
> 'Five or six.'
> 'How many are there in your section?'

'Only fifteen.'
'Any casualties among your officers?'
'No.'
'Any wounded officers?'
'No.'
'What did you join for?'
'I am a Britisher.'
'Were you on Gallipoli?'
'Yes.'
'You had a lot of casualties there?'
'Yes, but the Turks had more.' [27]

While it was against the Hague Convention to mistreat prisoners deliberately in order to elicit information from them, it was far more common for prisoners to receive offers of cigarettes, alcohol and displays of sympathy from intelligence officers attempting to lull them into a false sense of security. Private Claude Benson of the 13th Battalion was captured at Bullecourt on 11 April 1917 and was among the large body of prisoners taken to the village of Écourt-Saint-Quentin. About 150 of the 1170 men of the 4th Australian Division captured that day were singled out and examined at a château that served as the headquarters of the 27th (Württemberg) Division:

> On our arrival some German officers questioned us separately about our battalion. The treatment we received from these polite officers was good as they offered us cigarettes and told us to light up . . . I thought it better not to smoke as I had been taught to take no risks if taken prisoner, really doubting what the cigarettes might contain.[28]

Intelligence officers focused their efforts on the officers and NCOs, who by virtue of rank and experience knew more about the AIF and its operations than the other ranks held separately in the château yard. Corporal Lancelot Davies of the 14th Battalion observed that some of the British tank crew among the body of prisoners 'were reluctant to let their identity become known to the enemy, as each one feared reprisals . . . [but] their oil-stained begrimed faces and hands, and their khaki drill clothes, gave them away'.[29] Captain Joseph Honeysett was the first officer from the 47th Battalion to fall into German hands and 'was not surprised' when he was led inside the château for questioning. He was 'ushered into a comfortably furnished bedroom', where he met the German officer who would conduct his interrogation:

Figure 3.2 Officers and NCOs of the 4th Australian Division await cross-examination at the château at Écourt-Saint-Quentin, following their capture at Bullecourt earlier that morning on 11 April 1917. (Bpk-Bildagentur Nr. 50170607)

> Lying on the bed there was a most affable looking man of middle age, who in perfect English, promptly apologised for any discourtesy he appeared to show in receiving me in that manner! At the bedside, notebook in hand, was seated a very aristocratic looking young Lieutenant ... In French, he asked me to accept a cigarette and a glass of cognac.[30]

German intelligence officers found kind treatment such as this elicited results from prisoners, who often 'spoke more willingly even than the deserters'.[31] Showing care and sympathy was particularly successful within the first few hours of capture when prisoners were still suffering from the fear, shock and confusion of capture. One German officer described four Australians of the 22nd Battalion captured near Bapaume in February 1917 as being 'quite shocked that they are being treated so well ... particularly as they had been gripped by rumours of barbarism and rough treatment'.[32] Reassured that they would not be beaten or killed, the prisoners went on to discuss how pleased they were at the outcome of the first conscription plebiscite in Australia and were 'all particularly happy to have landed in captivity, through which they have escaped a heavy workload on frugal provisions'.[33]

It was not uncommon for intelligence officers to pretend that they knew more about Australian units than did the men themselves. One man captured at Passchendaele was stunned when he overheard a German officer positively identify his unit in perfect English. 'We had no numbers on our shoulder titles, but he recognised the battalion colours.'[34] A 51st Battalion man captured at Mouquet Farm lied about his unit's identity, claiming to be from the 151st: 'But he showed me that he was better informed than I had bargained for. He could tell me that our Battalion had been formed up in Egypt from old Gallipoli hands and reinforcements, and he knew General Cox and our Brigadier by name.'[35] A signaller from the 14th Battalion was adamant that 'I gave them no authentic information, but for giving false information I was imprisoned apart from the others in a cold shed for five days at Ribecourt'.[36]

Captured airmen were better prepared against confidence tricks such as these. On 2 October 1917, Second Lieutenant Ivo Agnew of No. 2 Squadron AFC became separated from his patrol during an engagement with a German twin-seater over Villers-Outréaux. Having lost his bearings and developed engine trouble, Agnew was captured when he mistakenly landed his Airco DH.5 scout on a German airfield outside Valenciennes.[37] He wrote in his diary that he 'was treated well' that night, 'had dinner with the officers of the 42nd Squadron' and was given a tour of the airfield where he was shown a number of German aircraft, 'mostly Albatross scouts, though there were 4 of ours among them resplendent in black iron crosses'.[38] This treatment might have partially reflected the chivalry of the air war, but it was also a deliberate attempt by German pilots to lull Agnew into a false sense of security before handing him over for cross-examination. Despite receiving preferential treatment, Agnew remained tight-lipped on operational matters when he was questioned at Le Cateau several days later. He made 'a good military impression' on his German examiner and was thought to be 'considerably better educated than average soldiers who stem from the English colonies'.[39]

Because they had been trained in counter-intelligence methods, captured airmen were often subjected to more subtle forms of cross-examination. Australian pilots were usually detained in châteaux with their captured British counterparts before they were sent to a prison camp in Germany. The idea was that they would discuss aircraft, squadrons and operational details while intelligence staff listened in. Lieutenant Wentworth Randell of No. 4 Squadron AFC 'found two microphones hidden in the wall' of the locked room he shared with two other airmen at Lille, as did Lieutenant Archie Rackett of No. 2 Squadron AFC, who spent time at the Europäischer Hof 'listening hotel' at Karlsruhe after arriving in Germany.[40] Knowing a 'dictaphone' was 'cunningly concealed in the walls', Rackett was put in with a French pilot 'who spoke no English. We managed to purchase a pack of cards and thus we amused ourselves without hardly speaking.'[41] Captain William Cull of the 22nd Battalion had been at the 'listening hotel' some months earlier; oblivious that a device was most likely recording his conversations, he was nevertheless conscious that a 'quiet listener outside the door might hear something to his advantage'.[42]

A similar technique was sometimes used at prisoner collecting stations in the forward areas, where German soldiers dressed in British uniforms would listen in on prisoner conversations. One man captured at Mouquet Farm reported 'a German who claimed to be a New Zealander' who tried to befriend him at Cambrai. 'He may have been "dinkum", but I had my suspicions and I "sang dumb".'[43] Another man recalled seeing a German soldier at a prisoner cage at Sailly-le-Sec in April 1918 wearing 'a "Tommy" tunic beneath his own, which he wore unbuttoned'.[44]

Not all prisoners were treated so well. Some men reported being beaten and abused by German infantry before intelligence staff had questioned them formally. Charles Bean recognised that this sometimes happened, but these incidents were usually due to the 'stupidity and vindictiveness of certain "dugout" martinets' rather than a concerted effort by examining officers to use violence to extract information from prisoners.[45] Whereas troops of the 10th and 11th Battalions were 'almost happy' to have been captured at Mouquet Farm in August 1916, men of the 51st Battalion captured there on 3 September were treated with disdain.[46] The two different experiences reflected the bitter fighting and the temperament of the Prussian troops who occupied the Mouquet Farm defences in the latter attack. One captured Australian was 'knocked about the head with German stick bombs' for refusing to reveal the location of British and Australian artillery batteries that were then shelling the German positions.[47] Another was told he was obliged to give answers to all questions, and was kicked and beaten when he refused. A German officer 'threatened to shoot me. I tried to sleep, but they worried me all the time.'[48]

A German officer who examined a group of captured Australians in August 1918 concluded his report not knowing whether what they had said was 'pretence or truth ... [but] all were reticent and only after a lot of talking did their tongues become loose'.[49] Australians responded to questioning in many different ways, but if the Germans looked upon prisoners as the 'most valuable source of news in the western theatre of war', what intelligence did they garner from Australian prisoners?

The first cross-examination involving Australians in France occurred at Douai on 6 May 1916, the morning after the German raid on the Bridoux Salient. *Hauptmann* Fritz Lübcke, the intelligence officer for the German Sixth Army, questioned the eleven prisoners and later cross-examined Australians captured at Fromelles. From what the prisoners told him, Lübcke pieced together an accurate account of the 2nd Australian Division's activities in its first few weeks in France. He also established the location of its headquarters at Erquinghem, the effectiveness of German shellfire on dumps and communication trenches, and the strength and disposition of 5th Brigade defences.[50] The only officer captured in the raid, Lieutenant Norman Blanchard, was recovering from gunshot and shrapnel wounds in the Douai field hospital when Lübcke questioned him. Lübcke's report from their discussion details how Blanchard confirmed the 2nd Australian Division's order of battle, the presence of a 'Dictaphone' to intercept German telephone messages, and the names of several officers at brigade and battalion headquarters. Blanchard also revealed that 'a comprehensive English attack is planned for the foreseeable future'.[51] Lübcke did not record how this information was received or put to use, but his report would have gone on to OHL's intelligence branch for further analysis and action. Days later, line regiments in the German Sixth Army area received Lübcke's notes from the interrogation, telling them that the AIF had begun operations in France and included a drawing illustrating how Australian uniforms and equipment differed from those of other British troops.[52]

As well as issuing visual aids to front-line units, German intelligence officers often included 'mood pictures' in reports to capture snapshots of the war as it was being felt on the opposite side of No Man's Land. Reports on the interrogation of prisoners usually included accounts of service, comments on their state of mind, the prisoner's opinions and grievances, the relationships between Allied units, and remarks on the political and domestic situation at home.[53] Sometimes, intelligence officers made assessments of the character of Australian troops. Captured at Pozières on 26 July 1916, Private Ernest Fitch of the 5th Battalion made a 'first-rate impression as a soldier' on *Hauptmann* Friedrich Weber, an intelligence officer for the German First Army, who considered Fitch to be 'extremely intelligent' and was impressed by his 'considerable experience' on Gallipoli. [54]

Figure 3.3 Men of the 11th Battalion and 1st Pioneer Battalion following their capture in the Cordonnerie Salient near Fleurbaix in May 1916. The relaxed body language and smiles of the prisoners suggest that they had been sufficiently assured no harm would come to them. (Photo courtesy of Brett Butterworth)

Examining officers often went to great lengths to determine the number of *Gallipoli-Kämpfer* ('Gallipoli fighters') among the ranks of captured Australians.[55] Having questioned Australians captured at Pozières, Weber concluded that those who had served on Gallipoli made better soldiers than the reinforcements who had little or no combat experience. Weber believed the troops of the 1st Australian Division were 'a completely different calibre to the average English soldier ... Each and every man knows how to fend for himself in an emergency and even if the leadership completely disintegrated, they would still constitute an excellent unit, which is not the case for the English.'[56] In the following days, he questioned troops from the 1st and 2nd Australian Divisions and made tentative comments on the combat effectiveness of I Anzac Corps. 'Where something special has to be accomplished, the English leadership deploys Australian troops, amongst whom there is fierce competition for success at the battalion level.'[57]

Weber did not rate the 4th Australian Division highly, claiming that 'their officers are decidedly below the average English officer; they differentiate themselves only slightly from their troops, and in personal interactions pay no attention to the difference in rank'.[58] At Fromelles, Lübcke was struck by the 5th Australian Division's inexperience, reporting how 'the officers ... despite repeated protestations that their conscience as officers would not allow them to disclose military secrets, cheerfully dictated to us complete details of the planning and execution of the attack, and the dispositions of the units involved'.[59]

In spite of the reminders and official warnings, Australian troops were regularly captured with letters, diaries and other documents in their possession. Weber learned of the effectiveness of a German bombardment at Rozenburg Château near Messines on 1 July 1916 from the diary of an unknown soldier from the 25th Battalion who was either killed or captured at Mouquet Farm. The diarist described: 'We went forward through an old sap, crawling over the parapet and into a shell hole ... Then the real show began. [The Germans] set up a hellish barrage of shells and flares on us. I had never seen such a magnificent sight before.'[60] Private descriptions of the fighting could be used to determine the effectiveness of bombardments and raids against British positions and were a good indication of morale. A letter from a 37th Battalion man captured at Houplines in February 1917 was particularly revealing:

> A terrible and mighty push will be made during the spring, and this will probably end the war. Then we will go home forever and [I will] never leave Australia again. I have had enough of it. How often do I long to be with you all at home. I am sorry that I did not listen to your words and left you. Now I am paying for it. I wish it were all over ... I send you some tears with this letter.[61]

Other disclosures had greater operational significance. After the battle of Menin Road in Belgium on 20 September 1917, a German prisoner spoke of a British officer who had been captured the night before and had told them an attack was imminent. Lieutenant Harold Ferguson of the 7th Machine Gun Company was listed as missing and was later established to be the officer to whom the German prisoner was referring. When Ferguson returned to Britain from Germany in December 1918, he was arrested for 'scandalous conduct' on suspicion of having deserted to the enemy and disclosing plans for the attack at Menin Road – he is the only Australian identified in this study as having been questioned over the conduct of his capture.[62] After a month imprisoned at Warwick Square in London, AIF Headquarters reviewed Ferguson's repatriated prisoner statement and absolved him of any wrongdoing. He had bumped into a German patrol while scouting positions in No Man's Land the night before the attack. 'I immediately dropped to my knee and drew my revolver and rushed at the patrol, killing two of them.' Ferguson had tripped and fell into a shell hole, where he was rushed by a second party and captured. 'They then conducted me to a pillbox. On my way there I destroyed all papers ... they took my Sam Brown belt and private papers.'[63]

Despite Ferguson's attempts to destroy his orders – which should not have been in the forward area for this very reason – German troops were able to recover them and make hasty preparations for the Australian attack. Commanders of the Prussian 121st Division ordered 'annihilation fire' to be brought down along the I Anzac Corps front, striking at all approaches, staging areas, gun batteries and machine-gun positions as detailed in the recovered documents.[64] Neighbouring divisions were warned, and special counter-attack units further to the rear were prepared for fighting in the Westhoek sector. Although the Australian trenches were packed with infantrymen waiting for the attack to begin, the bombardment that came down upon them did not prevent them from carrying out their attack. Within hours of the documents being recovered, the 1st and 2nd Australian Divisions carried out an otherwise highly successful assault on the German positions, supported by enormous amounts of artillery firepower.

Ferguson did not intentionally reveal information to the Germans, but there were instances where captured Australians spoke openly and willingly about operational matters to curry favour with the enemy. One occasion involved the desertion of Private Allen Yeo of the 14th Battalion to the Germans on the evening of 1 December 1916. The incident is described in the official history, with Yeo being the unnamed Australian soldier described as having 'walked over to the enemy':[65] 'A captured German soldier told of a youngster of the 4th Australian Division who had come across saying that he could no longer bear the cold and mud and want of sunlight; the officer had taken him into his own dugout and talked to him for half-an-hour – "quite a nice chap", he said.'[66]

Yeo was one of just two men from the 4th Australian Division captured in the period referred to in the official history.[67] He was carrying orders and a barrage map for a brigade attack on the German position known as Fritz's Folly in the Gueudecourt sector when he was captured. Because of the inclement weather, the fighting by this stage had come almost to a standstill, but Fritz's Folly was a small salient that protruded into the I Anzac Corps front. Previous attempts to take it had been hindered by mud, poor weather and well-placed enemy machine-guns.

In the proposed attack, guns of six siege batteries with almost unlimited supplies of ammunition would bombard the salient for three hours so there was 'nothing living in the area' when the attack began.[68]

Zero hour was fixed for the evening of 4 December 1916, with 14th Battalion receiving orders to capture Fritz's Folly and two nearby positions, Hilt and Lard trenches. The battalion commander, Lieutenant Colonel Charles Dare, sent Yeo 90 metres into the forward area with the orders and map so that one of his company commanders could study them.[69] Yeo was returning the orders to battalion headquarters when he deserted to the Germans. Instead of making his way through the water-logged and mud-congested trenches of the Australian positions, he ran down the length of a sunken road that comprised No Man's Land in full view of both Australian and German sentries. Despite repeated warnings from Australian sentries that he was going the wrong way, Yeo turned towards the German trenches and was captured by Saxon troops of the 101st Reserve Infantry Regiment.[70] With the Germans aware of the coming attack, the attack on Fritz's Folly was cancelled and Dare was immediately relieved of command.[71]

Nothing more of Yeo's desertion is documented in Australian records, and he was not questioned by German intelligence officers, so he does not appear in the German records either. But the information he carried with him had little bearing on enemy activity in the area. Ironically, a German messenger carrying documents and maps stumbled into the Australian positions later that day. Those documents revealed that German commanders of the XII (Royal Saxon) Reserve Corps planned on abandoning Fritz's Folly as soon as a new position had been built further to the rear. The prisoner explained that troops of the 23rd Reserve Division favoured the salient because of its close proximity to British lines, which meant it was not as frequently shelled. As a precaution against the Australian attack, German artillery bombarded the sunken road and the ground in front of Fritz's Folly, and on 6 December 1916, German troops abandoned the salient in accordance with XII Reserve Corps plans.[72] Yeo told the Saxons that an attack was coming, but this had no bearing on their activities and they spared the lives of the 14th Battalion men set to attack it. It was mutually beneficial for I Anzac Corps, which ended up occupying the position without incurring any further losses.

The other occasion when captured Australians willingly disclosed intelligence to the Germans was not so innocuous. Twenty-three-year-old Private Charles Christiansen of the 44th Battalion was a first-generation Australian whose father had emigrated from Flensburg on the German border with

Denmark in the 1870s.[73] Christiansen enlisted in the AIF in 1914, had landed on Gallipoli with the 11th Battalion in the early hours of 25 April 1915, and was twice wounded by shrapnel. He returned to Australia and was discharged owing to his wounds, but he re-enlisted several weeks after returning to civilian life. He evidently had a change of heart by the time the 44th Battalion arrived on the Western Front where he would be expected to fight against the German Army. According to members of his platoon, Christiansen was 'always complaining' and 'seemed to think that as a result of his wound received on Gallipoli he was entitled to a position well in the rear of the line'.[74] His eccentric behaviour came to a head a few days after the battalion carried out a trench raid near Houplines on the night of 13 March 1917 – an enterprise that resulted in nine men killed and fifty-four wounded and missing.

Four days later, in the hours before dawn on 17 March 1917, Christiansen abandoned his sentry post and fled across No Man's Land. According to German records, Christiansen drew rifle and machine-gun fire until troops of the 23rd (Royal Bavarian) Infantry Regiment came to realise his intention to give himself up. He was taken to Lille, where he was cross-examined by Major Hermann Hagen, an intelligence officer at II Bavarian Corps headquarters, to whom Christiansen said that 'he did not particularly want to be part of the war in France' on account of his German heritage. Throughout his conversation with Hagen, Christiansen made a series of frank statements about what he knew about II Anzac Corps and its operations in the Armentières sector: 'He is obviously anxious to get across that he has important information. He states to have been particularly encouraged in his decision when he learned that undertakings against our positions will be made on the night of 17/18th and 18/19th March. He had wanted to warn us about those.'[75]

No further raids were planned in the days after Christiansen's desertion, showing that either he fed misinformation to the Germans believing it to be true or concocted the story in an attempt to secure better treatment.[76] During his interrogation, Christiansen revealed the arrangement of the 11th Brigade defences, which included the location of artillery and mortar batteries in Ploegsteert Wood, and referred to 'a rumour that Ypres will be attacked in approximately eight weeks'. Discontented with his platoon commander and regimental medical officer who had both rejected his request for a base job, Christiansen told Hagen 'the officers are supposed to have a compassionate attitude but they do not really understand anything'. In turn, Hagen looked upon Christiansen as a very unreliable intelligence source, reporting that 'statements he had uttered

with high certainty became more insecure. He makes contradictory statements that undermine his credibility.'[77]

The German records do not tell us what the Bavarians did with the
information Christiansen gave them, but, as Christopher Duffy writes, the
German Army did not look upon all deserters favourably. As upholders of
military virtue, intelligence officers regarded them with suspicion and
generally respected honest prisoners who resisted questions under cross-
examination.[78] While desertion to the enemy was rare in the BEF, OHL
was suspicious that men like Yeo and Christiansen were spies attempting
to feed misinformation in an attempt to disrupt German operational
planning.[79] Both Yeo and Christiansen returned to Britain after the
Armistice, but only Christiansen was arrested for deserting to the
Germans. He confessed to his crime at AIF Headquarters and was
imprisoned at Warwick Square, but was soon after admitted to hospital
suffering from mental distress. Despite the looming prospect of the
death penalty, Christiansen never faced a court martial. His charge was
dropped, and he returned to Australia, where he was discharged in March
1919.[80]

Figure 3.4 The barn at Allonville, destroyed by rounds fired from a long-range
German rail gun in May 1918. Bean described the incident as a warning to all
captured men about the dangers of talking to the enemy. (AWM A02631)

While the information Yeo and Christiansen revealed to the Germans had little effect on the AIF's operations, it still had the potential of killing and wounding Australian troops. On the night of 30 May 1918, several high-explosive shells from a long-range German rail gun were fired at a château at Allonville, several kilometres behind the Somme front near Amiens. Two shells hit a barn where two companies of the 14th Battalion were resting, killing eighteen men and wounding sixty-eight (see figure 3.4). Just the day before, a translated German intelligence document had been circulated throughout AIF divisions, revealing how captured men from the 9th Brigade had told the Germans the location of 3rd Australian Division headquarters at Allonville.[81] Charles Bean, then the official Australian war correspondent, visited Allonville the morning after the shelling and wrote of the incident in his diary: 'The Germans were really shooting for the château. They were told some time ago, apparently, probably by a man of ours who they captured, that this was 3rd Division headquarters ... If any man of ours gave this news to them he himself killed those 18 comrades as directly as if he clubbed them.'[82] Bean later referred to the incident as the 'Allonville disaster' and described it as a 'warning to all captured men against giving away information, or even talking of such things among themselves'.[83]

It is hard to refute Bean's comments that most captured Australians were 'sturdily determined' not to give away information that might be of value to the enemy, but 'comparatively seldom' did they refuse to answer when questioned. Whether or not prisoners talked willingly, German intelligence officers were able to elicit important information from their uniforms, the documents they carried into combat, and their thoughts of home and petty grievances. From these, the German Army was able to maintain an accurate order of battle, observe activities in British lines and make assessments of Australian troop morale. Prisoners of war were important for the German Army's intelligence network, but the revelations made by individuals rarely undermined AIF operations.

Captain Mills, the Australian officer captured at Fromelles, was imprisoned in Germany and was later interned in Switzerland, where he fastidiously worked to trace the whereabouts of Australian prisoners of war in Germany on behalf of the Australian Red Cross Wounded and Missing Enquiry Bureau. The orders he took with him into combat revealed to the Germans that the Fromelles attack was nothing more than a feint, undermining the very purpose of the operation. Despite knowing this, however, German commanders decided to retain their formations in the Lille area rather than risk transferring them to the Somme.[84] While the discovery of the orders had no bearing on German operational activity in the Fromelles–Lille area, Mills' transgression shows that divulging operational information to the enemy, either willingly or unintentionally, was indeed a reality of the Australian experience of captivity in the First World War.

CHAPTER | 4

SAVING LIVES

PATRIOTIC WOMEN, PRISONERS OF WAR AND THE AUSTRALIAN RED CROSS SOCIETY

As the military and economic situation deteriorated in Germany, so did the military's ability to respect the pre-war agreements on the humane treatment of prisoners of war. Shortages worsened throughout 1917 and 1918, causing all social classes to feel the effects of the war in the pits of their stomachs. Tens of thousands of Allied prisoners of war in Germany had no option but to rely on whatever their captors could feed them. Conditions were dire, but Germany was able to defray some of the long-term costs of feeding prisoners of war by granting some of them access to humanitarian aid from the Red Cross.[1] The food situation at Karlsruhe had become so desperate in 1917 that British officers imprisoned there were offered 30 pfennigs a day to forgo the German-supplied rations so that they could be used to feed starving civilians.[2]

The International Red Cross Committee was founded in the 1860s on the principle of international humanitarianism and was backed by both the Hague and Geneva conventions.[3] Historians have questioned the role humanitarianism played in relief work during the First World War, since it was not always in the interests of global altruism. German, French and British prisoners of war benefited from aid paid for and distributed by their respective patriotic organisations.[4] This included the Australian Red Cross Society, which worked tirelessly to tend to the needs of Australian prisoners of war in both German and Ottoman captivity. Although the International Red Cross Committee had been established decades before the First World War, it did not have control over Red Cross agencies established during the war as patriotic extensions of the national war effort.[5] These particular organisations did not further the idea of inter-national humanitarianism, but raised funds for and distributed comforts to soldiers of their own military forces.[6] British, French, American and Belgian prisoners in German prison camps were sent food and clothing from their respective branches of the Red Cross and, as a result, faced better odds of surviving. Without relief from home, Russian and Italian prisoners suffered terribly from malnutrition and disease and had a 5 and 6 per cent mortality rate respectively. Romanian prisoners experienced the greatest suffering in German captivity, with 29 per cent succumbing to typhus and tuberculosis.[7]

Between August 1917 and December 1918, the Australian Red Cross Society dispatched more than 200 000 parcels for captured Australians imprisoned in Germany, which, setting rank aside, amounted to 9.5 kilograms of food and clothing per man, per day.[8] For Australians, surviving captivity in Germany did not depend on mateship, bush skills or being part of the Anzac legend but on having access to humanitarian aid and assistance from the Red Cross. An ex-prisoner of war returning to England praised the work of the Australian Red Cross Society, saying that 'without the slightest exaggeration that had it not been for these [food parcels] I should not have been here to-day'.[9] Another believed 'the Red Cross Society should get the VC, because they save any amount of lives'.[10] As Private Frank Hallihan of the 21st Battalion explained:

> It is impossible for me to write what feelings have come over me when I have thought to myself what praise is due to our Red Cross Society and everybody connected with it. Not only by the food and clothes that they send to us and which helped us in demoralising the Germans, but also for the beautiful letter that we received from Miss Chomley ... Even a German officer told me one day that our Red Cross Society was the finest organisation in the world.[11]

The role of the Red Cross in assisting Australian prisoners of war must be seen in the context of patriotism at the outset of war in August 1914, when civilians volunteered to support the first Australian troops preparing to embark overseas. The public outpouring of patriotism led to two major developments that consequently benefited Australian prisoners of war. The first was the establishment of the Australian branch of the British Red Cross Society by Lady Helen Munro Ferguson, wife of the Governor-General, just ten days after Britain declared war on Germany. This led to the formation of more than 2200 Red Cross branches across the country and 102 000 patriotic volunteers contributing to the Australian war effort. Since 88 000 of them were women, it can be said that the Red Cross played an important role in involving women in the national war effort and in public life.[12] The second development was the establishment of channels that allowed the public to donate funds so that Australian Red Cross work could continue for the duration of the war. Between 1916 and 1918, more than £176 000 was raised by public subscription, which paid for 395 595 food parcels sent to Australian prisoners in Germany and the Ottoman Empire.[13]

This chapter looks at two branches of the Australian Red Cross Society that sought to bridge the gap between the home and Germany and worked tirelessly to improve the health and well-being of Australian prisoners of war. One was the Wounded and Missing Enquiry Bureau administered by Vera Deakin, the other the Prisoner of War Department under by Mary Elizabeth Chomley. These two branches facilitated what Jay Winter has described as a 'kinship bond' between families and organisations in wartime while offering hope and support and helping to 'burn away the fog of confusion, misinformation and stylised language' of military bureaucracy.[14] Some of the women who worked in the Prisoner of War Department saw themselves as surrogate family members, referring to Australian prisoners as 'our men', while prisoners regarded its secretary, Mary Chomley, as 'a mother to us all'.[15] Tending to the needs of prisoners might have required a degree of motherhood, but Red Cross work did not directly articulate women's traditional roles. It was, as Joan Beaumont writes, a 'patriotic extension to the Australian military machine'.[16]

When the casualty lists from Gallipoli were published in Australian newspapers in May 1915, anxious families of the missing turned to the Defence Department for news of their fate. Defence rarely knew more than whether they were dead, wounded, missing or prisoners, but the information relayed to families was often misleading and contradictory.[17] Some factions of the Australian public felt something had to be done to ease the burden of misinformation and uncertainty for distraught families. In July 1915, the Red Cross New South Wales branch appointed barrister Langer Owen, KC, to establish an inquiry office in Sydney to circumvent army bureaucracy and gather information from the British Wounded and Missing Enquiry Bureau then operating from Cairo. As a result of the fighting in France the previous year, the British Red Cross had devised a system of using searchers to interview officers in hospitals and camps to seek information about a missing man's last known whereabouts. For a while, the British office in Cairo endeavoured to answer Australian

Figure 4.1 Vera Deakin, youngest daughter of the former prime minister, and secretary of the Australian Red Cross Wounded and Missing Enquiry Bureau, c. 1915. (AWM P02119.001)

inquiries, but this was not widely known or advertised at the time. It was only when the Australian Red Cross established its own Wounded and Missing Enquiry Bureau in Cairo in October 1915, under the direction of 26-year-old Vera Deakin, that Australian families started learning what had happened to their missing loved one.

Melanie Oppenheimer and Joan Beaumont write that the patriotic women who volunteered for this war work usually came from middle-class backgrounds and held militaristic and imperial views.[18] This was true of many Australian Red Cross volunteers who gave valuable assistance to prisoners of war in Germany. The Red Cross was run by the aristocracy in Britain and the ruling elites in the dominions, with each of the Australian Red Cross state secretaries being the wives of state governors. Vera Deakin was the youngest daughter of the former prime minister, had a degree in English from the University of Melbourne and had spent a period before the war travelling through Britain, Germany and Hungary pursuing a career in music.[19] Returning to Australia in August 1915, she cabled the Australian Red Cross office in Egypt seeking opportunities for war work and was at once encouraged to travel to Cairo. She was accompanied by her friend, Winifred Johnson; they both arrived on 20 October 1915 and opened the Australian Wounded and Missing Enquiry Bureau in the British Red Cross offices at the Gresham House Hotel the following morning.[20]

The bureau's task of finding the missing really came into being when Deakin's office moved to London in June 1916, once the AIF had transferred to the Western Front. The fighting on Gallipoli had shown that families of the missing were the hardest affected, since they were living in limbo not knowing whether a missing loved one was either dead, wounded or a prisoner of war. Whereas hundreds of Australians were listed as missing on Gallipoli, the fighting on the Western Front resulted in tens of thousands vanishing without trace. In the single month of May 1917, Deakin's office received 5093 inquiries and sent 2800 letters and cables to anxious families and friends of missing Australian soldiers.[21]

Rita Wilson of Meningie in South Australia typified most such anxious families. In September 1916 she wrote to the Wounded and Missing Enquiry Bureau in Adelaide seeking clarification of her brother's disappearance at Fromelles. 'What is meant by "missing"? Does it mean that he is a prisoner?'[22] Many families like the Wilsons clung to the hope that their missing son, brother or husband was alive and a prisoner of war. Some received news from officers and NCOs who knew first-hand that this was so. Nora Harvey of Canning Town, London, for example, received a letter from her Australian husband's platoon commander, assuring her that he had been captured near Bapaume and 'his life will not be in any danger during the rest of the war'.[23] These letters intended to ease the emotional strain of families, but unconfirmed reports could often give families false hope when missing men were later confirmed to have died. The Tait family of North Ballarat spent two years grieving for their son, who was missing, believed killed at Pozières. In 1918 they saw a photograph of a group of Australian prisoners in Germany in the local newspaper and believed their son to be among them. The Taits were adamant that their son was alive, 'hit on the head by a bomb and his memory may be gone'. They urged the Red Cross to 'spare no expence [sic]' and 'leave nothing undone' to find him in Germany.[24]

Deakin and her staff worked assiduously to identify prisoners of war from the many thousands of Australian soldiers who had been listed as missing on the Western Front. Operating from a single office on the ground floor of the Australian Red Cross headquarters in Westminster, the Wounded and Missing Enquiry Bureau sought to be 'the eyes and ears' of the families of missing men. Important though this work was for distraught Australian families, Deakin's London office was little more than a 'clearing-house' for reports that the British Red Cross Society prepared on behalf of Australian families.[25] After receiving lists from AIF Headquarters of confirmed dead and wounded, Deakin's staff went about creating and updating inquiry lists that went out to British Red Cross searchers who combed hospital wards and convalescent homes interviewing men from the battalions about those who appeared on the list. Since the Australian Red Cross had just nine searchers in France and Britain, it was the army of British volunteers who did most of the work.[26]

Sick and wounded soldiers were an important source of information because they were often last to see a missing man alive or dead. Searchers had to be meticulous with their questioning to make sure witnesses were talking about a man on the inquiry list. In April 1917, British searchers conducted interviews with wounded men of the 42nd Battalion recovering from wounds in hospitals at Boulogne, South London, Norwich and Oxford, hoping to establish the whereabouts of two 42nd Battalion men who had disappeared after a German trench raid on their position near Houplines. One of the missing men was Reginald Hawkins, an Indigenous soldier and a well-known personality in 7 Platoon's Lewis gun section, who was known for his dark complexion and former occupation as a buck jumper in Queensland. Several men were able to pass on information to the Red Cross that suggested 'Hawky' was a prisoner of war. He was on sentry duty and was seen to 'run over the [fire] bay when the Germans raided and ran right into their arms'. They heard him 'call out in the darkness, as if taken hold of by the Germans', and a search party later found an Australian boot tied to the wire 'to let us know [the Germans] had got one of ours'.[27]

Eyewitness testimony alone did not confirm that a missing man was a prisoner of war. Deakin's office received tens of thousands of witness reports, and since the bureau was as much an auxiliary of the army as it was serving in the interests of Australian families, reports were usually passed on to AIF Headquarters as evidence for courts of inquiry. They were not forwarded to anxious families until they had been corroborated with other sources. As is the case with all eyewitness testimony, reports often proved contradictory and misleading. Mary Watkins of Waverley in

New South Wales received news that her missing son had been seen 'surrounded by 8 of the enemy' at Lagnicourt in April 1917. The witness assumed that her son 'must have been taken prisoner', but Mary Watkins received another report saying her son had been badly wounded and was recovering in hospital in England.[28] Having been twice assured her son was alive, it was later confirmed that he had died in a German field hospital days after his capture.[29]

Deakin had to be careful in managing the expectations of concerned families. Of the 36 000 individual cases handled by the Wounded and Missing Enquiry Bureau between October 1915 and November 1918, less than 10 per cent resulted in the missing soldier turning up in Germany as a prisoner of war. In January 1918, Deakin was compelled to write to volunteers at the enquiry office in Melbourne advising them to discourage relatives of soldiers rumoured to be captured 'from entertaining hopes which had no chance of being fulfilled'.[30] The Wounded and Missing Enquiry Bureau might have sought to be the eyes and ears of anxious Australian families, but it was sometimes better to retain unconfirmed reports than worsen the situation they were trying to assuage.

A missing man was officially known to be a prisoner of war once the London office received confirmation through formal channels. In accord with the 1907 Hague Convention, Britain, France and Germany each established prisoner-of-war inquiry offices that shared information about the whereabouts and well-being of captured men via the International Red Cross Prisoner of War Agency in Geneva, Switzerland. Official lists from Switzerland confirmed the transfer of prisoners between camps and hospitals, if, when and why they died, under what circumstances, and when and from where they escaped. Since the principle of reciprocity and the threat of reprisals ensured that the belligerents adhered to the pre-war agreements, Britain and Germany willingly shared information on the well-being of prisoners so that organisations like the Wounded and Missing Enquiry Bureau could notify the relevant authorities and next of kin. Deakin's office might have been an extension of the AIF, but its work clearly depended on broader concepts of international humanitarianism to function effectively.

The Australian Red Cross also received lists of prisoners from the German War Ministry, telegrams from the neutral Red Cross office in Denmark, notifications from either the British Central Prisoners of War Committee or AIF Headquarters, and letters from other captured

men.[31] With so many offices and agencies working through neutral intermediaries, it could sometimes take months for news to make its way from
Berlin to London. Captured men remained 'missing' during this time,
relying on German provisions. In some instances, prisoners were able to
circumvent the convoluted system of information-sharing by writing directly to family and friends in England, who would cable the Red Cross
and relatives in Australia.[32] Months after her Australian husband went
missing at Bullecourt, Lilian Ryan-Smith of Upper Holloway in London
learnt that he was alive and a prisoner when he sent a letter from a work
party behind German lines at the height of the reprisals in mid-1917. Since
his reassurances belied the realities of his deliberate mistreatment, his
letter passed the German censors in France: 'Do not worry or despair.
I am doing quite well and think the time is not far distant when we both
shall be doing our usual Sunday's walk together.'[33]

Sometimes, the double, triple and quadruple handling of information
through intermediaries increased the likelihood of mistakes that exacerbated the anguish of Australian families. Having been told by the Defence
Department that her husband had been killed at Fromelles, Catherine
Cahill of Clifton Hill in Melbourne received a cable from the International
Red Cross Prisoner of War Agency in Switzerland that said her husband
was alive and a prisoner of war. Having bypassed the Wounded and
Missing Enquiry Bureau where error would have otherwise been noticed,
the cable said her husband was 'in excellent condition of health' and
had written home just three weeks before.[34] After eighteen months of
mourning, Catherine Cahill was elated by the news that her husband was
alive. But instead of his letter, she received a cable six months later telling
her of a grievous error. Despite all good intentions, the Swiss authorities
had confused her husband with another Australian soldier captured at
Fromelles, meaning news of her husband's death 'may be assumed to be
correct'. In the end, Catherine Cahill mourned her husband twice over.[35]

Despite occasional administrative mishaps, Deakin's Wounded and
Missing Enquiry Bureau filled the void felt by many Australian families
anxious for news of their missing son, brother or husband. The most
fortunate were families of men who were later confirmed prisoners of war,
some of whom sent heartfelt letters of appreciation to Deakin and her
volunteers. 'I feel I cannot thank you enough for your goodness in finding
the whereabouts of my son. The happiness to know he is still alive is
great.'[36] The brother of one Australian prisoner of war in Germany felt
the Red Cross had 'lifted a great load of anxiety off my mind'.[37]

Figure 4.2 Mary Elizabeth Chomley OBE, secretary of the Australian Red Cross Prisoner of War Department, 1916–19. (IWM WWC D8–5 566)

Once a missing man was confirmed as a prisoner of war, the Australian Red Cross Prisoner of War Department set about sending him regular consignments of food and clothing for the duration of his captivity. Like Deakin, the department's secretary, Mary Elizabeth Chomley, embodied middle-class, militaristic and imperialistic values. She was the daughter of a Melbourne judge who presided over the County and Supreme Courts of Victoria (he had been assistant prosecutor in the trial of the notorious bushranger Ned Kelly) and was well known within Melbourne social circles for her charity and social work. Chomley was a strong and independent woman with a keen sense of moral responsibility, and her well-connected social network reflected nineteenth-century attitudes to voluntary action. She had been the inaugural secretary of the Australian Exhibition of Women's Work in 1907, a founding member of the Arts and Crafts Society Victoria, and was a long-standing member of the Victoria League, an organisation that promoted loyalty to the British Empire and offered practical assistance to people in need. At the age of

43, unmarried and without children, Mary Chomley had been on a year-long tour of Europe when war erupted in August 1914.[38] True to her patriotic convictions and loyalty to the British Empire, she joined the Voluntary Aid Detachment in London and worked as superintendent of domestic staff at Princess Christian's Hospital for Officers in Grosvenor Street. There, Mary Chomley was said to have been the 'leading spirit' for Australian officers wounded on Gallipoli and recovering in the Melbourne ward.[39]

Chomley was an important figure in the lives of Australian prisoners in Germany, but she did not work single-handedly or as independently as others have assumed.[40] She had very little to do with the formation of the Prisoner of War Department, which came about following public concern over how Australian troops would fare if they had the misfortune of falling into the hands of the 'Hun'. Although the Australian Red Cross was well established by the time Australian troops landed on Gallipoli, it was slow to respond to the needs of seventy-nine Australians captured in the campaign who were then languishing in Ottoman camps. With no other support, these prisoners had to rely on parcels from families and friends, who had no idea what to send or how much. Since Ottoman Turkey did not have a representative at the International Prisoner of War Agency in Switzerland, families were asked to send money to the American Ambassador in Constantinople, who was doing all he could to ease suffering of British prisoners of war.[41]

After the AIF transferred to the Western Front, the Australian Red Cross worked to provide prisoners of war with regular consignments of food and clothing. In July 1916, the Australian High Commissioner in London, Andrew Fisher, organised a delegation to visit the British section of the International Prisoner of War Agency in Geneva with a view to creating a system that shored up the welfare needs of captured Australians. Australian Red Cross work is usually seen as having been carried out by patriotic women like Deakin and Chomley, but three men comprised the Australian mission to Geneva: Colonel Frederick Fairbairn, chief commissioner of the Australian Red Cross in London, Brigadier General Victor Sellheim, commandant at AIF Headquarters, and Colonel Charles Ryan, a consulting surgeon at AIF medical headquarters, who as a younger man had served as a surgeon for the Ottomans in the Russo-Turkish War and had the distinction of enduring several months in Russian captivity.[42]

For eight days, the mission studied the inner workings of the International Prisoner of War Agency and spoke with British officers interned at Château-d'Oex. They concluded that 'the food and clothing supplied to [British] prisoners in Germany is not sufficient for the maintenance of health, and indeed of life itself in some instances'. In their report to the Australian High Commissioner, Fairbairn, Sellheim and Ryan recommended that a 'responsible body' organise and send regular consignments of parcels to make Australian prisoners of war wholly self-sufficient rather than dependent on the German-supplied provisions. Fairbairn was happy to offer the services of his patriotic Red Cross volunteers to do the work the AIF was either incapable of or unwilling to perform. He recommended that 'all individuals desirous of helping in this work should therefore be requested to apply to the Australian branch of the Red Cross Society. Their efforts would be appreciated in this way.'[43]

The Prisoner of War Department was formally established in the Australian Red Cross offices at 54 Victoria Street in Westminster in July 1916, largely based on the model the Canadians had developed the previous year.[44] At least six well-connected middle-class Australian women already in London volunteered. The department's inaugural secretary, Kathleen O'Connor, was the youngest daughter of a New South Wales senator and High Court judge; aged 30, she was a mezzo-soprano soloist 'of no small order'.[45] Annie Chirnside, wife of a respected Victorian cattle breeder, had previously been president of the Werribee District Red Cross and had raised funds for local soldiers serving abroad.[46] Ruth Oliver was the youngest daughter of the royal commissioner for the Australian federal capital, while the Fisken sisters, Lilly and Alice, were active in the District Nursing Society and Free Kindergarten of Victoria before travelling to England at the start of the war. Having volunteered at Robert Lindsay Hospital throughout 1915, they spent time as munitions workers at a Vickers Limited armament factory before joining the Prisoner of War Department in 1916.[47] Agnes Edwards and Irene Davis were also from well-to-do families whose social standing promoted voluntary action, and similarly offered their services to the new Red Cross department as soon as they heard the call for volunteers.[48]

Fairbairn would have been aware of the social standing of the volunteers working for the Australian Red Cross Society in London, since he was himself part of Melbourne society. A wealthy pastoralist educated at Cambridge, he was captain of the Geelong Golf Club, sat on the committee of the Victorian Racing Club, and was said to have been 'one of the best amateur cricketers of his time in England'.[49]

These initial volunteers might have been well positioned in Australian social life, but they were not all best suited for the task required of them. Within days of the department's establishment, the number of Australian prisoners in Germany swelled from nineteen to five hundred owing to the 5th Australian Division's disastrous action at Fromelles. O'Connor was reported to have done an exceptional job in running the department in its opening weeks, but the increased workload coincided with news that her brother had been killed while fighting with the New Zealand Expeditionary Force in France. This left her unable to respond to the department's needs, so Fairbairn invited Chomley to become the new 'superintendent [and] relieve Miss O'Connor of the responsibility'.[50] Not only did Fairbairn and Chomley move in the same social circles in Melbourne but also Chomley's experience in managing voluntary groups matched the skills needed to mobilise the Australian Prisoner of War Department. By November 1916, Chomley had nine workers and occasional helpers, who in a single month packed 5280 parcels of food, 1781 parcels of tobacco, 708 parcels of clothing and 81 special hospital packages for Australian prisoners of war in Germany.[51]

Figure 4.3 The Australian Red Cross Prisoner of War Department in London, c. 1918. Mary Elizabeth Chomley is seated centre in the front row, fifth from the left. (SLVIC H2013.234/7)

Several weeks after arriving at a prison camp in Germany, Australian prisoners of war could expect to receive a typed letter from Mary Chomley explaining what assistance they could receive from her Prisoner of War Department.[52] The department would send six food parcels a month, 160 cigarettes, more than a kilogram of tobacco, and as much soap as permitted by War Office regulations. Each food parcel was a veritable pantry compared to what they received from their German captors, containing tea, sugar, condensed milk, biscuits, beef dripping, cheese, oats, jam and three tins of meat.[53] Contents varied to avoid monotony, and since most tinned goods were coming from Australia, it would be fair to say that Australian prisoners of war in contact with the Red Cross ate better in quality and quantity than the troops still fighting in France. In addition to parcels, prisoners of all nationalities were added to a bread list and received three loaves a week from bakeries in Switzerland and Denmark, while the wounded were sent extra parcels containing milk powder, beef tea and infant formula. Mary Chomley also updated a man's postal address with AIF Headquarters so that his mail would be sent directly to Germany.[54]

Food parcels were a welcome relief from the insufficient German diet, but they had to be closely monitored to avoid wastage. The first dispatch of food parcels from Britain to Germany was sent in 1914–15 amid concerns within the War Office about inefficient relief to British prisoners of war. While the British public was concerned that prisoners were not receiving enough food and clothing, the War Office was concerned that they received too much, which resulted in the Red Cross tracking millions of parcels being sent by families and regimental and welfare committees. A census of parcels passing through the General Post Office in June and July 1916 found the overall quantity excessive and its distribution unequal, with some men receiving sixteen parcels a fortnight while others got none. In response, the War Office directed the Central Prisoners of War Committee to authorise, control and coordinate the numerous relief and welfare organisations and regulate parcels being sent from England.[55] By placing restrictions on aid distribution, the War Office turned a voluntary war effort into a regulated industry.

While the Australian Prisoner of War Department comprised patriotic volunteers who felt it their duty to assist the national war effort, the department itself was made to regulate the amount of food and clothing for prisoners of war in Germany as a subsidiary of the Central Prisoners of War Committee. Privates and NCOs could receive no more than 27 kilograms of food a month, whereas officers could be sent up to

Figure 4.4 British Red Cross volunteers in London packing food parcels for Australian prisoners of war in Germany. (AWM H00507)

100 kilograms.[56] British volunteers at Haymarket stores packed parcels for Australians in Germany to stem the flow of contraband such as compasses and maps being illegally sent by well-intentioned family members – some of whom clearly expected their loved ones to escape. Contraband risked disrupting regular parcel supply; soap was monitored to enforce the blockade of Germany, and pepper was prohibited because it prevented bloodhounds from following the scented trail of escaping prisoners. Tubes of toothpaste might contain maps, tooth powder might contain poison, and some brands of British cigarettes were restricted because of the offensive depiction of the 'Hun' on the accompanying trading card.[57] Chomley dissuaded families and regimental associations from sending parcels, explaining that they rarely got past the German censors and were returned if unsuitable.[58]

Clothing was also closely monitored. Chomley explained to the men that they could expect an emergency clothing parcel and two new uniforms every six months. The first consignment contained warm underwear, a woollen cardigan, braces, handkerchiefs, towels, toiletries, a sewing kit, 100 cigarettes, a pipe and enough tobacco to last a week. Once the department received a man's measurements from AIF Headquarters, two uniforms, including a greatcoat, cardigan and boots, were sent to them in Germany. Officers could wear the same AIF khaki tunics, breeches, boots and leggings, but other ranks had to wear a distinctive prisoner-of-war uniform made in Britain and based on the obsolete Kitchener Blue uniforms with khaki drill inserts – after industrial-grade washing and fumigation, the dyes in these khaki inserts had a tendency to turn a brownish red (examples held in the collection of the Australian War Memorial are roughly the colour of dried blood).[59] German clothing policies ensured that the other ranks assigned to work parties in Germany were kept visually distinct from the local civilians and less likely to escape, but, as Oliver Wilkinson argues, it also had a psychological effect on a soldier's identity: 'The replacement clothing labelled them as captives, with all the potentially negative connotations (defeated, victim, coward, deserter and so on).'[60] The German authorities issued prisoners of other nationalities with an assortment of civilian and military uniforms altered with canvas and calico inserts, but British regulations ensured that Australians and other British prisoners of war in Germany received uniforms straight from War Office stores.

There was a notable difference between prisoners receiving parcels and men not in contact with the Red Cross. An Australian prisoner who had spent six months behind German lines during the reprisals entered camp at Friedrichsfeld with a group of men who were 'dreadfully thin, while some inside the wire were just the reverse!'[61] Constantly moving between camps and hospitals in France and Germany, the wounded suffered immensely while they waited for parcels to arrive. William Barry lost 25 kilograms in the ninety-three days he spent in hospitals in France before arriving in Germany. 'This rapid weight loss made me weak and was aiding rather than easing the pain of dysentery, which remained in various degrees of acuteness most of the time.'[62] It might have been tempting for starving men to satisfy months of hunger when they received their first food parcel, but they had to resist the urge to gorge themselves or risk a condition known as refeeding syndrome, which was fatal if not managed properly.[63] It was common for prisoners to experience 'internal trouble' once their diet improved, so men who arrived in Germany resembling 'walking skeletons' were often kept on a diet of powdered milk and soft foods for a while before being slowly reintroduced to solids.[64]

Figure 4.5 The obsolete British Army Kitchener Blue uniform sent from War Office stores in London to all British and dominion other ranks in German captivity. Some Australian prisoners of war wrote to the Red Cross feeling 'quite smart' in their new uniforms. (AWM EF1219)

An anonymous piece of doggerel from one of the other ranks camps encapsulates the sentiments shared by many hungry prisoners of war who desperately waited for Red Cross parcels to arrive:

> I am a *Kriegsgefangener*
> I wish that I were dead
> It's all through drinking sauerkraut
> And eating mouldy bread.
>
> My bed is in the corner,
> I sleep upon the floor
> My back is nearly broken
> My ribs are very sore.
>
> And when the war is over
> And I settle down to rest,
> If ever I meet a squarehead,
> I'll smash his bloody chest.[65]

The Red Cross was not the only welfare support hungry prisoners could turn to for assistance. All large prison camps had a British Help Committee, which sought to assist all sick, wounded and men not yet receiving regular consignments from the Red Cross. Warrant Officer John Bannigan of the 2nd Field Artillery Brigade managed the Help Committee at Soltau, and his description of this in-camp welfare work shows just how important it was for British prisoners of war. Since the German authorities at Soltau lacked the resources and supplies to tend properly to the growing needs of prisoners, Bannigan administered the 'medicines, bandages, pills etc' he received from the Invalids Comfort Fund, and gave out 'condensed milk, Bovril, Mellin's food, Glaxo ... which we could feed the wounded and sick, whom hard food would surely have killed'.[66] Bannigan dedicated his time in captivity to alleviating the pain and suffering of his fellow prisoners. Following his repatriation in 1919, he was awarded the Meritorious Service Medal for 'devotion and duty' in captivity.[67]

Despite the naval blockade and the economic hardships affecting all German social classes, the principle of reciprocity and the possibility of reprisals against German prisoners in England ensured that the German authorities adhered to pre-war agreements and allowed the delivery of food to British prisoners. Armed guards escorted deliveries of parcels from Dutch and Danish ports to prevent them being tampered with or stolen, and German troops and civilians faced harsh penalties if caught stealing from prisoners. There were supply problems and petty restrictions imposed by local authorities, and guards and prisoners sometimes pilfered parcels from camp post offices. But Chomley estimated that 80 per cent of food parcels succeeded in reaching their intended recipients.[68] One man admired the German conduct regarding the delivery of parcels: 'From what I saw of the average German soldier, he was honest. What I particularly noticed was he would sooner starve than steal our food. This "honesty" was inspired by fear of punishment, which was very severe if he happened to be caught. He was even punished if caught accepting a gift and the giver would also be punished.'[69]

A consistent, nutritious diet restored famished men to health, but parcels also had an immediate influence on morale. Prisoners in contact with the Red Cross were also connected with the outside world and were assured that they would never again suffer chronic hunger. In spite of what the German clothing regulations might have intended, prisoners generally found a renewed sense of self-worth once they received new uniforms from Britain. As Wilkinson argues, these helped to continue a British military identity, even in captivity.[70] One man at Güstrow wrote to Mary Chomley in October 1917 thanking the Red Cross for 'the blue prisoner uniform with a brown stripe on the trousers', which made him feel 'quite smart'.[71] Another Australian on a farm in Western Pomerania overheard German civilians comment how stylishly dressed he was for a prisoner of war.[72] Other ranks regularly wrote to the Prisoner of War Department requesting colour patches, regimental titles and Rising Sun collar badges so as to distinguish themselves as Australians from the tens of thousands of other British prisoners in the camps and work parties. Access to the Australian Red Cross facilitated access to uniforms, regimental titles, colour patches and badges, and helped Australians to accentuate a distinctive national identity among other British and dominion prisoners of war.[73] One man at Sagan said the distinctively Australian collar badges he received 'make us look smarter still. That is our ambition here, to look as clean and smart as possible under the circumstances.'[74]

Chomley received hundreds of photographs from Australian prisoners in Germany eager to show how well they were faring thanks to the work of the Prisoner of War Department – these photographs were often arranged by the German camp administration, showing how well prisoners were faring in German captivity. If Deakin's Wounded and Missing Enquiry Bureau was the wartime proxy for families of dead and missing soldiers, as Jay Winter writes,[75] Chomley became something of a surrogate mother for Australian prisoners of war and an important figure in

Figure 4.6 Red Cross food parcels arrive at the camp for other ranks prisoners at Schneidemühl, East Prussia, c. 1917. (AWM P01981.009)

their emotional survival. Mail from Britain arrived more regularly than from Australia, so Chomley often took it upon herself to write to the men and became a nurturing presence in their lives. She periodically asked if they needed anything special to make their captivity less alienating and monotonous. 'This is one thing above all I would like', replied one Australian prisoner of war at Sennelager in December 1917. 'If you have a piece of Ali Baba's magic carpet on hand I would be pleased if you would send it per return.'[76]

As secretary of the Prisoner of War Department, Chomley spent most of her working day corresponding with AIF Headquarters, War Office subsidiaries and state-based Red Cross branches. But after hours, she wrote to hundreds of Australian prisoners of war imprisoned in camps across Germany and the Ottoman Empire. While aspects of Red Cross work were merely extensions of the broader Australian war effort, Mary Chomley saw it as her patriotic duty to lend emotional support to prisoners of war, who, as one man put it, had 'no friends nearer than Australia'.[77] Unlike the bureaucratic tone of formality that families received from the Defence Department and AIF Administrative Headquarters, correspondence between Chomley and prisoners seemed open and sincere. One man at Münster began a letter with an apology. 'Pardon my liberty in addressing you as "my dear friend" but you have looked after us so well out here that I cannot regard you in any other light.'[78]

The Prisoner of War Department received 20 000 cards and letters each month from Australian prisoners of war in Germany, and while many were receipts confirming parcels received, Chomley felt compelled to respond to individual letters. She made sure Australian prisoners working in East Prussia had enough cardigans, jerkins, gloves and thigh-length trench boots to see them through the cold winter, and also arranged a book scheme of distinctively Australian titles to stave off inactivity and boredom.[79] She also mediated some men's domestic problems, as was the case when she learned about the wife of an Australian prisoner in Germany who had abandoned their two children and remarried but was still drawing a portion of her first husband's pay while he was in Germany. Chomley arranged for his allotment to go to his children, then wrote to Helen Munro Ferguson, seeking to have them placed in the care of a local Catholic institution.[80]

Strong-willed and determined, Mary Chomley rarely let emotion cloud her judgement on the well-being of individual prisoners. When she learned of Charles Christiansen's desertion to the Germans, she refused to treat him any differently from the thousands of Australian prisoners seeking assistance from her department. She replied to the wife of an Australian officer who instructed the Red Cross to refuse him parcels, saying she would not pass judgement on a man who was not in a position to explain his actions. 'Of course we are still sending him parcels, and I hope that it may turn out that he has been misjudged.'[81] She often cared too much, as was the case with a group of Australian Army Medical Corps stretcher-bearers captured at Mouquet Farm in August 1916. Since the 1906 Geneva Convention deemed them non-combatants, they could not be held as prisoners of war, so Chomley facilitated their return to Britain in 1918. She aired her opinions to AIF Headquarters when two men elected to return to return to the fighting in France instead of returning home to Australia. 'They say quite plainly they will never allow themselves to be taken alive again. Had I known these men would have to be sent straight back to the firing line, with every prospect of being taken Prisoner a second time ... I certainly would never have taken the trouble that I have taken to get them exchanged.'[82]

When Australian prisoners were repatriated to Britain after the Armistice, many visited the Australian Red Cross offices to meet the Prisoner of War Department volunteers and thank them for the invaluable help they had given them. For several weeks there was a 'serial tea party' in a room overlooking Buckingham Palace gardens where ex-prisoners of war and volunteer workers conversed around tables with flowers, flags, sandwiches and 'real old-fashioned plum cake'.[83] Australian prisoners of war did not attribute their survival to characteristics that affirmed the Anzac legend, but pointed to the voluntary efforts of the patriotic women of the Australian Red Cross Society. Referring to Mary Chomley, one man captured at Bullecourt who endured the reprisals said, 'It is to her we owe our lives.'[84] Vera Deakin's Wounded and Missing Enquiry Bureau was just as important, being the conduit through which families discovered that their missing son, brother or husband was alive or dead. For their substantial contributions to the Australian Red Cross Society, both Vera Deakin and Mary Chomley were made officers of the Order of the British Empire (Civil) in March 1918.

CHAPTER 5

CHALLENGING THE HOLZMINDEN ILLUSION

THE MYTH AND REALITY OF ESCAPE

On the evening of 23 July 1918, twenty-nine British prisoners at the officers' camp at Holzminden in Lower Saxony escaped after spending nine months digging a tunnel beneath their enclosure. Among them was Lieutenant Peter Lyons, a Western Australian of the 11th Battalion, who had tried to escape from Holzminden on two other occasions. Armed with a compass, a map of Germany, some money and a cut of bacon, this time Lyons was successful and took off across Germany towards neutral Holland with two other British officers. Lyons recalled hiding in woods during the day and avoiding all major roads and villages by night. 'When night came and things were quiet, we would set out again ... we travelled in this manner for 12 days, covering 185 miles [298 kilometres].'[1]

Escapes like this offered the prospect of transforming what was essentially a story of surrender, inaction, confinement and oppression into an exciting battle of wits between captive and captor. According to Stephen Garton, prisoners of war who tried escaping were transformed from passive victims into 'heroic men of action in a lineage stretching back to the siege of Troy'.[2] This is especially pertinent in the way in which captivity in Germany during the First World War has been popularly imagined. In her account of the Holzminden escape, Jacqueline Cook writes that British prisoners of war turned their minds to escape as soon as 'the doors slammed shut and the key turned in the lock'.[3] But does this accurately reflect Australian prisoners' responses to captivity in the First World War? The dominance of escape narratives in Britain in the interwar

Figure 5.1 The exposed tunnel used in the mass escape from Holzminden in Lower Saxony on the evening of 23 July 1918. Despite the prominence of escape narratives in remembering captivity in Germany, the Australian prisoner-of-war experience during the First World War suggests that prison breaks like this were more myth than reality. (AWM H11791)

period reflected a tendency for captured officers to publish memoirs of their wartime experiences rather than the other ranks. Since officers generally fared better than other ranks in captivity, their imprisonment was often seen in terms of 'a kind of public school surrounded by barbed wire'.[4] One Australian officer described the sporting nature of escape. 'Here we were, surrounded by barbed wire, well-armed sentries and brilliant arc lights, and the problem was to get out!'[5] In marked contrast to the ordeals endured by the other ranks during the reprisals in German-occupied France, this seemingly light-hearted version of German captivity helped to reinforce later perceptions that the First World War was a 'curiously civilised war'.[6]

It might have been an 'officer's duty' to escape during the Second World War, but British and dominion prisoners in the First World War had no official guidance about what was expected of them if they had the misfortune of falling into enemy hands. The 1907 Hague Convention made reference to escaped prisoners not being punished if they were recaptured, but this alone did not impress upon officers and other ranks of the BEF how to act or behave as prisoners of war. *Field Service Regulations* gave clear instructions on how to handle enemy prisoners for the purposes of gathering intelligence, but there was no direction on what was expected if officers or men were captured.[7] The War Office was decidedly vague on how soldiers should behave in the hands of the enemy, lest the message implied that surrendering was a preferable alternative to fighting to the end. With this came a stigma associated with capture inherent in the *Manual of Military Law* (1907), which deemed it a capital offence for British soldiers to 'shamefully cast away arms ... in the presence of the enemy', 'treacherously ... give intelligence to the enemy', and 'misbehave before the enemy in such a manner as to show cowardice'.[8] It was therefore not an officer's duty to attempt escape in the First World War. The decision to escape ultimately rested with individuals who had to decide whether life on the outside was preferable to spending the rest of the war behind barbed wire.

Despite varying lengths of time behind German lines, all surviving Australian prisoners were sent to Germany and entered an enormous prison system that comprised 105 industrial-size 'parent' camps (*Stammlager*) and more than 1.6 million prisoners by mid-1916.[9] By October 1918, those numbers had swelled to 175 camps and 2.5 million prisoners of war.[10] Fortunately, by the time the first Australians arrived in Germany in May 1916, the primitive *ad hoc* camps that had been plagued by hunger and disease had been significantly improved. The early camps had been overcrowded and unhygienic, but the new camps could accommodate up to 20 000 prisoners and were distributed along the principal rail networks to facilitate distribution of labour to key industrial and agricultural areas.

Attached to each camp was a complex network of smaller, more mobile working camps (*Arbeitskommando*) where other ranks worked to support Germany's diminishing wartime economy. While the perception of captivity in Germany is of uniformed officers detained in camps surrounded by barbed wire fences, in reality only officers and sick and injured other ranks remained idle for any length of time. Due to the blockade and Germany's economic problems, tens of thousands of Allied prisoners went out 'on commando' (as many British and dominion prisoners described it), assigned to work parties with German civilians in agriculture, industry, mining, quarrying and land drainage. By 1916, more than 90 per cent of all prisoners of war in Germany were out working beyond the confines of their associated camps.[11]

Figure 5.2 The camp for other ranks at Güstrow in Pomerania during a bleak and miserable German winter, c.1917–18. (AWM P09691.152)

A feature of the German prison camp system was segregation of captives along ethnic, religious and social lines. The camp authorities made no national distinctions between the major European armies and Caucasian troops from the dominions, which were all treated alike. As British prisoners, Australian shared quarters and worked alongside other predominantly white Christian prisoners of war, which included the French, Belgians and later Americans, Italians and Portuguese. Muslims and colonial troops from North Africa and South Asia were held at special propaganda camps at Wünsdorf-Zossen near Berlin, where they were subjected to German attempts to stir anti-colonial sentiment in an effort to destabilise the imperial control of Britain, France and Russia.[12] A similar attempt was made against Irish prisoners who were transferred to Limburg an der Lahn in December 1914 in an unsuccessful attempt to raise a brigade to fight against the British in Ireland alongside nationalist Sir Roger Casement.[13] Further segregation occurred to minimise the spread of disease. Arrivals from France were fumigated and inoculated and spent several days in quarantine before entering a camp, where they were kept separate from Russians and Romanians, who had been exposed to typhus epidemics at home and on the Eastern Front.[14] Officers and other ranks were also segregated. From the start of the war, captured officers were held in specially designated *Offizierslager* where accommodation and facilities were much better than those for other ranks. The Hague Convention exempted officers from working, ensured that they were paid at the same level as their corresponding rank in the German Army, and permitted freedoms that included parole and walks beyond the prison walls.[15]

War Office records show that of the 3848 Australians captured by German forces during the First World War, only two officers and forty-one other ranks succeeded in escaping.[16] Those who made successful escapes represented 1.1 per cent of all Australians captured by German forces, which means that more than 98 per cent of Australians remained in German hands until the end of hostilities.[17] The figures show that Canadians were more likely to succeed in their escapes than Australians (2.6 per cent of Canadians in German hands), although Australians were twice as likely to succeed as Newfoundlanders and South Africans (both 0.5 per cent), New Zealanders (0.4 per cent), British (0.2 per cent) and Indians (0 per cent).[18] The sources do not reveal how many prisoners tried to escape and were recaptured, but they show that Australians and other British prisoners of war in Germany were nowhere near as successful in their escape attempts as what popular accounts suggest. The figures raise important questions about why successful escapes were so uncommon. Do they reflect the enormous difficulties faced by prisoners who tried to escape, or were the majority of prisoners resigned to their fate and happy to spend the rest of the war behind barbed wire?

It first needs to be established just how difficult escaping was – especially from Germany. The most significant challenge facing British and French prisoners of war attempting to return to their own forces was the Western Front itself. Spanning 700 kilometres from the North Sea on the Belgian coast to the German border with Switzerland in the south, the Western Front was a formidable physical impediment that comprised vast trench networks, barbed wire, machine-guns and hundreds of thousands of German soldiers, all of which made it virtually impossible to penetrate without detection. After breaking out of a guarded prison camp without raising alarm, escaping prisoners would have to make their way across German-occupied territory, penetrate No Man's Land and survive an encounter with friendly forces at the other end. They usually had to do so alone, since help from the civilian population was limited owing to the harsh and repressive measures of German occupation.[19] French and Belgian civilians harbouring escaped prisoners were treated as spies, as was the case with British Red Cross nurse Edith Cavell, who in 1915 was executed for assisting 200 British prisoners of war to escape into Holland from her medical clinic in occupied Brussels.

Notwithstanding the challenges facing escaped prisoners on the run, those who evaded their captors immediately after capture had the best odds of escaping owing to the relatively short distance between them and friendly territory. Escapes like this were more common in 1918 when the fighting was more fluid and mobile than it had been in static trench warfare. This was the case for two Australian prisoners who succeeded in overpowering their captors after a German raid on the 17th Battalion positions near Sally-le-Sec on Morlancourt Ridge in May 1918. One man was able to pick up a rifle from the battlefield and kill his captor as he was being led to the rear, whereupon he waited for nightfall before returning to Australian lines. Another was able to drop into a shell hole as machine-guns fired on and killed his captors, and he too returned under the cover of darkness.[20] Perhaps the best known example is that involving Lieutenant Joe Maxwell of the 18th Battalion, who was able to fight his way out of captivity in one of the last AIF actions on the Western Front. After surrendering to German machine-gunners in the midst of combat, Maxwell was led to the rear where he shot and killed his captors with an automatic pistol he had concealed inside his gas respirator case. Maxwell made his way back to British lines and rejoined the fighting, going on to silence several other German machine-gun positions. For his actions (and by clearly overlooking his surrender in the first place), Maxwell was awarded the Victoria Cross.[21]

Actions like these seemed to reinforce attributes about the Australian soldier that suited the Anzac legend – his inherent ability to outwit the enemy and reverse a seemingly hopeless situation with great dash and good humour. Daring though these were, they were not the norm, especially when escape attempts by unarmed prisoners could almost always have fatal consequences. Evidence suggests German sentries killed a group of Australians captured near Villers-Bretonneux on 5 April 1918 following an unsuccessful attempt to overpower them.[22] In the days after capture, it was much more common for prisoners to display a complex series of psychological processes that rendered captured men paralysed with fear, shock and confusion. An American sociologist who studied the psychological stresses in captivity during the Second World War described this as a time when prisoners 'remain silent with no apparent interest in anything, even escape'. Australian prisoners were similarly affected by what he called 'collection centre stupor', which concealed a basic fear of the unknown and, with it, the potential dangers that lay ahead.[23] One man captured at Mouquet Farm described the moment when German troops overran his position and 'flew at us with rifles and anything to take our lives. But we didn't care then, we were no more use.'[24] This was a man soundly defeated in body and mind and in no state to make a bold bid for freedom.

The odds of making a successful escape diminished further as prisoners of war were led from the battlefield and deeper into German-occupied territory. Those who endured the reprisals behind the lines in 1917 might have been just kilometres from Allied forces (including artillery) but were subjected to violence, neglect and abuse that significantly reduced their physical and mental condition. Prisoners working at the work camp at Marquion were more concerned with their next meal than hatching a plan to escape. One man described how 'a few minutes after [eating] the pangs of hunger are aggravated again & until the ravenous feeling wears off & the dull ache sets in again, it is sheer torture. One cannot think clearly & only grasp the meaning in a dull sort of way.'[25] Prisoners subjected to reprisals were probably physically and mentally less capable of escaping. Ravaged by disease and malnutrition in the German forward area, they became 'merely skeletons ... wretched and woebegone' within weeks.[26] An Australian officer realised that escape was virtually impossible when he was subsisting wholly on German-supplied rations. They were 'not sufficient to keep one healthy and strong, much less did they enable us to put by portions from time to time for use on a trek to the frontier'.[27]

Just five of the estimated 1400 Australians subjected to the reprisals succeeded in making a successful bid for freedom. The first were Lance Corporal Hamilton Parsons and Private George Stewart, West Australians of the 16th Battalion, who were captured at Bullecourt and escaped from the Marquion work party after six weeks in the hands of the Germans. Using a pair of wire-cutters to break out of their compound at night during a thunderstorm, they headed west towards friendly territory using the flares drifting over No Man's Land to guide them. They moved only at night to avoid detection, and spent their days hiding in woods, hedges, sunken roads and half-completed dugouts until they reached the front line, which they somehow passed without raising alarm. A British sentry detected the pair as they crossed No Man's Land, thinking they were Germans:

> Parsons was shot in the shoulder and someone called 'Halt!' We knew by the voice that it was a British sentry, and although he told us to put our hands up, we just rushed past him into our trenches, right into the Australians and near the same spot where we previously had been captured. We were, of course, well fed and quite happy.[28]

By sheer luck, Parsons and Stewart re-entered Allied lines at the very spot where they had been captured six weeks earlier after it had been captured by Australian troops in later fighting. Charles Bean later interviewed the men, and went on to publish a lengthy dispatch about how poorly Australian prisoners were faring in German hands.[29] Parsons and Stewart were both awarded the Military Medal for their successful escape, and returned to Australia in the following months. Parsons spent the rest of the war with the Western Australian Recruiting Committee, giving talks about his experiences behind German lines to help stimulate recruiting for the AIF.[30]

Their story was also used to stir resentment among Australian troops fighting on the Western Front, with Bean's dispatch appearing in print several days before II Anzac Corps went into action at Messines on 7 June 1917. As the then commander of the 3rd Australian Division, Major General John Monash made sure his assaulting companies had read the story so that the ordeal of the Bullecourt prisoners would raise their indignation in combat.[31] Bean says the story had no recorded effect on the performance of the 3rd Australian Division at Messines, but it did among men of the 4th Australian Division, who had suffered heavily in the Bullecourt attack and whose men were being deliberately mistreated behind German lines. One 47th Battalion man was 'nettled' after reading the story of the escaped prisoners, and went into action at Messines vowing not to take prisoners. 'Nothing wearing the German uniform was to be spared', he wrote. 'They all had to die ... if the Germans break all laws then we must do the same to get even with them.'[32]

Once prisoners of war were transported to Germany and entered the prison camps, the prospect of making a successful escape diminished even further. If successful, the likely destination for a prisoner on the run was neutral Holland or Switzerland. The German authorities expected escapes to be made from camps close to these frontiers and therefore bolstered their security. This included officers' camps in the Rhineland, where many British officers were concentrated in late 1917 as a reprisal against British and French aircraft bombing military and civilian targets in towns along the Rhine and the Moselle rivers. The policy was meant to deter future air raids, but it put many camps close to the Dutch border and they were obvious places from which officers might try to escape. Camps on the Rhine had more sentries, guard towers and barbed wire than most other camps in Germany, and sentries routinely and rigorously patrolled the border area on bicycles and with bloodhounds. In some areas, Dutch road signs were used to fool escaping prisoners into thinking they had crossed the frontier, while prisoners who were successful in reaching the border discovered they had to negotiate an electrified fence before crossing into neutral territory. Although the Hague Convention prevented the German authorities from doing so, there were often repercussions for men caught escaping. One Australian soldier imprisoned at Soltau did 'not personally know of any of our chaps escaping while a prisoner of war in Germany . . . Attempts at escape were not punished very severely unless the offender was found in possession of fire-arms. But it might mean being placed "on the list" for the salt-mines. And there was no joy in that.'[33] Another Australian was not so fortunate: he was caught trying to escape, tied to a tree and threatened with execution.[34]

Notwithstanding harsh penalties designed to dissuade prisoners from an attempt at flight, it was extremely difficult for escaped prisoners to flee from the large and secure prison camps. Some officers saw escape as a form of entertainment, but in many cases, the comfortable conditions in officers' camps was a good enough incentive for prisoners to remain where they were. By late April 1917, at least thirty Australian officers in Germany were concentrated at the all-British camp at Krefeld in the Rhineland, about 30 kilometres from the Dutch border, where the atmosphere was surprisingly relaxed in spite of the security and the presence of an entire regiment of German sentries. Formerly the barracks of a German hussar regiment, Krefeld was said to be 'undoubtedly the best' camp officers experienced in Germany.[35] Those imprisoned there spent their days playing sport, performing theatre, reading books, writing letters, playing games, gambling, attending lectures and going on walks beyond the prison walls. They also received Red Cross food parcels regularly and could write home every fortnight. Of his time imprisoned at Krefeld, Captain Joseph Honeysett observed, 'In those camps where the treatment of prisoners was good, fewer escapes were made.'[36]

Good treatment and comfortable living in the camps gave prisoners of war very little desire to return to trench warfare in France and Belgium. The reverse was often true of camps where prisoners were deliberately mistreated and the facilities deficient or restricted. At the peak of the German reprisals in mid-1917, British officers at Krefeld were moved to the 10th Army Corps district in Lower Saxony and imprisoned in camps at Holzminden, Clausthal, Schwarmstedt and Ströhen Moor, where they were subjected to an organised system of coercion, verbal abuse and excessive penalties for seemingly minor infractions. Lieutenant Herbert Johnson of the 21st Machine Gun Company transferred to Ströhen Moor after three weeks at Krefeld. 'We believed this was because the Germans had got wind of a concerted attempt to escape', he said.[37] Along with Johnson, most Australian officers in captivity at this time ended up at the *Straflager* (punishment camp) at Ströhen Moor in the bleak and miserable marshlands around Hanover, where prisoners lived amid cramped, filthy conditions and endured a dysentery outbreak under the punitive regime of *Hauptmann* Karl Niemeyer. One Australian officer described Ströhen Moor as 'a most disgustingly insanitary hole, overcrowded and verminous'.[38] Daily life was so bad that prisoners fared 'far worse than ... ordinary criminals'.[39]

The frequency with which Australian officers tried escaping Ströhen Moor exceeded that from any other prison camp in Germany. On the night of 26 September 1917, Captain John Mott and Lieutenant Henry Fitzgerald crept out of the barracks at Ströhen Moor and used a key Mott had fashioned from a piece of steel plating to unlock the gate to the wire enclosure. They crossed a potato field without detection, then crossed a peat bog towards the Dutch border. In six days they travelled 130 kilometres on foot, avoiding roads and resting in forests during the day. Fitzgerald's escape ended when the pair bumped into a bicycle patrol as they attempted to cross the Ems Canal near Schüttorf. Fitzgerald was recaptured and spent two weeks in solitary confinement at Ströhen Moor, but Mott was able to outrun the patrol, slip beneath the electric fence and cross the border into Holland, where he became the first Australian officer to escape German captivity in the First World War.[40]

Daring though it was, Mott's escape from Ströhen Moor was not an accurate reflection of what all captured officers experienced in captivity, because of the 148 Australian officers captured on the Western Front, only Mott and Herbert Johnson were successful in their bids for freedom. They were the exception, with both men possessing backgrounds that appeared to have affirmed aspects of the Anzac legend, which claimed that the Australian bush produced resourceful and independent soldiers. Mott was raised in the southern Grampians in Victoria and had studied mechanical engineering in Melbourne. Before the war, he owned a mine and ran a conveyance between Norseman and Esperance on the Western Australian goldfields. Newspaper articles celebrating his escape from German captivity described him as a 'fine specimen of an Australian' and attributed his success in escaping to many years of cultivating a living from the bush.[41] Johnson was also from regional Australia, having spent most of his formative years on a sheep station outside Stanthorpe in south-east Queensland. True to the vision of a German prison camp being much like a public school dormitory, Johnson had attended Brisbane

Grammar School before working as a clerk at the Australasian Bank.[42] For 'gallant conduct and determination displayed in escaping', both John Mott and Herbert Johnson attended investiture ceremonies at Buckingham Palace and were awarded the Military Cross by King George V.[43]

War Office statistics table only instances in which prisoners succeeded in escaping, but we know from the statements of repatriated prisoners of war that many others tried and were unsuccessful in their bid for freedom. The letter of a British officer written after the Armistice (presumably to support the recommendations of bravery awards) lists numerous failed escape attempts involving the Australian officers at Ströhen Moor, giving some idea of the proportion of successful escapes to failed ones. Lieutenant Alfred Brine, 12th Battalion, was caught hiding in a bin wheeled out beyond the confines of the camp. Captain Maxwell Gore, 50th Battalion, remained hidden inside the camp long enough for the Germans to think he had escaped before making his attempt at escape – he got through the wire and made his way to the Dutch border, where he was recaptured by German sentries. Captain George Gardiner, 13th Battalion, cut the wire in full view of two sentries and took off on foot, but was soon recaptured. Lieutenant Hugh Anthony, 7th Battalion, dressed as a British orderly and went to clean a nearby pigsty. Once outside the camp, he bolted before he too was recaptured.[44] The letter does not mention the failed escape of Captain Joseph Honeysett, 47th Battalion, who also ran off outside the camp but was shot in the leg and set upon by military dogs.[45]

Since Mott and Johnson were the only Australian officers in Germany to succeed in their escape bids (representing 1.3 per cent of Australian officers in German captivity), their stories show that either being caught or not trying in the first place was more representative of Australian experience of captivity in German during the First World War. These figures partly reflect the better conditions officers enjoyed in the German prison camps, which allowed them to lead a reasonably comfortable existence. The figures also reflect a lack of direction from the War Office and a mindset in men who had perhaps accepted their fate as prisoners of war and remained so until the Armistice. While some men had no intention of escaping owing to comfortable conditions, others seem never to have even entertained the thought.[46] Officers in camps other than Ströhen Moor continued to receive Red Cross parcels and mail every fortnight and were able to continue pastimes that broke the monotony of camp routine. This relatively peaceful existence would have otherwise been disrupted by an attempt at flight, successful or not. Minor freedoms were cherished so

Figure 5.3 Australian prisoners of war at an *Arbeitskommando* near Kassel, c. 1917. Of the forty-three Australians who escaped German captivity in the First World War, more than half were other ranks working close to the Dutch border. (AWM P03236.120)

much at Mainz and Clausthal that senior British officers banned escape attempts for fear of collective reprisals.[47]

Strict no-escape policies meant fewer parades and barrack searches and more opportunities to enjoy the minor liberties that prisoners of war received in German captivity. But officers pursued other clandestine activities that passed the time and relieved the melancholy and tedium of waiting for the war to end. Even in the worst camps, prisoners resisted their captors by collecting and hiding escape equipment: Johnson was able to make a compass from his wristwatch and a magnetised sewing needle, while Mott was able to acquire a pair of wire-cutters and a compass from a parcel his brother had sent from England.[48] By using a new writing nib wet with saliva, Mott wrote between the lines of a letter asking his brother to send escape equipment through the mail. The letter passed the camp censor and made its way to London, whereupon his brother applied diluted ink to reveal the secret message. A specially marked parcel arrived weeks later, which Mott intercepted by sneaking into the mailroom before sentries had searched it for contraband.[49] The British intelligence agency MI9 adopted a similar technique of getting escape material to British and dominion prisoners of war in Germany during the Second World War, but this practice was never formally adopted by any agency during the First World War.[50] To ensure the health and safety of Australians in Germany, the Australian Red Cross refused to send escape material in food or clothing parcels and prohibited relatives in Australia from sending parcels directly.[51]

Not that it needed to be sent via the post, because vast quantities of escape material had already made its way into the camps through German guards. Sentries and their families had endured strict wartime rationing, substitute foodstuffs and ever-increasing material shortages for years, making some items contained within Red Cross food parcels highly sought-after commodities. By 1918, restrictions on food were so severe that sentries would happily assist prisoners of war in return for butter, dripping, Bully Beef and cakes of soap. German civilians exchanged escape equipment and clothing for food, while in the winter months Russian prisoners, who did not receive consignments from home, were adept at acquiring almost anything for food and warm clothing.[52] Such was the black market trade at the officers' camp at Holzminden that an Australian orderly was able to acquire wire-cutters, a compass and enough photographic equipment to make 300 copies of a map for the mass escape attempt in July 1918.[53] As John Bannigan explained, prisoners remained the masters of hiding contraband:

> We had various ways of beating the German searchers. We found them fairly dull, which was helpful. Gold, sovereigns, etc, we generally hid in our mouths; paper money, and compasses we held in our hands; and revolvers we found a bit more difficult ... There were hundreds of ways of getting things through a search, but some of them are not for publication.[54]

Captivity for officers was characterised by extended periods of longing for a day when the war might finally come to an end. Things were very different for other ranks, all of whom were eventually sent to Germany and spent most of their time out 'on commando' in the countryside where they had more opportunities for an attempt at flight. By November 1918, two Australian other ranks had escaped to Switzerland, three to Russia (then gripped by civil war) and twenty-four to Holland. It was said in the

Second World War that escaping was an officer's duty, but the Australian experience shows that other ranks were more likely to escape captivity in the First World War (see table 5.1).

Table 5.1 Australian escapes from German captivity, 1916–18

	France & Belgium	Switzerland	Holland	Russia	Total
Officers	0	0	2	0	2
Other ranks	12	2	24	3	41
Total	12	2	26	3	43

Source: War Office, *Statistics of the Military Effort of the British Empire*, p. 329; *London Gazette*, 27 January 1920; POW statements, AWM30

One was Private Russel Badcock, a Tasmanian of the 26th Battalion, who succeeded in crossing the Dutch frontier from Westphalia in May 1918. Whereas Mott and Johnson experienced hardship at the officers' camp at Ströhen Moor, Badcock's experiences typified the experiences of the other ranks. Having been wounded on capture at Pozières in July 1916, Badcock spent several weeks in hospital at Göttingen before being sent to a work party where he worked long days on meagre provisions shovelling beets. He was moved first to Kassel, then to Altmorschen on the Fulda River, where he felled timber for several months before moving back to Kassel to work at the Henschel & Son locomotive factory. There, Badcock and two other prisoners fled for the Dutch border and got as far as Warendorf, 180 kilometres away, before being captured by German police. Returned to Kassel, they received nineteen days solitary confinement and received daily issues of bread and water. The sentries belted them on the slightest provocation, and Badcock was 'bludgeoned with a club'.[55]

Badcock was later sent to work in the garden of Herr Henschel, the factory's proprietor, who was 'by no means an unkind sort. Frequently his morning salutation would be "Well, Tasmanian, how are things today?"'[56] But their mistreatment resulting from their previous escape attempt seemed to stiffen Badcock's resolve to try again for the Dutch frontier. They collected food and hid supplies in multiple small caches hidden in the garden; they acquired civilian clothing from an exchanged German soldier who had been a prisoner of war in England and had been treated well. Badcock and his accomplice also saved biscuits, tinned sardines and chocolate from Red Cross food packages and procured sacks because 'in this quarter of Germany almost everyone carried a sack so that our carrying one was not likely to provoke attention'.[57] They sought civilian clothing and obtained other portions of their 'rig out' from French and Russian prisoners of war, also carefully unstitching the red cotton drill from their trousers that identified them as prisoners of war. They stole a road map from Herr Henschel's motor shed and acquired a compass before setting off through the streets of Kassel.

In fifteen nights they travelled 220 kilometres to Münsterland on the border, where, after wading through a lightly guarded swamp, they crossed the frontier and entered the Dutch village of Delden as free men.[58] For his escape, Badcock was awarded the Military Medal.

Although he had worked on a mixed dairy and cropping farm at Exton in Tasmania before the war, Badcock was described in newspaper reports as a 'sturdy young fruit farmer' – his rural background appearing to affirm aspects of the Anzac legend.[59]

Another Australian who escaped was Private Wesley Choat of the 32nd Battalion, who was described in Australian newspapers as being engaged in farming on the Fleurieu Peninsula in South Australia before the war.[60] Captured at Fromelles, Choat was attached to a small work party straightening a bend in a canal at Weidenbruch near Essen in 1917. Conditions there were rough: Choat reported how at one point he 'had become very weak owing to the shortage of food'. After a period in hospital suffering from rheumatism, Choat tried escaping from Weidenbruch but was caught by German sentries as he neared the Dutch border. He spent two weeks in solitary confinement and tried again as soon as he returned to work.

Along with Private William Pitts of the 50th Battalion, Choat broke out of the compound in the middle of the night and evaded a sentry too occupied flattering a German woman to catch the pair escaping. After taking a train to Kleinenbroich near Dusseldorf, Choat and Pitts set off on foot towards the town of Brüggen and a large pine forest 'in which we would have been hopelessly lost owing to the darkness had it not been for the use of the compass'. After three days of travelling through torrential rain, Choat and Pitts crossed the Dutch border without encountering any sentries, 'presumably thinking more about the effect of the weather on their skins than their duty'.[61] Both Choat and Pitts were awarded the Military Medal for the escape, their success made all the easier by the ineffectiveness of German sentries, the fact that they had no rivers to cross and, in spite of the torrential rain, relatively good weather. Preparation was essential for a successful escape bid in the autumn and winter months, when the weather, terrain, fatigue and hunger could sometimes prevail over a prisoner's desire for freedom.[62]

It sometimes was better for prisoners of war to remain where they were, however, for those who escaped to Russia during the civil war had the additional burden of finding their way back to England. Arkhangelsk was one of three major ports used by the British to send military assistance to their Russian allies on the Eastern Front but, towards the end of 1918, it was the only one not occupied by the Bolsheviks. Scheduling and the freezing conditions in the North Sea meant it would sometimes be several months before ships destined for England would port at Arkhangelsk. Having escaped with two Russian prisoners from a work party at Szittkehmen in East Prussia in May 1918, Private Joseph Newman of the 17th Battalion made his way to Arkhangelsk via Petrograd where he received some assistance from the British consulate. He took an icebreaker to Montreal, Canada, where he eventually sought a return passage to England.[63] Private Thomas Taylor of the 14th Battalion escaped to Russia from Heisburg in the final weeks of the war and was unable to return to England for five months after the Armistice.[64]

Since the majority of Australian other ranks prisoners either failed in their escape bids or chose to remain in captivity, the experiences of Badcock, Choat and Newman do not represent what most Australian prisoners of war endured in German captivity. This raises important questions about why so many remained where they were. Since going out 'on commando' gave other ranks more opportunities to escape, why did so few make a dash for freedom? It is true that violence, neglect and mistreatment stiffened the resolve in men to try to make it back to friendly or neutral territory – Badcock's second attempt seemed motivated by his brutal beating. While those who did escape have been celebrated and remembered for their actions, it is just as important to recognise that there were incentives for some prisoners of war groups to remain where they were.

This was especially true for other ranks assigned to work parties in the agricultural sector, since the use of captive labour was mutually beneficial for farmers and prisoners. Farm work was less strenuous and gave other ranks more opportunities to lead a fit and healthy life alongside German civilians. Farmers preferred captive labour because it was much cheaper than civilian contractors, and prisoners preferred farm work because they could supplement a diet of Bully Beef, tinned stew and dripping from Red

Cross parcels with fresh produce and outdoor exercise.[65] At a time when tens of thousands of civilians were starving in metropolitan areas, one Australian prisoner working on a farm near Minden wrote to the Red Cross saying he was in an 'excellent position as far as food is concerned'. Every Sunday, his breakfast consisted of porridge, milk, sugar and two biscuits, while lunch was mashed potatoes with dripping, a pound of sausage, onions, boiled potatoes, cabbage and turnips. For dinner he ate sheep's tongue, fried vegetables, and biscuits with honey, jam and butter. 'How's that?' he boasted. '*Très bien*, eh?'[66]

With better food and plenty of exercise, prisoners on farms often possessed the mental and physical stamina required to attempt an escape. But few actually did. Many working in rural areas discovered German civilians to be kind and decent people and not all that different from those at home. With most German men of military age being drafted into the military, prisoners of war could often be integrated into households as proxy members. An Australian on a farm near Dülmen worked for a widow and her five children. In a letter to Mary Chomley, he described how 'we are a cheerful lot and keep ourselves well and truly alive when the day's work is over with any foolery we can think of'.[67]

Australian interactions with German civilians will be discussed later, but it is worth recognising that other ranks were often granted opportunities that made them less than eager to escape. Prolonged incarceration, a monotonous diet and infrequent contact with women tended to suppress sexual urges of prisoners in the camps, but there are instances of prisoners on farms fulfilling needs left unattended by the absence of German men. Since British prisoners of war were able to procure practically anything from hungry civilians in exchange for soap, chocolate and British cigarettes, some Australian prisoners were repatriated to Britain after the Armistice suffering minor venereal complaints.[68]

The great irony of the popular escape narratives is that more Australians crossed the borders with Switzerland and Holland with German consent than by a great escape. In accord with the principle of reciprocity, Germany adhered to the 1906 Geneva Convention, which permitted captors to transport sick and wounded prisoners whom they had no desire to retain to either neutral Holland or Switzerland, where they would be interned until the end of the war. Around a hundred Australian officers and other ranks went before a medical commission at Heidelberg and, if deemed unsuited for further military service, were approved for

Figure 5.4 British and Australian prisoners of war at Aachen (known to the French and British as Aix-la-Chapelle), crossing the border under German supervision for internment in neutral Holland, c. 1918. (AWM P01322.007)

internment in Switzerland. This included amputees, the blind, the physically impaired and men suffering from 'shell shock' and tuberculosis who would otherwise be dependent on the German medical system.[69] Captain William Cull was passed for internment in 1918 and described a sense of relief of knowing 'we were at least leaving Germany and all its Teutonic devilries behind, but taking with us a memory of brutalities so bitter that they are never likely to be obliterated'.[70]

Psychological casualties received greater consideration following a bilateral agreement between Britain and Germany in July 1917 whereby officers and NCOs who had been in captivity for longer than eighteen months were eligible for internment in neutral Holland. If individual prisoners had not made considerable improvement after three months, they would be eligible to full repatriation to England.[71] Working on the basis that those who had endured captivity the longest would be the first interned, the agreement helped the belligerents to manage psychological conditions that manifested in prisoners affected by prolonged incarceration. By November 1918, around 260 Australian officers and NCOs had crossed the border into Holland in accord with the agreement, which in the end, somewhat ironically, amounted to around seven times as many as did so by escaping.[72]

Figure 5.5 Wounded internees in fresh AIF uniforms at Hotel Jungfrau at Mürren, Switzerland, in 1918. The woman in the centre is believed to be Lady Grant Duff, wife of the senior British Red Cross delegate in Switzerland. (AWM H01921A)

Having crossed the border either by escaping or exchange, what freedoms were there for prisoners interned in the neutral countries? Some 27 000 Allied prisoners benefited from the agreements to be interned in Switzerland by the end of 1917: finally free from the oppressive prisoner-of-war camps of imperial Germany, they were housed in hotels, boarding houses and sanatoria at Meiringen, Interlaken, Mürren, Château-d'Oex and Montreux-Vevey. British officers were quartered in cottages separately from the other ranks, and since there were no guards, they could be joined by their families, if they could afford it and so desired. There was at least one Australian family living in Switzerland at this time. The violinist Leila Doubleday had been performing in Vienna when war was declared and spent two years in exile at Montreux-Vevey with her brother and grandmother. The family performed concerts for interned Australians in Switzerland and provided 'goodness to every poor, battered, derelict Australian they chanced to meet'.[73]

Internment in Switzerland might have initially seemed picturesque and idyllic, but internees could not stray further than eight kilometres from their barracks: they had a curfew at midnight, and were periodically concerned about food.[74] An Australian private interned at Château-d'Oex described rations being 'passable in quality but scarce in quantity. I was still getting my Red Cross parcels. I had received none at Constance but the food there was considerably better than it had been at Soltau. We got meat five times a week and there was an additional ration of potatoes.'[75] The Swiss authorities also did what they could to ensure that internees would return home from the war ready to play a full part in the social and economic life of their community.[76] All ranks were expected to work, and were categorised according to skills and physical abilities. Men on light duties became camp barbers and tailors, and some made slippers for a local relief organisation. Vacancies were made for internees to attend classes on motor skills, leather-working, carpentry, tailoring, watch-repairing and French polishing, and at least three Australians worked for the Peter, Cailler, Kohler, Chocolate Company at Vevey.[77] Working kept the men busy and prepared them for civilian life, but it was loathed by the men as being excessive, tedious and unpaid.[78] Some objected to being treated the same as the German internees.[79] As the senior AIF representative in Switzerland, Captain Charles Mills reported: '25 per cent of our men are doing something or other. Another 25 per cent are under medical care, the remaining 50 per cent are wasting their time.' Some were offered jobs cutting grass, 'but very few accepted'.[80]

Figure 5.6 A reminder of what escaping prisoners of war believed they were returning to. Australian dead in the wire at Anvil Wood near Péronne, France, 2 September 1918. (AWM E03149)

Internment in Switzerland was probably just as tedious as the prison camps of Germany, yet conditions in Holland were hardly any better. Officers were interned at Scheveningen and other ranks at Leeuwarden, with most interned Australians similarly engaged in camp duties, classes and workshops aimed at preparing them for civilian life.[81] Other than studying French and German, and carrying out administrative duties to support the AIF representative in Holland, the eight Australian officers quartered at Hotel Zeerust had little else to do. On the night before the Armistice, one was arrested for drunkenness and conduct unbecoming of an officer; the others were charged with disobeying regulations and being found at a 'night café' after curfew.[82] Drunkenness was frequent, as were gambling and insubordination, and at least three Australian other ranks were hospitalised with venereal disease.[83] Australian prisoners of war might have been granted the opportunity to leave Germany and enjoy freedom in Switzerland and Holland, but the idea of spending the rest of the war 'virtually prisoners' in a neutral country probably seemed a good enough reason to stay where they were in Germany.[84]

Lieutenant Peter Lyons, the West Australian who succeeded in escaping the officers' camp at Holzminden in July 1918, spent thirteen days on the run with his British accomplices. But like so many other escaping prisoners of war, he too was recaptured, just as he crossed a river near the Dutch border. He 'never forgot the terrible feeling of frustration as I was hauled back a prisoner of war'.[85] Most prisoners of war did not make successful escapes; for Australians, at least, captivity was more an endurance test than a light-hearted game.[86]

When considering why so few Australians succeeded escaping, it is worth remembering what it was they were returning to. After escaping from Ströhen Moor in September 1917, Captain John Mott elected to join his battalion in France, where he was awarded a Military Cross for command and leadership in fighting at Proyart during the Hundred Days Offensive in August 1918. Months later, he received a bar to his Military Cross for his successful escape from Germany. Mott clearly felt the need to return to the war during one of its most critical stages, but he was among a handful of Australian prisoners who felt like this. After repatriation to Britain and a mandatory four weeks furlough, escaped prisoners of war were given the option of repatriation to Australia or returning to France. With the exception of Mott and one other man, Private Henry Thomas of the 30th Battalion (as well as the repatriated AAMC stretcher-bearers referred to in chapter 4), all Australian prisoners who escaped German captivity elected to return home and discharge from the AIF.[87] There is no evidence suggesting prisoners of war were aware that they might have the option of returning home if successful, but the thought that escaping would mean a return to the trenches and all it entailed was probably the greatest of all incentives to remain where they were.

Australian prisoners in Germany were not as resourceful and persistent in escaping as the Anzac legend suggests, nor did any perceived notions of mateship lure them back to the fighting. When conditions were good and treatment fair, there was little reason for Australian prisoners to want to try to made a bold bid for freedom. Australian prisoners in German captivity did not make heroic escape attempts that affirmed their place in popular memory. They endured German captivity as best they could, as many possessed little desire to return to the mud and blood of the trenches.

CHAPTER 6

WELL FED AND PLENTY OF FREEDOM

AUTONOMY AND INDEPENDENCE IN GERMAN CAPTIVITY

Six months after his capture at Fromelles, Captain Charles Mills was at a camp for Allied officers at Hanoversch Münden in Lower Saxony, where he wrote to his commanding officer describing life as a prisoner of war. 'Our daily life is much as we make it. Daily routine is in our own hands, and except for a roll call at 9.30 morning and night, we are left alone, which suits us very well.' Mills spent his days reading, exercising, studying French and German, and enjoying walks beyond the prison walls. His captors were 'uniformly courteous', and the food was decent and better than expected. His greatest concern was the uncertainty of the war's duration. 'Time hangs! Day after day with absolutely nothing to do! I have led a busy and active life and find this enforced lack of occupation very trying.'[1]

While officers enjoyed better living conditions and food than other ranks, every day was a battle against monotony and the uncertainty of when, or whether, they would see their loved ones again. Conditions for other ranks were different, with thousands 'on commando' in factories, forests and mines facing a similar struggle on top of the privations and occasional danger that characterised their daily lives. One man at a limestone quarry at Wülfrath in the Rhineland wrote to the Red Cross saying he and his fellow prisoners were 'thin and downhearted' owing to the heavy work, abuse and the meagre daily issue of bread and ersatz coffee: 'The work is killing the poor boys. The Germans are bent on getting the last drop of blood.'[2]

Notwithstanding vastly different conditions officers and other ranks experienced in German captivity, there is a sense of congruity in that prisoners of war across all ranks endured hardship, anguish and deprivation during their time in Germany. Their plight often reflected the deteriorating material conditions in Germany that worsened the longer the war continued, although Roger Chickering writes that the decentralised and ill-coordinated military bureaucracy had a tendency to show little compassion towards prisoners of war.[3] British prisoners of war generally experienced better conditions than other prisoner nationalities. For example, pre-existing colonial attitudes in Germany heightened by mass-market fiction and wartime propaganda contributed to a stereotype that condoned the German mistreatment of Russian prisoners. Russians were seen as dirty, lazy, inferior Slavs, used to hard work and severe reprimands because they were said to have been 'accustomed to iron coercion in their homeland'.[4]

Local factors also influenced the day-to-day lives of prisoners, such as the strict regulations of local military authorities, the effectiveness of camp administrators, and the personalities of individual commandants and work party overseers. One neutral inspector of the German prison camps observed that the complaints from prisoners could usually be anticipated from the attitude of camp administrators: 'If the commandant is influenced by humane principles and a kindly spirit, one may expect to find the entire camp with this atmosphere,' he wrote. 'If, on the other hand, the commandant is a military martinet with brutal and inhumane instincts, the whole atmosphere of the camp ... is harsh and inhumane.'[5] Captain Pius Stengel ran the officers' camps at Freiburg and was clearly among the former. In September 1918, he gave Lieutenant Maurice Burke of the 29th Battalion the privacy of his office upon learning that Burke's brother had been killed in France.[6]

While the treatment of prisoners could at times be severe, conditions varied throughout the country so much that no two prison camps, hospitals or work parties were ever alike. This resulted in a diverse range of experiences among prisoners of war, some of whom experienced exceptionally good treatment while others exceedingly poor. Captivity is often seen as outside the heroic and masculine archetype of the Anzac legend, yet the letters, diaries and repatriation statements by Australian prisoners of war reveal a universal determination to see the war through in the best possible way. An Australian private wounded and taken prisoner at Mouquet Farm had an exceptionally difficult time in a hospital at Grafenwohr but ended up on the estate of Bavarian nobility north of Regensburg. There, with a few Russians, he did little work and they had 'the time of our lives'.[7] Experiences like this make it difficult to generalise about how prisoners fared in German captivity, but the relatively low mortality rate – especially among British prisoners – suggests that the neglect was neither widespread nor as severe as post-war accounts suggest.

What distinguished the otherwise disparate array of experiences among Australian prisoners was the way they coped with the everyday stresses of confinement. Very few Australians in German captivity saw themselves as having surrendered manhood.[8] Capture might have appeared less humiliating in France and Belgium when one's captors were white and Christian as Australian troops predominantly were – an aspect of captivity that differed significantly from those who fell into the hands of the 'unspeakable' Muslim Turk.[9] In Germany, once prisoners started receiving Red Cross food and clothing parcels and mail from home, captured Australians generally overcame the stigma of capture and began to exert themselves as the autonomous, masculine and disciplined soldiers they had previously been. Lieutenant Arthur Dent of the 19th Battalion spent six months detained at a former health retreat beside a small lake outside Neubrandenburg where German captivity was 'not so monotonous as one would imagine it to be'. The camp was peaceful and serene, making daily life relaxing and enjoyable. 'Conditions are just what they make them,' he explained. 'Our camp was a little community in itself, surrounded, of course, by barbed wire.'[10]

Prisoners took pride in their health and appearance, attended daily parades and respected the rank of their captors and fellow captives. Some even augmented their dark-blue prison tunics with AIF shoulder titles, colour patches and Rising Sun hat badges in an effort to retain a sense of soldierly and national identity. These men do not fit the often-perceived image of the prisoner of war as a 'discontented mopey creature, who sits all day bemoaning his fate', as Lieutenant Dent wryly put it.[11] Rather, they were soldiers who regarded survival a personal triumph amid the uncertainty of everyday life in captivity. While it is important to recognise the challenges that prisoners of war faced, it is important to move beyond the perception of prisoners of war as traumatised victims and look at the many ways prisoners sought to be active during their captivity and the way they used the freedoms afforded them to shape the best possible conditions.

Figure 6.1 Private Alfred Jackson, 54th Battalion, at Alten-Grabow near Hanover, c. 1918. Having overcome any perceived stigma that came with surrender, men like Jackson took pride in their appearance and often exerted themselves as confident, masculine soldiers defined by more than their imprisonment. (AWM P03236.030)

How prisoners coped with captivity adds a new dimension to recent scholarship on the emotional challenges combatants faced during the First World War. Writing on the way British soldiers overcame the war's psychological demands, Michael Roper argues that a man's family, especially his mother, was vital for his emotional survival. Letter-writing, in particular, drew British civilian-soldiers back into the lives they left behind and helped them to articulate and make sense of their strange, trench-dwelling existence. Maintaining this connection, fighting a so-called secret battle between home and the trenches, went some way to help British soldiers survive the emotional turbulence of combat on the Western Front.[12]

Life for prisoners of war was very different, for the nature of their confinement meant they were unable to maintain ties with home as readily as the men who remained in the trenches.[13] To abide with German regulations, other ranks could send just three postcards and two letters home each month, while officers were permitted an additional postcard and slightly longer letters.[14] The German authorities censored all outgoing mail for details on living conditions, location of work parties and accounts of violence and abuse; these were deleted in a heavy black ink to avoid the prospect of reprisals against German prisoners in British hands. Mail from Britain could take up to three weeks to arrive and six months from Australia. Not only was all outgoing mail restricted in volume and content but also sentries at each of the parent camps searched all parcels for contraband and censored incoming letters. Some took umbrage with the content of letters, leading to reprimands. An orderly at the officers' camp at Karlsruhe 'received 6 days "jug" because he *received* a letter in which his sister referred to the Germans as "Huns"'.[15] As well as reassuring loved ones that they were alive, healthy and faring well – even when they were sick and hungry – prisoners struggled to articulate the tedium and uncertainty of daily life in the camps. 'I have not the foggiest idea of what I shall write', one Australian officer confessed in a letter to his parents, likening news at Karlsruhe to 'vegetation in the Sahara'.[16] One man working at Nuremberg wrote to Mary Chomley saying that 'there is nothing fresh to report from this side, life goes on as usual with occasional outburst of startling news, of which we never hear the true facts. The worst part of this life is the close confinement, during the last four months we have been no more than 300 yards from our work.'[17]

Mary Chomley's letters helped to fill the emotional void in the lives of Australian prisoners in Germany. Not only did she know what influences affected their health and well-being but also she was consciously aware of the issues and sensitivities specific to the lives of individual prisoners. She knew what not to write about, so correspondence from her office in London was more likely to pass the German censor's desk quickly. Chomley's correspondents described details to her that offer a unique insight into the psychological cost of prolonged imprisonment, including arguments between prisoners who had lived for too long in overcrowded barracks, and men 'not in the best of health' and suffering 'fearful headaches' at night.[18] 'The barbed wire fever does not do me any good', confessed one man feeling the long-term effects of his imprisonment at Friedrichsfeld in August 1918.[19]

Swiss doctor and International Red Cross representative Dr Adolf Vischer inspected many of the camps and observed that the psychological cost of captivity manifested itself in a disorder similar in nature to neurasthenia called *Stacheldraht-Krankheit* ('barbed wire disease'). Its primary causes included the monotony and stagnation of camp life, the lack of privacy, constant contact with the same people, and feelings of isolation brought on by limited interaction with the outside world.[20] Chomley helped mitigate these symptoms in Australian prisoners who, in some cases, possessed enough freedom to overcome the demoralising effects of barbed wire disease. As other historians have shown, singing songs, reading books, learning languages, producing theatrical performances, publishing newspapers and playing sport all helped prisoners of war to assert themselves as humans defined by more than their state of imprisonment.[21] Edmund King makes the point that if prisoners of war were kept busy in pursuits of this sort, their minds, at least, were free.[22] Prisoners of war generally drew upon practices familiar to them in civilian life, which had the added benefit of serving as timely reminders of home. Some pursuits were not always enjoyed for the betterment of individual well-being. Gambling was particularly popular among British and Australian officers at Krefeld, as Captain Joseph Honeysett observed: 'Roulette, poker, *vingt-et-un*, baccarat, bridge and innumerable other gambles all had their adherents ... many played for stakes considerably above their means. Settlement of debts was made by cheques (negotiable after the war!) which were made out on any odd scrap of paper!'[23]

Figure 6.2 British and Australian prisoners of war 'on commando' at an asparagus farm near Cologne in the Rhineland, c. 1918. (AWM P00063.028)

Important to all prisoners, irrespective of rank, was the quantity and availability of Red Cross food and clothing, which in the context of Germany's dire economic situation, helped prisoners destabilise the traditional captor–captive relationship. Richard Radford observed the economic organisation of prison camps in the Second World War, writing that scarce and unobtainable commodities such as cigarettes, soap, choc-olate, tinned meat and warm clothing were bartered on the black market among prisoners as well as with German civilians and guards.[24] Highly sought-after products in Red Cross food parcels let prisoners improve their living conditions and their chances of survival. The sheer amount available to British prisoners also highlighted the failure of Germany's unrestricted U-boat campaign and its inability to stem the global flow of resources into Britain and France, and made clear to captors and prisoners the insur-mountable strategic advantage the Allies possessed in the last eighteen months of the war.[25] This had a powerful impact on morale among prisoners of war, who could see from the rapidly deteriorating conditions around them that the war would not last much longer. Private Ernest Chalk of the 15th Battalion realised this when he arrived at Minden, and was being marched to the other ranks camp on the other side of town:

> One thing we noticed was the bareness of all the shop windows. There was not a pound of food for sale in any of them, and this we tried to cheer each other up with. 'Well, Cobbers, we won't be here for long, anyhow. Jerry can't last much longer. Why look he has nothing left to eat. He will soon be starved into giving in.' It seemed strange to me afterwards that we did not think at the time, that if Germany starved we should do the same.[26]

Such were the demands on Germany that most other ranks were assigned to work parties either in agriculture or in industry. Agriculture was likely to mean participation in a relatively small work party under conditions that varied depending on the location, season and the employer. Farm work in particular had the advantage of greater access to fresh produce, exercise and contact with German civilians, while security tended to be more relaxed, making it easier for prisoners to try their hand at escape – if they so desired. One Australian prisoner reported being 'well fed and allowed plenty of freedom' while engaged in farm work near Schneidemühl in East Prussia, showing little desire to return to the trenches of the Western Front.[27] Prisoners also mined coal and iron, quarried chalk and limestone, and extracted diatomaceous earth from swamps for the manufacture of explosives. The latter contravened the legalities of using captive labour for war work, but paled in comparison to the reprisals in France and the use of prisoners in the production of munitions in strict violation of the Hague Convention.[28]

The use of prisoner labour in Germany's industrial sector exposed a problem with local army commanders who did not always adhere to internationally accepted standards.[29] The worst offenders were those in charge of labour camps involving industrial work, which was dirty, unpleasant, dangerous and physically demanding. Conditions in the Rhineland and Westphalia were particularly severe owing to the reluctance of coal and steel barons to grant access to neutral inspectors inquiring into the welfare of prisoners, fearful that they would reveal 'trade secrets' to overseas competitors.[30] Guards and civilian contractors tended not to show compassion for the mental and physical well-being of prisoners, making life 'on commando' more bleak and miserable than anywhere else in Germany for other ranks prisoners.[31]

The Rheinische-Kalksteinwerke stone quarry at Wülfrath near Düsseldorf typified the conditions under which other ranks lived and worked in industrial Germany. A party of twenty-five Australians captured at Pozières and Mouquet Farm were sent to Wülfrath in late 1916, where they joined 700 British, French and Russian prisoners in cramped, underground quarters, and worked under the punitive regimen of a *Feldwebel* who flogged prisoners with a cane. 'You did just what you were told ... for you didn't know what [the sentries] were capable of doing. It might be the cold steel of the bayonet or a gentle reminder with the butt of his rifle.'[32] For months the men worked twelve-hour shifts, six days a week, swinging pick axes and sledgehammers to fill as many 2-ton trucks with limestone as possible. 'We knew that the *posterns* were bribed at the rate of 50 pfennigs to force five and six wagons a day.'[33] Accidents from falling rock and tunnel collapses were common, and prisoners rarely received food parcels from the nearby camp at Friedrichsfeld.[34] Heavy labour, an irregular diet and constant abuse contributed to a rapid decline in mental and physical health among these prisoners. Many resorted to harming themselves in an effort to escape the quarry's privations: 'The men were breaking up with the strain, and with not sufficient food to do it on. So they put their hands under the wagons and let them to be run over; their feet likewise. They scratched their legs with stones and put stuff on to poison them – anything at all to get away from this Kommando.'[35] One man shared a similar experience at a mine near Münster in the Rhineland:

> The bosses in the mines are all powerful and frequently order men who are prisoners of war to work 2 shifts [16 hours underground] ... they are abused without the slightest provocation ... those who are ignorant of the language and mining alike have been beaten with stick and slapping the face with the hands is a common occurrence and you have to consider the name swine a term of endearment.[36]

Life at the Golpa-Nord coal mine at Bitterfeld in Saxony was just as demanding, with the added unpleasantness of prisoners spending up to eighteen hours a day underground. There they risked choking on coal dust, getting caught between trucks or being buried under rock.[37] Captured at Bullecourt and spending months behind German lines in France, Private Norman Gordon of the 15th Battalion was hit and killed by a train not long after he had arrived in Germany. The German authorities sent a report to the Red Cross in London claiming that Gordon 'was proceeding along a narrow path alongside the railway lines. In stepping aside to avoid a train he slipped and fell under the wheels. It has been proved that the occurrence was entirely accidental.'[38] There were no witnesses, but the local authorities were eager to rule Gordon's death an accident for fear of shedding light on conditions at the Golpa-Nord coalmine and risk losing 'trade secrets'. After the Armistice, repatriated prisoners reported that Gordon 'had been getting a bad time from the Germans' and alluded to the likelihood that he had died attempting to harm himself in an effort to avoid returning to the coalface.[39]

Not all attempts by prisoners to try to shape better conditions were as desperate as at Wülfrath and Bitterfeld. Elsewhere, prisoners were able to resist their captors by attempting to escape, staging strikes and feigning illnesses to avoid work (a crime called *Faulkrank*), which usually resulted in sentences involving food restrictions, solitary confinement and a punishment called 'stilly-stand' (*Stillstehen*) – prisoners were made to stand to attention, exposed to the elements, for extended periods. Those too weak to work were often more susceptible to beatings from sentries, who let fly with fists and rifle butts. One man injured in a coalmine at Alton near Essen could barely walk when reassigned to an iron foundry at Duisburg. He was forced to work – quite literally – 'at the point of the revolver'.[40]

Sending thousands of other ranks into the countryside solved the issue of overcrowding in the camps, which had caused significant problems in Germany in the earlier stages of the war. Using prisoners as a labour force also made up the shortfall in manpower caused by growing demands on the German economy and the call-up of workers for military service. For prisoners who had languished for months behind barbed wire, the prospect of working outside was a welcome change. 'It got very tiresome looking at barbed wire all day long', claimed one man who had been imprisoned at Münster for more than a year.[41] Working could be harsh and unforgiving, but prisoners held in the camps for long periods often saw the prospect of work as an antidote to barbed wire disease.

Those who had been forced to work at gunpoint amid filthy and depressing conditions held the opposite view, bitterly resenting being made to work for the Germans. It might have been lawful, depending on the work involved, but some prisoners viewed it as supporting the enemy's war effort.[42]

The conditions under which some other ranks worked highlighted the problem with forced labour productivity. Prisoners rarely make a motivated workforce, even when they found themselves assigned to work parties performing tasks similar to their trades in civilian life. Having worked as an iron moulder on the railways before the war, an Australian prisoner wrote to the Red Cross describing tracklaying at Müncheberg. He commented how 'the work we are doing now is exercise out in the fresh air. Work on the rails will do us good although it goes against the grain to work for the [Germans].'[43] Prisoners would often work slowly, or tried to avoid work if it was seen as supporting the German war effort, but this was not a universal experience because some prisoners found themselves employed in tasks they thoroughly enjoyed. One man working as a gas stoker in Hamburg went about his duties so efficiently that he had to decline a job offer when his civilian overseer learnt of the Armistice.[44]

Those who had no choice but to remain in camp still found a sense of masculine, soldierly pride in harassing their captors by dodging work, malingering and hampering productivity through sabotage, resistance and interference. None of these were unique to the prisoner-of-war experience, as Nathan Wise writes of Australian attitudes to work during the First World War, although Wise argues that Australian soldiers often took masculine pride in a job well done when engaged in work in the British forward area.[45] In captivity, prisoners digging peat broke shovels, timber-cutters broke axe handles and labourers buried spades while planting crops. Fed up with the tirades of a civilian overseer, prisoners at Bohmte near Osnabrück sabotaged the harvest by cutting the eyes from the potatoes they were planting.[46] On the Rhine near Dülmen, a foreman in charge of British and French prisoners engaged in canal works came to notice more prisoners than available wheelbarrows. 'On reporting the matter, it was decided to empty the canal of water to investigate. The Germans found over six hundred wheelbarrows and their contents, which had been tipped into the canal by the prisoners.'[47]

Finding a sense of soldierly pride in retaliating against their German captors was a way prisoners could let off steam, and was just as common among officers as the other ranks.[48] Although it did not overtly affect Germany's ability to continue the war, resistance was good for morale, and was a practice British prisoners of war in Germany during the Second World War came to know as 'goon baiting'.[49] Towards the end of 1917, British and Australian officers at Ströhen Moor kept spirits high by resisting a German *Feldwebel* in feuds over curfews on the camp canteen and restrictions on the distribution of mail and parcels. An outburst against 'the evils of standing on parade with hands in pockets' prompted the prisoners to do just that: 'Our comedian refused to dismiss *appell* this morning until everyone took their hands out of their pockets. But as nothing happened in five minutes, he gave in.'[50]

The officers at Ströhen Moor were also ordered to contribute to the collection of scrap metal by forfeiting the steel helmets prisoners still had with them since falling into German hands months before. Realising that they were destined for the foundry to feed Germany's demand for steel, the prisoners commenced an extraordinary crusade of hiding them throughout the camp.[51] Most ended up in the latrine pit in the centre of the camp where, once discovered, a sentry was made to recover them with a stick:

> When he had pulled out two [helmets] in one hit, an officer sneaked up and threw them in again. The Boche chased him and caught him, and straight away he was jugged. While the dragging was still in progress, another officer crept up to the pit with a stick, a piece of string, and a bent nail, and started fishing.[52]

The Hague Convention permitted the German authorities to use captured men as a labour force, but was less clear on whether the regulations extended to NCOs. The issue came to a head at Mindenin in April 1916, following reports that German authorities were using the camp to punish British NCOs who refused to work for their captors. The situation deteriorated to the point where visiting neutral inspectors reported the punishment of prisoners being on the 'verge of real intentional cruelty'.[53] After Australians began arriving in Germany, reports of an alleged shooting of a German prisoner at the Torrens Island Internment Camp near Adelaide in 1915 gave the authorities at Stuttgart reason to force British and Australian NCOs to work so as to 'bring the sons of convicts to heel'.[54] There remained a widespread belief among prisoners that they could not be made to do so against their will. The Hague Convention made no specific reference to NCOs and work, but the principle of reciprocity was such that both Britain and Germany came to a bilateral understanding that resulted in work being purely voluntary for all captured NCOs. Knowing this, other ranks scrounged chevrons on the black market to masquerade as lance corporals, corporals or sergeants to avoid work.[55] The opposite was true for NCOs, some of whom realised the benefits of working beyond the wire and volunteered in the hope of making a bid for the Dutch border.[56]

Figure 6.3 Australian officers at Krefeld in the Rhineland, which many considered 'undoubtedly the best' camp in Germany, c. 1917. (AWM P08451.002)

The understanding between British and German authorities over the treatment of captured NCOs gave these prisoners the right to refuse working for their captors. The policy was adhered to in many camps, but changed during the war as the economic situation in Germany worsened. By 1918, there were severe repercussions for NCOs who refused to work, particularly for men in the infamous 10th Army Corps district near Hanover. NCOs imprisoned in this area were subjected to the same level of torment suffered by British officers at Ströhen Moor and Holzminden. NCOs imprisoned at Bohmte, Hamelin and Soltau endured punishments until they were coerced to work. Arriving at Bohmte in September 1917, a party of Australians captured at Bullecourt joined several hundred British prisoners in an existing protest against working. Food parcels and mail were restricted, and the prisoners were given eight hours of 'stilly stand' each day, where they were verbally abused, threatened by sentries with fixed bayonets and a *Feldwebel* who frequently ran at them with a drawn sabre. The prisoners held out for six weeks before they finally relented owing to lack of food.[57] A similar situation unfolded at Lechfeld in Bavaria, where NCOs who refused to work were made to live on barley, water and horse meat until they 'volunteered' to work.[58]

The most obvious role for NCOs in the prison camp system was to supervise the other ranks men who remained in the parent camps, many of whom were too sick or wounded for manual labour. NCOs maintained morale and discipline in much the same way as they did in their units before capture, but in Germany they became responsible for hundreds, if not thousands, of other ranks at any given time. As senior soldiers, NCOs formed a buffer between the German camp administration and the rest of the prison camp population. In some locations, a Senior British Officer (SBO) mediated between the two groups, relaying orders from the camp administration and managing issues that arose from the prisoner population. This included Warrant Officer John Bannigan who was the SBO at the all-NCO camp at Grossenwede in the Hanover marshlands before his presidency of the British Help Committee at Soltau. For six months in 1917, Bannigan represented the interests of more than 2000 British prisoners amid horrible conditions. He stood his ground over German attempts to work the men under his command, which on one occasion resulted in the commandant 'rushing ... straight at me and waving his sword over my head'. Food parcels were suspended, mail was stopped, and the men faced further penalties if their refusal to work continued:

> I told him to get on with the 'strafing' because the NCOs were not
> going to work. So the game went on, from day after day. Sometimes we
> got food, and sometimes we did not. But we always had enough
> stomach to defy the Germans. We considered it our duty to do it. We
> were in the war to win it, and we knew that the smallest inconvenience
> we could put them to would help.[59]

Prisoners like Bannigan succeeded in overcoming the perceived stigma of having surrendered manhood through capture by dedicating their time in captivity to the needs of the camp. Others worked in mail rooms, cookhouses and toilets, and helped to create lives of martial routine where they showed a sense of regimental bearing and pride in improving the lives of other prisoners. NCOs at Nuremberg who refused to work for the Germans happily delivered parcels and war news to the other ranks working at surrounding labour camps.[60] Men who could speak German and French worked as translators and communicated between the

Germans and other prisoner nationalities. Others worked as orderlies for British officers at nearby camps, and those with medical skills worked in camp hospitals (known as *Lazarettes*), bathing and bandaging sick and wounded prisoners.[61]

Officers also found ways to help their fellow prisoners. Owing to his wounds, Captain Charles Mills was among the first Australians exchanged to Switzerland where he spent the remaining twelve months of the war as the senior representative of approximately a hundred interned Australians. During this time, Mills was dedicated to finding missing members of the AIF whose names appeared on prisoner-of-war lists from Berlin, and relaying their whereabouts to London via the International Red Cross Office in Berne. After the Armistice, Mills went back to Germany and spent eight months working with the German War Office to locate the graves of Australian prisoners and arrange photographs for their next of kin. He was perhaps motivated in this work by his 'serious error of judgement' in revealing sensitive operational information to the Germans at Fromelles. Upon returning to Australia in late 1919, however, he was made an Officer of the Order of the British Empire 'in recognition of valuable services'.[62]

Figure 6.4 Life in the barracks at Güstrow, 1918. On the left is Sgt William Groves, 14th Battalion, who endured the reprisals and published a serialised account of his experiences in *Reveille* in the mid-1930s. Once moved to Germany, Groves was not compelled to work for his captors owing to his rank. (AWM P09581.155)

Aside from living with ever-present barbed wire, sentries and guard towers, prisoners who worked camp duties were more successful in creating an atmosphere of domestic normality when they had very little contact with their captors. After enduring the reprisals, Private Ernest Chalk of the 15th Battalion spent twelve months in the washhouse in Dülmen and wrote of being 'fairly left well alone by the Germans. We had two roll calls each day, but apart from that we were not troubled by them, and for this we were very thankful indeed.'[63] Another man wrote home saying he had led 'a gentleman's life' working in the camp postal room at Friedrichsfeld. 'The summer was glorious, with long sunny days and twilight lasting till 9 o'clock and later. We got books and footballs, etc from England and things altogether took on a brighter hue.'[64] In some camps such as Dülmen and Friedrichsfeld, prisoners could lead lives free from the daily torments of the bullying sentries and corrupt civilian contractors. But the depression and uncertainty of never knowing when the war might end still had a profound effect, particularly on men already struggling with the physical and mental trauma of combat and abuse in captivity. Private Vernal Cousins of the 48th Battalion was captured at Passchendaele and hospitalised at Soltau suffering from dysentery before being moved to a ward reserved for 'shell shock' cases. He took his own life with a razor in February 1918 and was one of two Australian prisoners of war known to have committed suicide in German captivity.[65]

The unique position of Private Douglas Grant of the 13th Battalion demonstrates the ability of some men to stave off the chronic effects of barbed wire disease while trying to retain a sense of duty and military pride. Grant was one of twenty known Indigenous members of the AIF captured on the Western Front. Born around 1885 in the Australian Indigenous nations of the rainforests of northern Queensland, he has a unique pre-war story of being orphaned as a result of a frontier massacre. Adopted and raised by a Scottish taxidermist who worked for the Museum of Australia, Grant attended public school in Sydney and worked as a draughtsman and wool-classer before joining the AIF in 1916.[66] Having first overcome racist regulations that prevented Indigenous Australians from leaving the country without government approval, Grant arrived on the Western Front in February 1917 and was captured at Bullecourt two months later. He spent several weeks recovering from grenade fragmentation wounds in a field hospital in France before passing through a number of camps in Germany. In a letter to Mary Chomley, Grant described himself as 'a native of Australia, adopted in infancy and educated by my foster parents whose honoured name I bear, imbued me with the feelings and spirit of love of home, honour and patriotism'.[67]

In January 1918, both Grant and another dark-skinned Indigenous Australian, Private Roland Carter of the 50th Battalion, were sent to the special *Halbmondlager* ('crescent-moon camp') for Muslim prisoners at Wünsdorf-Zossen near Berlin.[68] Carter was a labourer before the war and was the first Ngarrindjeri man to enlist in the AIF from the Port McLeay Mission Station on Lake Alexandra in South Australia. Wounded in the shoulder and captured at Noreuil on 2 April 1917, Carter was treated at a German field hospital at Valenciennes, where he discussed Ngarrindjeri healing methods with German doctors.[69] By the time Grant and Carter were transferred to Wünsdorf-Zossen in January 1918, the camp contained Chinese and Vietnamese who had been lumped in with French colonial prisoners: Moroccans, Algerians, Tunisians and Senegalese. Sikhs, Hindus and Punjabis of the British Indian Army shared quarters with Nepalese Gurkhas, Afghans and men from the British West Indies. They joined smaller numbers of Canadian, Newfoundland and British prisoners of war who were moved there around the same time.

The exotic mix of prisoners within a short distance of Berlin's universities gave German anthropologists a rare opportunity to study non-Europeans on European soil – some considering a visit to the camp 'as worthwhile as a trip around the world'.[70] With support from the German Army and a variety of government ministries, a steady stream of researchers, artists and photographers visited the camp for research purposes. One project was the Royal Prussian Phonographic Commission led by philosopher and psychologist Professor Carl Stumpf and linguist Wilhelm Doegen, whose teams regularly visited the camp to record dialects as prisoners sang folk songs, read Bible verses and recited excerpts from literary works.[71] The commission recorded the voice of one Australian prisoner of war, Private William Grigsby of the 51st Battalion, as he recited the Parable of the Prodigal Son from the New Testament (Luke XV: 11–32): 'Let's have a feast and celebrate. For this son of mine was dead and is alive again; he was lost and is found.'[72]

Leonhard Adam, a German researcher associated with the Prussian Phonographic Commission, first met Douglas Grant at Wünsdorf-Zossen in early 1918. Reflecting on his work during a radio interview in Australia in the 1950s, Adam remembered Grant as a likeable and intelligent man who could emulate a thick Scottish brogue and with whom he shared his passion for English literature. Having benefited from a privileged upbringing in white Australia, Grant was 'unable to give me any information that we did not already know' about Indigenous Australians, because 'his attitude to his own people was exactly that of a white person'.[73] Neither Grant nor Carter was recorded by the Phonographic Commission, but both men sat for portraits by photographer Otto Stiehl and a variety of artists, including Thomas Baumgartner and Max Beringer. Grant caught the eye of German sculptor Rudolf Marcuse, who was invited to the camp to make bronze busts of 'interesting types' and made one of Grant.[74] Decades after the war, Marcuse fled to England to escape the Nazi persecution of European Jewry and took his collection of works with him. The bust is today held in a private collection in the United Kingdom.[75]

In spite of the continuous procession of scholars and artists and the somewhat degrading nature of their visits, the prisoners at Wünsdorf-Zossen retained a remarkable degree of freedom inside the camp and out. In a letter to his family at Port Mcleay Mission in South Australia, Carter described good treatment and being in 'fairly good health'.[76] Christian prisoners were permitted to attend regular church services, which Carter 'liked very much', and were frequently given parole after promising they would not escape: 'I went in the town to see the moving pictures. All the Native prisoners of war went.'[77] Another prisoner recalled Grant being allowed to travel to Berlin where 'being black, he couldn't get away'. As well as visiting local museums and libraries, it was said Grant was 'photographed and his skull measured' at a Berlin university. 'He was measured all over and upside down and inside out . . . he was the prize piece, the prize capture.'[78]

(a)   (b)

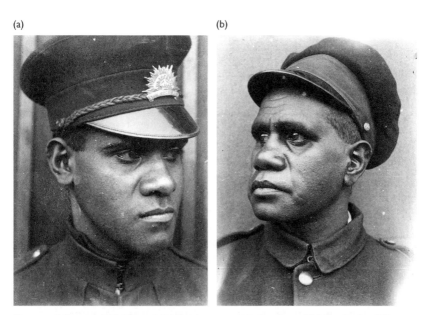

Figures 6.5a and 6.5b Otto Stiehl's photographic studies of (a) Pte Roland Carter, 50th Battalion, and (b) Pte Douglas Grant, 13th Battalion, at the *Halbmondlager* at Wünsdorf-Zossen in 1918. (BpK Bildagentur H33029617 & H30029794)

German scholars and artists might have seen Grant as an ethnic curiosity, but their inquiries did not define the nature of his captivity or the way he responded to it. Instead, the work he carried out highlights the degree of agency that prisoners possessed in captivity. Not long after arriving at Wünsdorf-Zossen, Grant volunteered to work in the parcel room where he helped to distribute mail, food and clothing to British prisoners. His literacy and impeccable copperplate handwriting led to his election as president of the British Help Committee. Grant gave special consideration to a group of Sikhs, Hindus, Punjabis and Gurkhas sent to work in the potash works at Steinförde bei Wietze more than 150 kilometres away, where there had been little consideration for their cultural needs. Since a majority of soldiers in the British Indian Army were semi- or non-literate, Grant corresponded with civilian internees and translators attached to the work camp. He arranged for the Red Cross to send the men regular supplies of goat, beef, fish, ghee, lentils, gur, rice, atta, spice and tea, as was appropriate for their religious customs.[79] The most significant tradition for the Muslim prisoners at Steinförde was Ramadan, which was observed throughout June and July 1918 owing largely to Grant's efforts.[80] He described this work to Mary Chomley, explaining that he had found consolation in being 'of service inasmuch as a prisoner of war'.[81]

Grant's unique experience demonstrates that prisoners who spent the rest of the war in the large parent camps possessed the means to shape better conditions for themselves and other prisoners. But nowhere else in Germany were prisoners more successful in carving out a comfortable existence than on farms. For some men, life became not all that different from their pre-war lives, and in some cases, prisoners took an active interest in learning German farming methods in preparation for a working life after the war. A grazier in civilian life, Herbert Horner spent the last year of the war on farms where he took scrupulous notes on the methods employed by his captors because 'it helped to pass the time away'.[82] After the war, Horner included his observations as an appendix to his published account of captivity in Germany to help educate returning soldiers seeking agricultural work after discharge from the AIF. Although it is not explicit in archival records, the number of Australians who had been labourers and farm workers in civilian life and ended up working in the German agricultural sector is significant, indicating that there might have been some attempts by the German authorities to match prisoners' pre-war skills with selection for agricultural work.

This could have been the case at Osteroude near Göttingen, where other ranks were taken to a local market, which one man wryly described as 'a revival of the slave market'.[83] Since farmers found prisoners cheaper than civilian contractors, it made practical and economic sense to select men already physically used to farm work.[84] But whether or not they were skilled hands, farm work also proved beneficial for prisoners, who were usually motivated by the prospect of fresh air, exercise and access to fresh food to supplement their Red Cross diets. Raymond Ayres from the 13th Battalion, who had been a clerk before the war, spent the last year of the war near the village of Shakenhof in East Prussia, where he ate more in a single day than in a week during the reprisals the year before. 'Incredible as it may seem ... I had put on 4½ stone in weight [29 kilograms]. I was now heavier than ever before.'[85] Some prisoners were granted free time. Once a week, the Australian prisoner happily working at the gas works in Hamburg was 'allowed to go into the city and spend what money I had'.[86]

Another aspect of life in Germany that helped captured men persevere involved interacting with German civilians. Prisoners 'on commando' in rural areas intermingled with civilians and could go days – even weeks – without so much as seeing a sentry. Security was more relaxed in rural areas and offered greater prospects of escape, but the country's growing manpower shortage meant that prisoners often worked unsupervised alongside German women similarly engaged in large numbers. Interacting with women and children could be a timely reminder of life before the war, helping them to overcome Roper's concept of the 'secret battle' in captivity.[87] But relationships were not always cordial. Near Nuremberg, one Australian soldier captured at Mouquet Farm worked alongside German women dressed in mourning. 'These people had a most intense hatred towards prisoners. Their outlook was affected by having sons and brothers dead in the war, [so] some of this could be justified.'[88] Children threw rocks and called him an 'English pig', and the farmer's wife threatened to beat him with a shovel for his inability to understand German.[89]

Treatment like this could be particularly alienating, especially when individuals assigned to farms found themselves the only English-speakers in the district. But it is important to establish that prisoners 'on commando' in rural areas still managed to exert themselves in ways that challenged the traditional prisoner–captor relationship. Because they received plenty of exercise and ate better than any other prisoners in Germany, other ranks working in the agricultural sector tended to possess enough strength and confidence to stand up to their civilian overseers, some going so far as getting into fistfights with them. One man 'bogged' into his civilian overseer at Tessin during a village scramble for free coal briquettes. The German farmer shoved the prisoner in front of the local villagers, which was 'the last straw which broke the camel's back. I lost control of myself completely and whipped around like a flash.'[90] Another man engaged in forestry work near Schneidemühl had 'another row with the Guard [who] threatened to use his rifle on me, but when I took up the axe he changed his mind'.[91]

Although food was more abundant in rural areas, the paucity of imported goods in Germany owing to the naval blockade made some items in fortnightly consignments of Red Cross parcels highly sought-after. Soap in particular was not freely available in Germany in the last year of the war, and could fetch a high price on the black market. At Billenhagen near Rostock, an Australian who haggled with a German soldier on home leave set the exchange rate for soap at ten fresh farm eggs. '[He] smelt it, and gazed on it for a while, and asked how long it would last.'[92] At Schackenhof, Australian prisoners could not bear to see the pitiable state of the hungry village children: when parcels came in from Schneidemühl, the prisoners would give them tinned milk, cocoa, sugar, rice and butter, then share the rest of their parcels with starving Russian prisoners.[93] Sharing food and British-made cigarettes with demoralised and hungry Germans helped to smooth over any hostility that existed between the two groups and could mean the difference between shivering under a blanket on a cold winter's night and having wood for a fire. Raymond Ayres and the other prisoners at Schackenhof became inte-grated into village life. The district's military overseer bought tea from them every fortnight, and local women periodically offered their bodies in exchange for soap.[94]

The nature of the repatriation statements meant that few former prisoners of war described wartime romances with German women. Those who wrote about this aspect of their lives in captivity show that some prisoner groups were better placed to uphold a virile identity than others. Soldiers engaged in the fighting on the Western Front had grown accustomed to the single-sex environment of life in the trenches (although there were brothels in the *estaminets* behind the lines and in the major towns and cities), yet there was a growing concern among some prisoners who feared that, having being captured men, they would lose their virility and grow passive in confinement.[95] The problem was par-ticularly severe among officers and NCOs who spent most of their captiv-ity incarcerated in the parent camps without contact with women so they perhaps felt their chronic absence most. At Holzminden, an unknown AFC officer corresponded with a German woman who worked in the commandant's office. Owing to a circuitous delivery route to avoid detection by German sentries, the letters were intercepted by other prisoners, who transcribed and circulated news of the affair throughout the camp.[96]

As Adolf Vischer observed during his visits to the camps, men adorned their bunks with lewd and suggestive pictures, and tried to keep memories of past encounters alive by speaking openly about sex and their relationships with women. This was not a unique experience among prisoners of war but soldiers of the First World War more broadly. In captivity, friendships developed between men who enjoyed each other's company and rarely went further than companionship and sharing parcels.[97] That said, prisoners who dressed in drag for light-hearted theatrical performances would sometimes attract 'admirers' among other prisoners.[98] It was far more common for Australian prisoners to express their virility in writing, where they either flirted in their written exchanges with Mary Chomley or wrote to female acquaintances at home. The limited contact with women and the near absence of intimacy was probably the most emasculating aspect of captivity. One young Australian clearly felt he had missed the prospect of long-term happiness by sitting out the war behind German barbed wire. He wrote self-pityingly: 'I often wonder what it will be like when I return home to find all the best of you girls married or engaged ... It looks like my luck being out in regard to getting married, but I guess I will be able to pull through as a bachelor.'[99]

Because of their greater sense of freedom, better diets and unsupervised contact with women, other ranks working on farms exhibited their masculine selves more than other prisoners of war. As Lisa Todd writes, domestic laws made it illegal for German women to have affairs with prisoners – and, conversely, for prisoners to fraternise with civilians – but because of the absence of German men and the evolving gender roles that disrupted pre-war norms, romantic and sexual relationships inevitably developed.[100] Private Frank Sturrock of the 16th Battalion, for example, was captured at Bullecourt and spent the last year of the war as one of the few men in a small rural community 100 kilometres east of Schneidemühl. In marked contrast to the experiences of officers and NCOs in the camps who yearned for women through pictures and conversation, Sturrock's diary documents his daily interactions with dozens of Prussian women with whom he lived and worked. The following excerpt highlights the degree of freedom the other ranks sometimes experienced: '26.5.18: Sunday – went to Salinowo. Had a good time dancing with tarts ... 4.6.18: After tea had a tiff with Prakseda. Next day squared things when she gave me a rose … 6.6.18: Howing spuds with married sister. After tea another tart came home and had High time with the three.'[101]

Captivity was usually a stifling and oppressive experience that had a profound impact on the minds and bodies of the men who had no other option but to endure it. For many, the chronic effects of barbed wire disease proved their most harrowing and prolonged ordeal of the war. But the experiences of prisoners varied dramatically according to chance, circumstance, rank, their ability to work, and the deteriorating situation on the German home front.

Whether one was an officer who spent his days writing letters and goon-baiting to keep spirits high, or a private who deliberately crushed his foot to escape the privations of a Westphalian coal mine, the daily lives of Australian prisoners of war show that men who had been forced to surrender on the battlefields of the Western Front still possessed enough agency to shape better conditions and improve their chances of survival. British soldiers engaged in the fighting on the Western Front might have yearned for contact with home in an effort to survive the emotional cost of combat, but the realities of captivity were such that prisoners too had to find ways to overcome the secret battle of emotional survival.

CHAPTER 7

HUN HAUNTED?

REPATRIATION, HOME AND AFTERWARDS

Throughout September and October 1918, Allied forces made a series of offensives that threatened and destabilised the last of the German Army's defensive positions on the Western Front. The BEF broke through German lines between the Schelde and the Sambre rivers in early November, leading to the capture of hundreds of German prisoners and scores of field and heavy siege guns. Suffering a series of defeats from which it could never recover, the German Army collapsed. An armistice was signed at Compiègne on 11 November 1918, bringing an end to four years of fighting on the Western Front. German sailors of the High Seas Fleet had by then mutinied at Kiel, Kaiser Wilhelm II had abdicated and moved to Holland, and Germany was in the midst of revolution. The war had ended, and for 2.5 million Allied prisoners in German captivity, the day of being released after years of deprivation and hardship had finally arrived.

As with prisoners of war of all nationalities, Australians were both relieved and excited by the prospect of returning home. Lieutenant Les Ward of No. 2 Squadron AFC witnessed the collapse of imperial Germany from inside the officers' camp on the island of Dänholm near Stralsund on the Baltic coast. He wrote in his diary, just hours before the Armistice: 'We are all quite excited here ... We heard a lot of shouting & cheering at Straslund about 7.50 pm & this morning one of the officers obtained an *Extrablatt* [special paper] ... saying that the Revolution has taken place ... We are now waiting for developments so things should be very exciting.'[1] The guards who had watched over them for the previous six months absconded during the night, and by morning 'a man holding the rank of Sgt Mjr & does office work here is now commandant of the camp'.[2] At Heilsberg in East Prussia, other ranks

> awoke one morning & to our surprise in the place of the familiar German flag flying over the guard's quarters we saw a red flag in its place. There had been no rioting or shooting & everything had seemed to be going along as usual. We were surprised to see that no officers wore their uniforms or NCOs wore their rank. One of the guards who had been a lance corporal was now in entire charge of the camp.[3]

In accord with the Armistice terms, all British, French and Italian prisoners of war in Germany were immediately released and began the process of repatriation. German prisoners of war in France and Britain, however, remained in captivity until the Treaty of Versailles came into effect in January 1920 – a clear violation of the principle of reciprocity that had shaped the lives of millions of prisoners of war over the previous four years. Collection camps were established for British prisoners at Friedrichsfeld, Limburg, Darmstadt, Mannheim and Rastatt; from these camps, German authorities transported prisoners in north and central Germany to the Baltic and North Sea ports where they were formally handed over to a Commission of Reception of Prisoners of War. Over the following weeks, prisoners interned in Holland returned to England via Rotterdam, while those who ended up east of the Elbe River at the Armistice returned to England via Copenhagen in accord with the Danish Scheme.[4] Those in southern Germany went by rail into Switzerland, then proceeded to the French channel ports at Le Havre and Boulogne. Those who found themselves on the left bank of the River Rhine were recovered by Allied forces advancing to occupy the Rhineland.

But after years of not knowing when the war would end, it was difficult for some prisoners of war to comprehend the reality of returning home. An Australian prisoner of war described the stunned silence and pent-up emotion among a group of British prisoners at Danzig when they first saw the transport ship that would take them to Denmark. 'Neither a shout nor a cheer was heard. This prompted one man to say with a catch in his voice, "Anyone would think it was a bloody funeral. Don't you chaps know the boat's come to take you home?"'[5] Within a month, more than 70 000 British prisoners had returned from German captivity, with an additional 4000 men arriving at Dover, Leith and Hull every day until repatriation was complete in April 1919.[6] By then 163 199 British and dominion soldiers who had endured the ordeal of captivity had survived and returned home.

They represented 93 per cent of the total number of British prisoners captured on the Western Front.[7] Among them were 3541 Australians who had spent up to two and a half years in captivity at a time when massive improvements had been made to the overcrowded, disease-ridden prison camps that had housed prisoners in Germany in earlier parts of the war.

Figure 7.1 Australian ex-prisoners of war in the courtyard of AIF Administrative Headquarters in London, following their repatriation from German captivity, c. December 1918. (AWM D00117)

After landing at Dover, Leith or Hull, British prisoners returning from Germany spent two days at dispersal camps before heading to London to receive back pay, new uniforms and an extended period of leave.[8] Nearly 3000 Australian officers, NCOs and other ranks passed through the camp at Ripon after arriving at Hull in November and December 1918. There was no formal process of rehabilitating the mental and physical health of returning prisoners as there was during the Second World War, although Australian prisoners returning from Germany were required to undergo a medical examination to screen for communicable diseases before being permitted leave. Buoyed by the immediate prospect of back pay and freedom after such a prolonged period of uncertainty, returning prisoners were usually inclined to race through their medical examination without properly acknowledging injury or illness that afflicted them in captivity. 'I am not suffering from any disability due to or aggravated by war service, and feel fit and well', one man claimed after spending more than two years in the hands of the Germans. Another said he was 'now fit & capable of resuming civil occupation'.[9]

Having the men pass through the reception camps also gave the War Office and AIF Headquarters an opportunity to establish whether captured officers had acted in the face of the enemy in accordance with the British *Manual of Military Law*.[10] The Australian War Records Section recognised the value of written statements on the experiences of individuals in German captivity for 'historical record purposes', and these constitute a key source for this study.[11] Each statement varied in tone and length, and many other ranks simply added their names and signatures to group reports. Within several weeks, AIF Administrative Headquarters collated around 2500 statements on the circumstances of capture and how Australians had fared in the hands of the Germans. As well as commenting on life behind the front lines and conditions in the camps, they also recorded cases of neglect, abuse and needless suffering. One man captured at Fromelles described being marched to Lille on the afternoon of his capture in July 1916:

> There were some badly wounded men amongst us, but we were
> given no rest at all. Any man who fell out of the column of route [*sic*]
> would be promptly kicked back into it again by the German soldiers
> escorting us. The Uhlans were especially brutal. Marching through
> Lille, a crowd of populace, mainly women and children, crowded out
> into the streets to have a look at us ... the Uhlans lowered their lances
> and rode the people down. Women and children were sent sprawling
> under the horses' feet.[12]

Paucity of food and proper medical attention was a common theme. An Australian soldier blinded by grenade fragments at Hollebeke in Belgium in 1917 underwent surgery at Ghent where the medical treatment was so bad 'I had to scrape my running eye socket with my fingers to clean it out'.[13] A wounded officer reported a German major at Bullecourt robbing him of his belongings before forcing him to drink large quantities of paraffin. 'They were determined that I should drink this liquid, and to that end held me down and tried to force me, but without success.'[14] Once in Germany, Australians saw British prisoners arrive in camp 'merely skeletons' after working behind the lines.[15] One man shared his Red Cross parcel with a fellow Australian who arrived in camp on the brink of starvation: 'He made a rush at [a tin of Bully Beef] and grabbed it. After he had finished he simply sat down and cried like a kid.'[16]

Recognising these hardships, the Australian authorities offered former prisoners of war the choice of priority return to Australia or two months leave in Britain.[17] Those who went on leave used the time to decompress after a prolonged period of imprisonment, spending time sightseeing, visiting family and friends, as well as calling on the Australian Red Cross office in London to thank the volunteer workers for all that they had done to improve the lives of Australian prisoners of war. Others enjoyed the temptations of bars and brothels, which in turn resulted in soldiers over-staying their leave, contracting venereal disease and having altercations with military law. A handful of ex-prisoners of war who felt they had missed out on participating in the eventual Allied victory sought a discharge from the AIF to volunteer to serve with the British Army as part of the North Russia Relief Force.[18] Some who had been born in Britain sought discharge from the AIF and returned home to their British families.

With an eye towards the future, some former prisoners of war utilised the AIF Education Scheme, which sought to prepare Australian soldiers and nurses awaiting repatriation for life in the civilian world. Prisoners had benefited from their long periods of captivity to study and acquire new trades (admittedly, some while forcefully working for their captors) and, like all soldiers returning to Britain, also took up offers of non-military employment in Britain arranged through the Department of Repatriation and Demobilisation. One repatriated prisoner of war who worked as a motor engineer before the war spent three months working on a steam trawler in the fish industry in Aberdeen; another who worked as a railway porter completed a clerical training course at Clark's College in London.[19] In time, all repatriated prisoners of war returned to Australia in accord with the repatriation process for the rest of the AIF. They passed through depot camps in southern England and returned to Australia as part of much larger drafts of returning soldiers. Within several months they were discharged from the AIF and left to pick up the pieces of the civilian lives they had left behind.

Accounts of alleged mistreatment in German captivity reverberated throughout the British Empire as tens of thousands of returned prisoners of war arrived home. By February 1919, the Australian Defence Department had published the two-volume booklet *How the Germans Treated Australian Prisoners of War*. Drawing on excerpts from the most confronting repatriated prisoner-of-war statements collected at the reception depots, the booklet followed in the tradition of the 1915 British Bryce Report on alleged German atrocities in France and Belgium, which affirmed the wartime stereotype of the beastly German Hun. Reviewers considered the report a 'damnable indictment' and concluded that Germany had treated captured Australians with 'extreme brutality'.[20] At the time of its publication, Prime Minister William Morris Hughes was attending the Paris Peace Conference seeking war reparations for Australia. The Defence Department publication was far from a balanced assessment of life in German captivity, but its bias towards abuse and trauma helped Hughes to illustrate an aspect of the 'blood price' his nation had paid during the war.[21] In some small way, the reports from Australian prisoners of war helped to strengthen Australia's bid for a mandate over German New Guinea, then considered a strategic buffer against the threat of imperial Japan, and added weight to existing Allied attempts to impose criminal charges on the German Army for violating pre-war agreements.[22]

Figure 7.2 Captain William Cull's return to Northcote, Vic, after eighteen months in German captivity, c. October 1918. With him are his parents, John and Janet, and his nephew, also named John. Severely wounded in the hip by a German hand grenade, Cull was among a small number of wounded Australians who returned home via Switzerland before the Armistice. (Photo courtesy of Christine Webb, David Cull and Catherine McNamara-Wren)

The Defence report shed light on what was ultimately a little-known aspect of the Australian wartime experience, briefly generating public interest in a minority who had the misfortune of falling into the hands of the enemy. First-hand accounts from returned prisoners of war soon followed, with six men publishing accounts of their experiences in German captivity by 1920. Three were by officers and two had escaped, but all had otherwise endured misery and hardship that echoed a narrative of victimhood and trauma.[23] One of them was William Cull, wounded and captured near Bapaume, who summed up his time in German captivity as a 'continuity of agonies, mental and physical … [with] every little happening indelibly stamped on the mind'.[24] William Groves published a serialised account of his experiences during the reprisals in the New South Wales Returned Servicemen's journal *Reveille* between 1932 and 1934, and was probably the last Australian prisoner of the Germans to do so before the Second World War. For Groves, captivity evoked 'memories of broken men, broken spirits [and] a broken enemy nation … melancholy memories, memories not to be brooded upon'.[25]

This narrative of victimhood and trauma was cold comfort for the families of men like Private Findlay Fraser of the 48th Battalion who had died as a prisoner of war in Germany. Having been wounded in the leg upon capture at Bullecourt, Fraser suffered heart failure while under aesthetic at the prisoner-of-war hospital at Dülmen in May 1917.[26] As Oliver Wilkinson explains, the memory of prisoners of war who died in captivity was subsumed by collective memories of the war dead, who had seemingly died heroically in battle for a worthwhile cause and formed a central part of the war's remembrance.[27] In 1923, the bodies of those who had died in the German prison camps and associated hospitals had been recovered from outlying cemeteries and reinterred in one of four large cemeteries established in Germany and maintained by the Imperial War Graves Commission: Cologne Southern, Hamburg, Niederzwehren and Berlin South-Western. The post-war narrative of victimhood and suffering among prisoners of war was at odds with an otherwise heroic narrative of Australia's gallant war dead. Findlay Fraser's mother thanked AIF Base Records office for the details of her son's reinterment at Cologne Cemetery but concluded by saying, '[W]e have not much interest, considering our son is laying in a German prison grave yard. Not wishing to be unkind, but it hurts.'[28]

Bleak stories of captivity were raw, immediate, and confronting to readers who had known little of this aspect of the fighting on the Western

Figure 7.3 The grave of Private Clarence Mason, 13th Battalion, at Berlin South-Western Cemetery. Captured at Bullecourt and enduring reprisals, Mason was sent to an *Arbeitskommando* on the Baltic island of Rügen after being transported to Germany. He died of pneumonia and was initially buried at Altenkirchen. An Australian prisoner wrote to the Red Cross reporting that a 'German parson officiated. Flowers were planted on his grave and we arranged for [a] cross to be erected.' Mason was reinterred in Berlin South-Western Cemetery in 1925. (Author's photograph)

Front, but they were far from an accurate reflection of life in German prison camps. Memoirs became an important source for historians to study wartime captivity, largely owing to the absence of most other archival material documenting the lives of prisoners of war.[29] The keeping of diaries was forbidden, letters were heavily censored and personal items were usually lost as prisoners moved between camps and work parties. Like all first-hand accounts, the dependence on memories without corroborating sources created problems of misinterpretation, limited perspective and the distortion of recalled events. Hindsight and introspection made unpleasant memories seem more vivid than happier and less threatening ones, such as boredom, relief and acts of compassion, which were all just as prominent in the lives of prisoners of war.[30]

Veterans who wrote about captivity also tended to cast themselves as victims at the expense of other wartime experiences that did not fit the wretched self-image of the returned prisoner of war. Although some reported kind treatment from their captors, these experiences did not form part of the emerging prisoner-of-war narrative. Former prisoners of both the Germans and the Ottomans also did in print what they could not do in captivity: lash out at their captors. Others have noted that Australians in Ottoman captivity tended to assert a sense of racial superiority by overstating instances of abuse and deceit, which they saw as characteristics of an inferior Ottoman culture. Thomas White's classic wartime memoir of Ottoman captivity, *Guests of the Unspeakable* (1932), 'cashes in on the reading public's long-standing orientalist prejudices alluding to the sexual depravities of the Turks'.[31]

Race had little bearing on the memoirs written by Australian prisoners of the Germans, who saw themselves as racial equals to their white Christian captors. They instead exerted moral superiority over wartime archetypes that reviled German brutality. In his account, tellingly titled *In the Hands of the Hun* (c. 1920), Alfred Gray described being paraded before a crowd of civilians after ten days locked in the casemates of Fort MacDonald in Lille. He described a French woman approaching the column of Australian prisoners before she was intercepted by a German soldier and killed with a bayonet thrust.[32] William Cull recounted a conversation with a sentry who spoke candidly about raping and murdering civilians during the invasion of Belgium in 1914.[33] Very few prisoners of the Germans wrote about captivity, but those who did found their stories of victimhood and trauma at odds with an overly heroic narrative espoused by other soldier-writers, who, as Robin Gerster writes, 'strove assiduously to keep the AIF escutcheon blemish-free'.[34] Within time, the unique experiences of Australian prisoners of war were subsumed by the tragedy of 60 000 war dead whose memory formed the centrepiece of Australia's First World War remembrance. Captivity had become a story of surrender and inaction, at odds with the Anzac legend and a national memory that – with the exception of Gallipoli – gave prominence to victories over defeats.

In accordance with the penalties imposed on Germany under the Treaty of Versailles, former members of the imperial German armed forces were arrested and stood trial over their alleged breaches of international law during the course of the war. Amid mounting pressure from the Allied leaders to extradite as many as 900 Germans to face trials in Allied courts, the German Government insisted on having the alleged war criminals tried in the Reichsgericht (Supreme Court) in Leipzig. Reluctantly accepting this in May 1920, the Allies presented a much shorter list of forty-five suspects and the details of their alleged crimes to the German authorities, which included former prison guards who had deliberately mistreated British and French prisoners of war. The list was accompanied by a note stating that the first list of suspects was a test of the Germans' self-commitment to the rigours of inter-national law, even when not all accused could be traced or had credible evidence against them.

Just twelve men faced trials in Leipzig between May and July 1921 in legal proceedings the British press deemed a 'farce' and 'a hollow mock-ery' of the war crimes trials.[35] Five of the twelve were found guilty of mistreating prisoners of war and received prison sentences of less than a year. None had been involved in the reprisals in France during the spring of 1917 nor were responsible for the mistreatment of Australians in the German prison camps. With Britain and France discontinuing any form of cooperation with the Reichsgericht owing to its leniency, the trials ended quietly owing to the lack of sufficient evidence. The failure of the Leipzig war crimes trials was an important lesson for the Allies, who vowed never again to allow national courts try to punish their own alleged war crim-inals. At Nuremberg in 1945 and 1946, judges from Britain, France, the Soviet Union and the United States presided over the hearings of twenty-two Nazi war criminals.

A major limitation of this study is that the repatriation statements and written accounts by Australians who endured German captivity do not record the long-lasting consequences of imprisonment. Surrender and spending the rest of the war behind German barbed wire might have spared some Australians from any further fighting on the Western Front, but how did this relatively small group of returned servicemen fare in the post-war years? The mortality study identified twenty men who died in the period between the Armistice and the disbandment of the AIF in March 1921, showing that the consequences of the war did not end with the Armistice in November 1918. One of them was Private Thomas Marsh of the 51st Battalion, who committed suicide four weeks after his return to Australia. He was found in a suburban street in Fremantle in Western Australia 'lying on his back in a pool of blood' with a beer bottle and a razor nearby.[36] It is not clear whether the death of Thomas Marsh was linked to his captivity or his war service, but his tragic demise so soon after his return home fits within a body of scholarly work on the men and their families who were irreparably affected by the consequences of the First World War. Not all examples are so raw and immediate. Private Alfred Holton of the 33rd Battalion had been captured near Morlancourt in May 1918 and described the sense of alienation upon returning home to Australia: 'I found it hard to settle down and used to go to Sydney now & again for a drink or two ... I [eventually] settled down to a quiet life in the bush, which I did appreciate. I gave up the drinking within 12 months and I did not touch it until I joined the Army in 1939.'[37]

The existence of these so-called 'shattered Anzacs' contests the Anzac legend and its proponents who view Australia's involvement in the First World War as a defining nation-building event. As well as illustrating the cost of war on the minds and bodies of whose who endured it, the stories of Marsh and Holton add a personal dimension to medical studies published after the Second World War that reported psychological conditions among returned prisoners of war.[38] While Australian repatriation history is a fairly well-trodden field, the existing works are skewed towards returned servicemen who experienced combat, not captivity.[39] Studies examining the long-term effects of captivity focus almost exclusively on the 22 000 Australian prisoners from the Asia Pacific in the Second World War – they show that men who endured extreme deprivation and suffering in Japanese captivity experienced a host of health, work and financial difficulties well into old age. Kate Ariotti's study of sixty-seven Australian prisoners of the Ottomans who sought assistance from the Repatriation Department is the only attempt to consider the long-term effects of captivity in the First World War. Her findings are an important point of comparison when considering the post-war experiences of Australians captured on the Western Front.

The collective experience of 264 men of the 13th Battalion captured by German forces in France and Belgium gives some idea how former prisoners of the Germans fared after their return home. Raised in Sydney in September 1914, the battalion's members were drawn principally from Sydney's suburbs and the nearby regional areas of New South Wales. After the war, returned servicemen often returned to their communities and drew benefits from the New South Wales Repatriation Department (the archival records of which are held centrally in the National Archives of Australia repository in Sydney). Since a number of the 13th Battalion prisoners of war had previously served in South Africa during the Boer War of 1899–1902, in German New Guinea with the Australian Naval

Military Expeditionary Force in 1914, and on Gallipoli with the Australian Imperial Force in 1915, there is the possibility that problems arising in the post-war period might not have arisen from captivity alone. But all men in the sample had been infantrymen who endured the rigours of trench warfare on the Western Front and experienced combat during which they had been captured. A significant number were captured at Bullecourt (223), although some were taken prisoner at Mouquet Farm (28) and in trench raids, patrols and smaller actions with German forces in both France and Belgium (12).

The sample comprised 11 officers, 46 NCOs and 206 other ranks, many of the latter group having been subjected to the reprisals of spring, 1917. Twelve men of the 13th Battalion died in German dressing stations, hospitals and camp *Lazarettes* suffering from wounds received in battle, disease and the lingering effects of their conditions. The remaining 251 experienced a broad range of conditions in captivity until the Armistice of November 1918, whereupon they were repatriated to Britain and then Australia. Private Hamilton Warrell was one 13th Battalion prisoner of war who came home affected by his war service. Captured at Mouquet Farm while suffering a gunshot wound to his lower abdomen, he developed rheumatic fever in captivity and went on to spend more than six months in hospital after his return to Australia. 'All that could be done for me was done, yet I never regained my health', he wrote.[40]

Since the very nature of the human experience meant that each man reacted to combat, captivity and the return to civilian life differently, not all returned prisoners of war developed into shattered Anzacs. In the decades after the First World War, returned servicemen who believed their war service had affected their health, relationships and ability to earn an independent living sought assistance from the Repatriation Department (colloquially known as 'the Repat'). The Australian Government implemented a scheme for pensions, benefits and ongoing medical treatment as early as 1914, and over time it was improved to meet the growing needs of returned servicemen and their dependants. The Repatriation Department was established in 1921 to take over the running of military hospitals after the disbandment of the AIF, but came to assist disabled and incapacitated veterans through the provision of ongoing medical treatment. It was also responsible for rehabilitating veterans through war gratuities, vocational training, war service homes, veteran hospitals and hostels, and state-based soldier settlement schemes.[41] While the Repat was primarily concerned with returned servicemen, assistance became a family matter. Families struggled to live with war-damaged soldiers and suffered through their loss of esteem and income. In some instances, wives played a crucial role in the family economy and advocated for their husband's rights on top of their expected domestic roles.[42]

Official records show that 90 389 returned soldiers were receiving war disability pensions within two years after the end of the war; a decade later, the number had dropped to 74 578, with an estimated 780 returned servicemen dying from war-related causes each year.[43] A 1936 inquiry into the welfare of the 'burnt-out digger' found an average age of death among returned servicemen six and half years younger than other Australians.[44] To recognise that veterans were dying in middle age before reaching the age of 60 (when the aged pension was available), a service pension was introduced for permanently unemployable veterans turning 55. This was calculated in percentage terms according to the effect of the disability on a man's earning capacity, additional sums being paid for the maintenance of a wife and dependent children.

The pension undoubtedly improved the lives of returned servicemen incapacitated by war service, but there was an undercurrent of public scepticism towards the enormous expense of the Repatriation system that made some men less inclined to seek financial and medical assistance.[45] Veterans sometimes saw assistance as a sign of weakness and felt that it was best left to those who really needed it. Donald Muir, who had been wounded in the leg and captured in the botched trench raid at Piccadilly Farm in September 1916, was repatriated in April 1919 having 'no disability' and 'fit to resume former occupation'.[46] He returned to Forbes in New South Wales where he worked for many years as a labourer and never sought Repat assistance. The department's only record of him is a single-page report documenting his death from prostate cancer in Balmain Hospital in 1956, aged 87.[47]

Of the 264 members of the 13th Battalion captured on the Western Front, 191 contacted the Repatriation Department seeking financial and medical assistance in the decades after returning home. The individual case files of those who sought assistance often reveal the private and often debilitating long-term consequences of combat and captivity on individuals and their families. But as a historical source, the Repat case files must be used with caution. Returned servicemen seeking benefits often had to demonstrate a nexus between the illnesses, injury, wounds or incapacity they were suffering and their war service. If unsuccessful, the applicant was granted the right of appeal, which was rigorously tested by a medical board that set out to prove beyond reasonable doubt his condition was not due to or aggravated by war service. The Repat files are inherently skewed towards tales of woe, and, as Stephen Garton writes, 'are more likely to be a repository of complaint rather than compliment'.[48] Nor are the records complete or easy to use. Many were destroyed upon the death of the beneficiary while those that survive are scattered across state repositories of the National Archives of Australia where vast quantities are not yet publicly available.

Former prisoners of war seeking repatriation benefits found it extremely difficult to prove a link between ill-health and captivity, since many of the ailments affecting them were not immediately visible. The situation was not helped by the destruction of detailed AIF medical records in London in 1919 and the near impossibility of acquiring medical records from Germany. Sometimes the only medical records the Repat could draw on for prisoners of war were those from medical examinations at the dispersal camp at Ripon, where recently released prisoners of war, excited by the prospect of freedom, leave and back pay, reported feeling 'fit & capable of resuming civil occupation' rather than drawing attention to the lingering effects of wounds, nerves and illness.[49]

Over time, former prisoners of war began pointing to deliberate mistreatment, unsanitary conditions and insufficient medical treatment while in German captivity to assist their bids for financial and medical assistance. Consistent with Ariotti's findings, 'ex-prisoners tapped into those impressions of captivity made popular during the latter years of the war ... to portray their experiences of imprisonment as a time of great suffering that necessitated compensation'.[50] This included former prisoners of war from the 13th Battalion. Alfred MacNab explained to the Repat that he had 'remained a prisoner for two years and was employed in a factory burning some substance to produce a powder, and also employed in the salt mines. After being repatriated to England I suffered from a fistula which appeared after an operation for perineal abscesses.'[51] MacNab was granted a 50 per cent pension for a host of bowel problems attributed to his time in captivity, and later sought help when his 'heart went bung'; he then began experiencing 'sleepless nights – splitting headaches, irritable and despondent and very vivid dreams'. This resulted in an increase to his pension to help support his wife and two children, but MacNab went on to seek another increase, describing how he had been 'struck in the mouth by a prison guard with the handle of a bayonet'.[52]

Not all former prisoners of war felt comfortable seeking assistance. Having lied about his age to enlist in the AIF in August 1915, Private Hubert O'Meara was just seventeen years old when he was captured at Bullecourt nursing shrapnel wounds to his scalp. Deemed unfit to work behind the lines during the reprisals, O'Meara was sent to a hospital at Soltau near Hanover where he spent the rest of the war too sick to go out 'on commando'. When he returned to Maroubra in March 1919, friends and family noticed a marked difference from the 'strong healthy boy' who had gone off to war four years before. Having been a prisoner of war for twenty months, O'Meara was 'in a very run down state but being young and worrying about the future he was anxious to get a start on some training'. O'Meara trained as a pastry cook under the auspices of a scheme run by the Repatriation Department and found stable, long-term employment at Ireland Bakeries in Surry Hills and Gartrell White in Newtown. He married in 1921 and appeared to be making the most of post-war life.

O'Meara's health deteriorated soon after; he began suffering from boils and stomach trouble that would often cause him to spit up blood. He sought health benefits through membership of a Friendly Society or 'lodge', but his application was denied on the basis that 'his health had been ruined by his treatment as a prisoner of war'. Rather than turn to the Repatriation Department, O'Meara preferred to visit the outpatients department at Prince Henry, Sydney and St Vincent's hospitals, where he was told the miserable German provisions that sustained him in captivity had gravely affected the lining of his stomach. Although his condition waxed and waned over the years, O'Meara self-medicated through diet and daily doses of olive oil and visits to the outpatients whenever he needed, forever concerned 'that he could not do his job'. He served part-time in the Voluntary Defence Corps during the Second World War and was active in his local branch of the Returned Sailors', Soldiers' and Airmen's Imperial League (RSSAILA, the precursor to the Returned Servicemen's League) but persisted with the condition, later diagnosed as chronic dyspepsia, until ill-health forced his retirement in 1954. Ongoing medical costs amid a loss of income finally drove O'Meara to the Repat nearly thirty-six years after his return from captivity: 'I am 56 years and I am a member of the Maroubra Sub-Branch RSSAILA. This continued hospital treatment is both expensive and inconvenient and I feel I am entitled to consideration and medical treatment from the Repatriation Commission. I have never previously applied for or received any treatment. I have the Dr's prescription to verify this statement if necessary.'[53]

The Repatriation Department seemed more sympathetic towards former prisoners of war in the 1950s and 1960s, when men like O'Meara were moving beyond middle age. This, in part, reflected their increased medical needs during a period of better financial stability, but the Repat was perhaps being influenced by tropes of captivity from the Second World War. These recent claims for assistance from First World War prisoners coincided with the establishment of a £250 000 Prisoner of War Trust Fund in 1952 to assist in the rehabilitation of former prisoners of war from both the Asia Pacific and European theatres during the Second World War. The Australian Government funded further grants throughout the 1960s and 1970s, distributing more than $1 million by the time the trust fund ended in 1977. While grants were made available to assist former prisoners who suffered 'distress or hardship as a result of any major disability (physical and mental) directly referable to the conditions of captivity, or as a result of any material prejudice directly referable to such conditions is in need of such payments to overcome such distress or hardship', they were only available to veterans who had endured captivity in the Second World War.[54] Other than the pension from the Repatriation Department, no other scheme existed to assist returned servicemen who had been prisoners of war in the First World War.[55]

Figure 7.4 Oswald McClelland with his grandchildren at a family event at Pyree, NSW, in 1964. Proudly wearing his Returned from Active Service badge, McClelland was one of a number of returned servicemen from the 13th Battalion who suffered as a prisoner of war but did not fit the 'shattered Anzac' archetype. (Photo courtesy of Glen Newing)

Private Oswald McClelland was captured at Bullecourt and endured the reprisals behind the lines and other hardships in captivity. He returned to the small dairy community of Beaumont near Nowra in New South Wales where he married and raised three daughters in the guesthouse he built on Cambewarra Mountain. There he ran a refreshment shop where he and his wife Alma made 'the best ice cream south of Sydney'.[56] McClelland was actively involved in the small rural community and travelled to Sydney to march with the 13th Battalion Association each Anzac Day. Although he had been involved in establishing RSSAILA subbranches at Nowra and Greenwell Point, he rarely spoke about the war to his wife and daughters, and reviled spinach, which reminded him too much of the boiled stinging nettles that sustained him during the bleak months at the Marquion engineering dump in 1917.[57] In 1944, McClelland moved his family to Greenwell Point, where respiratory problems seemed to affect him less in the coastal air.

McClelland managed his condition as best he could until 1956 when his respiratory and continuing back problems affected his ability to continue working as a caretaker at Crookhaven Holiday Park. 'I wish to state that whilst a prisoner of war in Germany I was bashed in the back with the butt of a rifle held by a guard and was unable to work for a fortnight', he wrote.[58] A series of medical examinations by his local doctor in Nowra confirmed to the Repatriation Department that McClelland was suffering from a fused vertebrae and chronic bronchitis, but there was no evidence linking his respiratory problems with war service: his repatriated prisoner statement detailing his treatment in German captivity had been lost, and the medical report from his examination at the dispersal camp at Ripon deemed him 'fit for service'. The Repat gave McClelland the benefit of the doubt. He was unlikely to find employment less physically demanding so they approved him for a 50 per cent war pension and continued medical treatment. He died of a heart attack exacerbated by bronchitis and emphysema in 1965, aged 71.[59]

Neither Donald Muir, Alfred MacNab, Hubert O'Meara or Oswald McClelland neatly fit the archetype of the 'shattered Anzac' that has dominated Australian scholarly literature on the First World War in recent years. Just as they had in German captivity, these former prisoners of war were able to overcome the challenges they faced in their civilian lives and survive to the best of their ability. There were some men in the 13th Battalion sample who did not fare well, and others who died prematurely, but it cannot be said that war service or captivity was the root cause of all cases. Private Daniel Kruger was crushed by a ferry while

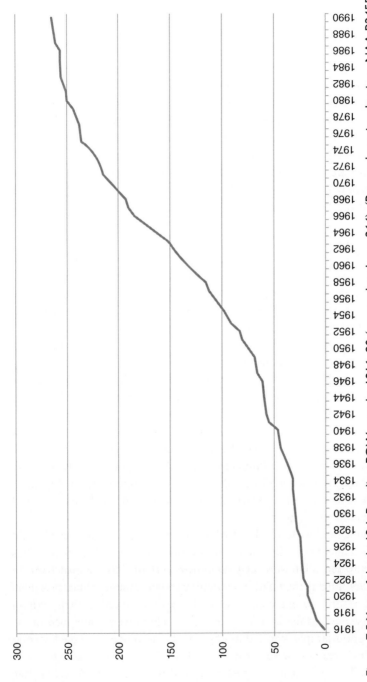

Figure 7.5 Year of death, 13th Battalion POW sample, 1916–90 (accumulated; n = 264). (Personal service dossiers, NAA B2455; Repatriation Department case files, NAA C138; Ancestry.com)

working as an engineer at Garden Island in 1920; Private Aubrey McClintock shot himself in the main street of Temora in 1922; Private John Ashmore died in a 100-ton rock fall at the Mount Pleasant colliery in 1927, and Private Alexander Stevenson was aboard a fishing trawler lost off the coast of Iceland in 1937. Indigenous soldier Private Douglas Grant struggled with racism on top of bouts of unemployment, alcoholism and psychiatric problems attributed to war service. His post-war hardships featured in *World War One: A History in 100 Stories*: 'Living unhappily on a pension, he was never able to find steady work, marry, or successfully negotiate the space between black and white Australia. He was often seen drinking alone or in the company of other "burnt out" diggers. Douglas Grant died "in loneliness and obscurity" in the Prince Henry Hospital, La Perouse in 1951.'[60]

Some men came home from the war deeply traumatised by their wartime experiences, but not all. Positive stories of returned servicemen doing well in life and society are not so well covered by historians. Newspaper reports, Soldier Settlement Loan files and the Repatriation Department case files often refer to a man's time in German captivity to explain away instances of ill-health, anti-social behaviour or altercations with the law, but are not always an accurate reflection of the impact of war on individuals and their families. Some men harboured problems beyond the realms of their wartime experiences. Captured in the Bridoux Salient trench raid in May 1916, Corporal David Austin of the 20th Battalion was arrested in 1923 for the indecent assault of a 10-year-old girl and spent eighteen months imprisoned in Long Bay Gaol. A psychiatrist gave evidence at his trial, claiming that Austin was 'Hun haunted' and 'on the borderland of insanity. Most soldiers who had been held prisoners by the Germans for any length of time ... had always been found to be abnormal.'[61]

Without ignoring the presence of shattered Anzacs within the 13th Battalion sample, the stories of hardship and privation in the years after the war do not neatly reflect their collective post-war experiences. Since half of the sample was still alive in 1960, there is a sense that servicemen were able to put their wartime experiences and any associated hardships behind them: they were able to find work, have families and go on to lead productive lives well beyond middle age. The statistics might not reflect the quality of life, but they show that former prisoners from the 13th Battalion had an average life expectancy of sixty-six years, which, according to figures by the Australian Institute of Health and Welfare, was about the same as the national average for men of their age group at the end of the First World War.[62] Notwithstanding the hardships faced during the war and after, former prisoners of war from the 13th Battalion were neither better off nor worse off than men of their age group who had not fought in the First World War.

Many of the 13th Battalion prisoners were active in the RSSAILA and were included in social gatherings and annual battalion reunions in Sydney. Douglas Grant was an active participant: in September 1929 he gave an address to 300 veterans attending the battalion reunion at the Burlington Hotel in Haymarket about his unique experiences at the *Halbmondlager* at Wünsorf-Zossen.[63] In 1938 and 1939, Captain George Gardiner arranged a reunion of ex-prisoners of war in Sydney to commemorate the twentieth anniversary of the escape of British officers from Holzminden in July 1918. The view was to have an annual prisoner-of-war reunion, but there appeared to be little interest. Since few returned prisoners had been part of the Holzminden escape (Gardiner had been in the camp at the time), most attendees seemed satisfied with annual

Figure 7.6 Returned servicemen of the 13th Battalion Association march past the Cenotaph in Martin Place, Sydney, on Anzac Day in 1946. Many former prisoners of war from the battalion were actively involved in battalion reunions and their local RSSAILA subbranches. (AWM 127107)

battalion reunions and membership of the much more inclusive RSSAILA.[64] In 1935, a Prisoner of War Club in Adelaide hoped 'to help each other in the claims of any suffering sickness from war causes' but had disbanded by 1946 when an Ex-Prisoner of War and Relatives Association was established for veterans of the Second World War.[65]

Forty-one men from the 13th Battalion sample went on to serve during the Second World War, mainly in garrison battalions and the Volunteer Defence Corps based in Australia owing to their age. Captain Arthur Fox commanded a battery of field guns from the 13th Field Regiment during the Battle of Buna-Gona in New Guinea in 1942–43, and Captain Donald Wells served with the 35th Australian Works Company. He went to Singapore with the rest of the 8th Australian Division and very narrowly avoided capture when the British garrison surrendered to the Japanese in February 1942. Private Percival Gosper lied about his age in both world wars, overstating it in the first and understating it in the second. A lance sergeant in the 2/1st Battalion, he served in the Middle East and fought at Bardia, Greece and on the island of Crete. Gosper was killed fighting German *Fallschirmjäger* when his rifle company assaulted a fortified olive oil factory near Retimo airfield on 23 May 1941. Just as captivity had saved Gosper from being killed or wounded twenty-four years earlier, his death on Crete spared him the ignominy of surrendering a second time in his life. Allied forces were evacuated in the following days, and the Wehrmacht seized control of the island. The Germans captured 12 000 Allied soldiers, which included 3000 Australians, who spent the next four years in captivity in Austria and Nazi Germany.

Private Donald Fraser died at the age of 94 in January 1990 and was the last surviving member of the 13th Battalion taken prisoner on the Western Front. He had fought on Gallipoli, been wounded in the arm by grenade fragments before his capture at Bullecourt, and was repatriated to Britain in 1919 without complaint of illness or wounds. Fraser returned to Bourke in remote north-western New South Wales where he lived and worked before the war, outwardly appearing 'none the worse for the sufferings and privations he experienced while in the hands of the enemy'.[66] He managed the East Toorale Hotel for a while, marrying Rose Walklin in 1925 with whom he had the first of their ten children. At Binburra near East Torrale, Fraser grazed sheep on a block of land allocated to him under the government Soldier Settlement Scheme, but failing productivity from the dry, rocky land yielded little return and strained the family financially through the years of the Great Depression.[67]

Figure 7.7 Donald Fraser at his home in Bourke, NSW, following an oral history interview with Tasmanian researcher David Chalk in December 1985. Neither a victim nor a hero, Fraser did the best he could to pick up the threads of his life after returning home from captivity. (Photo courtesy of Ian Chalk)

After selling Binburra to his older brother, Fraser purchased land closer to Bourke on the flat open plains astride the Darling River and established Kinchella Station in 1935. This venture proved much more prosperous. Grazing sheep while battling through long periods of drought and intermittent rainfall during the late 1930s and into the 1940s, Don Fraser worked hard to expand his property into 60 000 acres of fertile, well-irrigated land that stood the family in good stead before the wool boom of the 1950s. Fraser bought a house in San Souci in Sydney so that his younger children would receive a decent education; he lived there intermittently with his wife and children while regularly flying back to Kinchella to manage the property with his older sons. Deeply proud of his Scottish heritage, he holidayed in Argyllshire for six months in 1955 with his wife and four of his children in the village where his father had been born and raised before emigrating to Australia.

A reserved and humble man who seldom raised his voice or spoke his mind, Donald Fraser never said much about his wartime experiences to his wife and children. He encouraged them in all their endeavours and often showed a willingness to help others less fortunate than himself. Determined to make a go of it on his own, Fraser was among seventy-three former prisoners of war from the 13th Battalion who did not seek financial and medical benefits from the Repatriation Department. In between trips to San Souci, Fraser was active in Bourke community life, and was a member of a long list of local associations, such as the District Hospital Committee, the Carnival, Rodeo and Show Committee, the Pastures Protection Board, the United Farmers and Woolgrowers Association, the Masonic Lodge and the Bourke RSSAILA subbranch. Community work, farming and family life might have kept his wartime demons at bay, but there were two events in Donald Fraser's post-war life that left him devastated. Leslie Blacker, a farmhand from Binburra station whom Fraser treated as surrogate son, ignored his advice and enlisted in the Second AIF in 1940. Blacker served with the 2/1st Battalion and fought in Libya, on Crete and in New Guinea, and was accidentally killed at Aitape in February 1945. The other traumatic event was the death of his beloved youngest son, Rob, in a car accident on Kinchella Station in January 1966.

Donald Fraser was president of the Bourke RSSAILA subbranch for many years and, in October 1945, organised a reception in the Council Chambers for a group of servicemen and women returning home from the Second World War. Some of them had been prisoners of the Italians, Germans and Japanese. To them he said: 'I was a prisoner of war for 18 months and I know their form. I extend a welcome to you on your return to your native town and hope you will pick up the threads where you left off prior to going away.'[68] Fraser's advice accorded precisely with the way he had lived his own life: devoted to work, family and community. He had returned home from the First World War neither a victim nor a hero, and did the best he could to resume the life he left behind. One of the last moments Fraser had with his daughter before he died was spent reminiscing about conditions at a mine near Soltau where he had worked to extract potassium salt in 1918.[69] Memories of captivity might have been with Donald Fraser as he reflected on the totality of his life, but he was defined by much more than the privations he endured as a prisoner of war.[70]

CONCLUSION

This book has argued that Germany's treatment of Allied prisoners during the First World War was neither brutal nor benign, but somewhere in between. Through the experiences of Australian prisoners of war captured on the Western Front, we see that Germany largely adhered to the pre-war agreements as best it could. Although there were cases of deliberate mistreatment, ex-prisoners of war testified that their captors had largely treated them humanely, provided them with food, shelter and medical assistance, and respected the rank of captured officers.

Once in Germany, Australian prisoners of war benefited from assistance from the Red Cross, primarily in the form of generous quantities of food and clothing that made most prisoners of war self-sufficient rather than dependent on the German-supplied provisions. The neglect and abuse experienced by Australian prisoners of war did not always reflect a formal German policy of mistreatment. With the exception of reprisals affecting the other ranks captured in mid-1917, the hardships endured by Australian prisoners of war were largely a consequence of Germany's declining ability to care properly for the 2.5 million Allied prisoners in its camps by the end of the war – a reality exacerbated by a war being fought on multiple fronts, critical food shortages, and an economy hampered by naval blockade. The Australian experience of German captivity supports Uta Hinz's argument that the First World War was 'not a total war that negated each international law or humanitarian norm'.[1] Had Germany not abided by the pre-war agreements, more prisoners would have suffered and the mortality rate would have probably been higher.

Yet things were very different behind the lines in German-occupied France, where the protecting powers of neutral countries could not police the pre-war agreements. Since the humane treatment of prisoners could not always be ensured, the German Army treated captured Australians in accord with a principle of reciprocity that sought to improve conditions for German prisoners of war in British and French captivity. German troops accepted the surrender of Australians to prevent the reciprocal killing of captured Germans, and wounded Australians received medical treatment in the German casualty evacuation system knowing that German casualties received treatment in British and French aid stations just the same. Moreover, the principle of reciprocity also seemed to legitimise the abuse of prisoners while violating the terms of the pre-war agreements. This aspect of the Australian experience of German captivity supports Heather Jones' assertion that the belligerents disregarded and undermined the laws established to protect the well-being of captured soldiers. These worsening cycles of violence set new precedents for the Second World War, when British and dominion prisoners of war continued to endure violent reprisals in German captivity.[2]

In addition to these themes, this book has highlighted the value of prisoners of war to the armies that capture them. Captured Australians were an important part of the German Army's intelligence-gathering network, where kind treatment and friendly conversation had the potential to yield important operational information on the AIF and its activities on the Western Front. Once prisoners of war were sufficiently assured that no harm would come to them, they often spoke openly and candidly about military matters and disclosed important information about morale, strength and the disposition of the AIF and its operations. Prisoners of war were also valued as a workforce amid a growing manpower shortage in Germany and its collapsing domestic economy. Prisoners of war rarely made a motivated workforce, but the men who spent the remainder of the war imprisoned in Germany recognised the value of working beyond the wire as a relief from the tedium of camp life and the prospect of exercise, better food and contact with women.

Captured Australians also found ways to overcome the challenges of German captivity. They immensely benefited from the Australian Red Cross Society, almost all its volunteers being British and Australian women. Vera Deakin and the Wounded and Missing Enquiry Bureau relieved the anxiety of Australian families by confirming that a missing man was alive in German captivity, while Mary Elizabeth Chomley's Prisoner of War Department sent regular consignments of food and clothing that sustained them throughout their time behind German barbed wire. Chomley personally helped prisoners to overcome the battle for emotional survival by fulfilling the role of a surrogate mother. Australian prisoners of war might not have made heroic escape attempts to the extent remembered by popular memory, but thousands of Australian prisoners of war possessed enough freedom in captivity to shape the best possible conditions to improve their chances of survival. Some malingered and resisted their captors while others busied themselves with camp duties. For Australians, the war behind German barbed wire was nowhere near as violent or traumatic as the trench warfare in France and Belgium. Some came home traumatised by their wartime experiences, defining the rest of their lives – and those of their families – by the violence of combat and abuse endured in German prison camps. But many were able to put the war behind them and moved on in life, leading happy and fulfilling lives well into old age.

The Australian experience of captivity in the First World War has all but faded from public memory, eclipsed by the tragedy of 60 000 war dead and the immense suffering and hardships of the much greater numbers of Australians captured in the Second World War. But those who were captured in the fighting on the Western Front fought a battle radically different from the ones that hold central place in the memory of Australia's proud military past. Australian soldiers who had the misfortune of falling into German hands struggled to survive the extreme violence of trench warfare, then the cruelty of their captors and the depravity of the enclosures that defined their very existence. Nulla pitied the sight of the 'poor beggars' towards the end of *Somme Mud*, but this depiction of the 'scarecrows on legs' was not an accurate reflection of how all Australians fared in German hands.[3] Plenty of Australian prisoners of war received medical treatment, food and shelter in accord with the pre-war agreements, and were treated fairly by a captive nation struggling to support its own people.

No single Australian narrative emerged from captivity on the Western Front, but the way prisoners of war regarded survival as a personal triumph united their otherwise disparate array of experiences. Australians survived captivity not by virtue of nationality, or because they were fit and young and had the skills and attributes of bushmen, such as improvisation and resilience, as the Anzac legend purports. Those who had the misfortune of falling into German hands largely overcame the stigma of surrender – most resigned themselves to their fate and found ways to use the minor freedoms available to them to improve their chances of survival. A few made heroic escapes, but most remained where they were until the end of the war, withstanding the dreary monotony of camp life, the ever-present threat of beatings and reprisals, and not knowing when or whether they would see their loved ones again. German captivity in the First World War was neither brutal nor benign, but one long endurance test that most Australians survived, which might not have been the case had they remained fighting on the Western Front.

Australians who died in German captivity, 1916–21

The cemeteries where Australians who died as prisoners of war are buried often bear no geographic relation to the places of their imprisonment. Initially buried near where they died, they were exhumed in the mid-1920s and reinterred in the nearest cemetery created and maintained by the Imperial (later Commonwealth) War Graves Commission. Australians who died in the prison camps and associated *Larzarette* in Germany were consolidated into the Cologne Southern, Hamburg, Niederzwehren or Berlin South-Western cemeteries. The end date has been extended to 31 March 1921, the day the Australian Imperial Force was formally disbanded, to give some sense of the number of former prisoners of war who died while returning and after returning to Australia.

Rank	Surname	First name	Unit	Date of death	Cause	Buried/commemorated
Lieut	Dobie	Meldrum	1 Pnr Bn	28 May 1916	Wounds	Cabaret-Rouge British Cemetery, France
Pte	Goodrich	William	25 Bn	23 Jun 1916	Wounds	Pont-du-Hem Military Cemetery, France
Pte	Fogden	William	25 Bn	30 Jun 1916	Wounds	Aciet-le-Grand Communal Cemetery Extension, France
Pte	Thornburrow	Edward	31 Bn	2 Jul 1916	Wounds	Cabaret-Rouge British Cemetery, France
Pte	Braganza	Louis	9 Bn	4 Jul 1916	Wounds	Cabaret Rouge British Cemetery, France
Sgt	Barry	Harold	9 Bn	4 Jul 1916	Wounds	Australian National Memorial, Villers-Bretonneux, France
Sgt	Croft	Harold	14 Bn	8 Jul 1916	Wounds	Lille Southern Cemetery, France
Pte	Pflaum	Raymond	32 Bn	19 Jul 1916	Wounds	Fromelles (Pheasant Wood) Cemetery, France
Pte	Jenkin	George	57 Bn	19 Jul 1916	Wounds	VC Corner Cemetery Memorial, France
Pte	Goulding	John	31 Bn	19 Jul 1916	Wounds	Australian National Memorial, Villers-Bretonneux, France

(cont.)

Rank	Surname	First name	Unit	Date of death	Cause	Buried/commemorated
Pte	Mason	James	31 Bn	19 Jul 1916	Wounds	Australian National Memorial, Villers-Bretonneux, France
Pte	Davidson	Percy	29 Bn	20 Jul 1916	Wounds	Cabaret-Rouge British Cemetery, France
LCpl	Dyke	Thomas	32 Bn	20 Jul 1916	Wounds	Cabaret-Rouge British Cemetery, France
Pte	Pearce	Harold	30 Bn	21 Jul 1916	Wounds	Cabaret-Rouge British Cemetery, France
Pte	MacKenzie	Alan	31 Bn	21 Jul 1916	Wounds	Cabaret-Rouge British Cemetery, France
Pte	Thomas	William	54 Bn	21 Jul 1916	Wounds	Cabaret-Rouge British Cemetery, France
Pte	Lawson	William	54 Bn	21 Jul 1916	Wounds	Lille Southern Cemetery, France
Pte	Ash	Cyril	32 Bn	22 Jul 1916	Wounds	Cabaret-Rouge British Cemetery, France
Pte	Hook	Roy	32 Bn	22 Jul 1916	Wounds	Cabaret-Rouge British Cemetery, France
Pte	Freeman	Norman	55 Bn	22 Jul 1916	Wounds	Cabaret-Rouge British Cemetery, France
Pte	Thomas	William	31 Bn	22 Jul 1916	Wounds	Douai Communal Cemetery, France
Sgt	Colless	Frederick	32 Bn	23 Jul 1916	Wounds	Lille Southern Cemetery, France
Pte	Scrimgeour	Thomas	29 Bn	23 Jul 1916	Wounds	Valenciennes (St Roch) Communal Cemetery, France

Rank	Surname	Forename	Unit	Date	Cause	Cemetery
Pte	Thomas	Walter	3 Bn	23 Jul 1916	Wounds	Australian National Memorial, Villers-Bretonneux, France
Capt	Arblaster	Charles	53 Bn	24 Jul 1916	Wounds	Douai Communal Cemetery, France
Pte	Tate	Charles	54 Bn	24 Jul 1916	Wounds	Douai Communal Cemetery, France
Pte	Copley	Allan	8 MG Coy	25 Jul 1916	Wounds	Valenciennes (St Roch) Communal Cemetery, France
Pte	Reay	John	55 Bn	26 Jul 1916	Wounds	Cabaret-Rouge British Cemetery, France
Pte	Lawrence	Francis	55 Bn	27 Jul 1916	Wounds	Cabaret-Rouge British Cemetery, France
Pte	Knight	James	31 Bn	27 Jul 1916	Wounds	Douai Communal Cemetery, France
Pte	McKinnon	Daniel	32 Bn	28 Jul 1916	Wounds	Douai Communal Cemetery, France
Pte	Crouch	Sidney	8 MG Coy	29 Jul 1916	Wounds	Valenciennes (St Roch) Communal Cemetery, France
LCpl	Sainsbury	Noel	28 Bn	29 Jul 1916	Killed	Australian National Memorial, Villers-Bretonneux, France
Pte	Holmes	Leslie	26 Bn	30 Jul 1916	Wounds	Lebucquiere Communal Cemetery Extension, France
Pte	Newman	John	25 Bn	1 Aug 1916	Wounds	Le Chateau Military Cemetery, France

(cont.)

Rank	Surname	First name	Unit	Date of death	Cause	Buried/commemorated
Pte	Herbert	William	26 Bn	2 Aug 1916	Wounds	Achiet-le-Grant Communal Cemetery Extension, France
Cpl	Horrocks	Stephen	28 Bn	2 Aug 1916	Wounds	Achiet-le-Grant Communal Cemetery Extension, France
Pte	Gibbs	Bertrand	23 Bn	2 Aug 1916	Wounds	Caudry Old Communal Cemetery, France
Pte	Cahill	James	32 Bn	3 Aug 1916	Wounds	Douai Communal Cemetery, France
Pte	Eaves	Joseph	54 Bn	14 Aug 1916	Wounds	Valenciennes (St Roch) Communal Cemetery, France
Pte	Smith	William	25 Bn	15 Aug 1916	Wounds	Niederzwehren Cemetery, Germany
Sgt	Jackson	Harry	13 Bn	15 Aug 1916	Wounds	Valley Cemetery, Vis-en-Artois, France
Pte	Elmore	Frederick	26 Bn	21 Aug 1918	Wounds	Le Château Military Cemetery, France
Pte	Powis	Charles	30 Bn	23 Aug 1916	Wounds	Niederzwehren Cemetery, Germany
Pte	McPherson	John	31 Bn	23 Aug 1916	Wounds	Niederzwehren Cemetery, Germany
Capt	Kennedy	Arthur	23 Bn	26 Aug 1916	Illness	Niederzwehren Cemetery, Germany

Rank	Surname	First name	Unit	Date	Cause	Cemetery
Pte	Lewis	Herbert	51 Bn	26 Aug 1916	Wounds	Caudry Old Communal Cemetery, France
Pte	Clarkin	William	7 Bn	26 Aug 1916	Wounds	Caudry Old Communal Cemetery, France
Pte	Deakin	Percy	26 Bn	28 Aug 1916	Wounds	Caudry Old Communal Cemetery, France
Pte	Heyen	Henry	21 Bn	31 Aug 1916	Wounds	Achiet-le-Grand, Communal Cemetery Extension, France
Pte	Hickey	Bernard	16 Bn	1 Sep 1916	Wounds	Adanac Military Cemetery, France
Pte	Metcalfe	Joseph	13 Bn	2 Sep 1916	Wounds	Lebucquiere Communal Cemetery Extension, France
Pte	Wolff	Edward	32 Bn	5 Sep 1916	Wounds	Douai Communal Cemetery, France
Cpl	Argall	John	10 Bn	9 Sep 1916	Wounds	Cologne Southern Cemetery, Germany
Pte	Zachariah	David	32 Bn	10 Sep 1916	Wounds	Niederzwehren Cemetery, Germany
Cpl	Murphy	James	51 Bn	10 Sep 1916	Wounds	Caudry Old Communal Cemetery, France
Pte	Johnstone	Frank	51 Bn	17 Sep 1916	Wounds	Caudry Old Communal Cemetery, France

Rank	Surname	First name	Unit	Date of death	Cause	Buried/commemorated
Pte	Nash	Charles	58 Bn	19 Sep 1916	Wounds	Cabaret-Rouge British Cemetery, France
Pte	Nairn	William	10 Bn	21 Sep 1916	Wounds	Niederzwehren Cemetery, Germany
Lieut	Dabb	Reginald	8 Bn	26 Sep 1916	Wounds	Cologne Southern Cemetery, Germany
Sgt	Hooper	John	18 Bn	1 Oct 1916	Wounds	Hooge Crater Cemetery, Belgium
Sgt	Reed	Arthur	51 Bn	1 Oct 1916	Wounds	Caudry Old Communal Cemetery, France
Pte	O'Neill	Clarence	28 Bn	5 Oct 1916	Wounds	Cologne Southern Cemetery, Germany
Pte	Fairweather	Andrew	55 Bn	16 Oct 1916	Illness	Hamburg Cemetery, Germany
Pte	Hislop	Allan	25 Bn	18 Oct 1916	Wounds	Niederzwehren Cemetery, Germany
Pte	Ramseyer	Frederick	21 Bn	25 Oct 1916	Wounds	Niederzwehren Cemetery, Germany
Pte	Bowler	Charles	51 Bn	26 Oct 1916	Wounds	Niederzwehren Cemetery, Germany
Pte	Carriss	Henry	27 Bn	11 Nov 1916	Wounds	Port-de-Paris Cemetery, France
Pte	Ratcliffe	Sydney	13 Bn	12 Nov 1916	Wounds	Niederzwehren Cemetery, Germany
Pte	Taylor	William	27 Bn	18 Nov 1916	Wounds	Port-de-Paris Cemetery, France

Rank	Surname	Given	Battalion	Date	Cause	Location
Pte	Cane	Arthur	55 Bn	23 Nov 1916	Illness	Cologne Southern Cemetery, Germany
Pte	Ransley	George	26 Bn	28 Nov 1916	Wounds	Port-de-Paris Cemetery, France
Pte	Butcher	Reginald	27 Bn	29 Nov 1916	Wounds	Port-de-Paris Cemetery, France
Sgt	White	Roy	10 Bn	6 Dec 1916	Illness	Hartley South New Cemetery, England
Pte	Althorp	Algar	10 Bn	15 Dec 1916	Wounds	Cologne Southern Cemetery, Germany
Lieut	Parker	Harold	37 Bn	30 Jan 1917	Wounds	Rue Petillion Military Cemetery, France
Pte	Poeppel	George	15 Bn	2 Feb 1917	Wounds	Achiet-le-Grand Communal Cemetery Extension, France
Pte	King	Leonard	15 Bn	4 Feb 1917	Wounds	Flesquieres Hill British Cemetery, France
Pte	Oliver	Thomas	15 Bn	4 Feb 1917	Wounds	Ontario Cemetery, France
Pte	Lake	Charles	15 Bn	9 Feb 1917	Wounds	Port-de-Paris Cemetery, France
Sgt	Crowther	Travis	15 Bn	11 Feb 1917	Wounds	Australian National Memorial, Villers-Bretonneux, France
Pte	McAtee	John	15 Bn	11 Feb 1917	Wounds	Australian National Memorial, Villers-Bretonneux, France
Pte	Moore	Alexander	15 Bn	11 Feb 1917	Wounds	Australian National Memorial, Villers-Bretonneux, France
Pte	Waters	Edward	15 Bn	16 Feb 1917	Wounds	Port-de-Paris Cemetery, France

Rank	Surname	First name	Unit	Date of death	Cause	Buried/commemorated
Pte	Grant	Lionel	28 Bn	22 Feb 1917	Illness	Port-de-Paris Cemetery, France
Pte	Peacock	William	22 Bn	26 Feb 1917	Wounds	Douchy-les-Ayette British Cemetery, France
Pte	Littleboy	George	42 Bn	26 Feb 1917	Wounds	Australian National Memorial, Villers-Bretonneux, France (believed to be buried at Rue Petilon Cemetery, Fleurbaix)
Pte	Conquest	Arthur	37 Bn	27 Feb 1917	Wounds	Rue Pettlion Military Cemetery, France
2 Lieut	Ahnall	Karl	28 Bn	2 Mar 1917	Wounds	Douchy-les-Ayette British Cemetery, France
Pte	Lawler	Timothy	17 Bn	2 Mar 1917	Wounds	Mory Abbey Military Cemetery, France
Lieut	Massie	Hugh	22 Bn	8 Mar 1917	Wounds	Douchy-les-Ayette, British Cemetery, France
Pte	Down	Clarence	23 Bn	23 Mar 1917	Wounds	Hem-Leglet Communal Cemetery, France
Pte	Yates	Alfred	17 Bn	7 Apr 1917	Wounds	Valenciennes (St Roch) Communal Cemetery, France
Pte	Beecken	Herman	10 Bn	8 Apr 1917	Wounds	Cabaret-Rouge British Cemetery, France

Rank	Surname	Forename	Unit	Date	Cause	Cemetery
Pte	Freeman	Fred	10 Bn	8 Apr 1917	Wounds	Ontario Cemetery, France
Pte	Osborne	Bertram	50 Bn	9 Apr 1917	Wounds	Valenciennes (St Roch) Communal Cemetery, France
Pte	Brown	Herbert	16 Bn	11 Apr 1917	Wounds	HAC Cemetery, France
Pte	Stewart	John	13 Bn	11 Apr 1917	Wounds	Australian National Memorial, Villers-Bretonneux, France
Pte	Brown	George	46 Bn	11 Apr 1917	Wounds	Australian National Memorial, Villers-Bretonneux, France
Pte	McKellar	Duncan	46 Bn	11 Apr 1917	Wounds	Australian National Memorial, Villers-Bretonneux, France
Sgt	Collins	Francis	14 Bn	12 Apr 1917	Wounds	Vis-en-Artois British Cemetery, France
Cpl	Jones	Ralph	14 Bn	12 Apr 1917	Wounds	Vis-en-Artois British Cemetery, France
Pte	Meginess	William	16 Bn	13 Apr 1917	Wounds	Cabaret-Rouge British Cemetery, France
Pte	Levett	Albert	48 Bn	13 Apr 1917	Wounds	Cabaret-Rouge British Cemetery, France
Pte	Muir	Rollo	4 LTMB	13 Apr 1917	Wounds	Hamburg Cemetery, Germany
Lieut	Kirkland	George	4 MGC	13 Apr 1917	Wounds	Hem-Lenglet Communal Cemetery, France

(cont.)

Rank	Surname	First name	Unit	Date of death	Cause	Buried/commemorated
Pte	Grant	Archibald	48 Bn	13 Apr 1917	Wounds	Hem-Lenglet Communal Cemetery, France
Pte	Gardner	William	48 Bn	13 Apr 1917	Wounds	Ontario Cemetery, France
Sgt	Murray	Robert	15 Bn	13 Apr 1917	Wounds	Valenciennes (St Roch) Communal Cemetery, France
Cpl	McLeod	Wallace	47 Bn	13 Apr 1917	Wounds	Valeciennes (St Roch) Communal Cemetery, France
Pte	Jeffs	Clarence	48 Bn	13 Apr 1917	Wounds	Vis-en-Artois British Cemetery, France
Cpl	Marshall	Frederick	48 Bn	13 Apr 1917	Wounds	Vis-en-Artois British Cemetery, France
Pte	Chamberlain	Frederick	15 Bn	14 Apr 1917	Wounds	Ontario Cemetery, France
Pte	Guest	William	14 Bn	15 Apr 1917	Wounds	Cabaret-Rouge British Cemetery, France
Cpl	Hogan	James	14 Bn	15 Apr 1917	Wounds	Cabaret-Rouge British Cemetery, France
Sgt	Robinson	Cecil	48 Bn	15 Apr 1917	Wounds	Cologne Southern Cemetery, Germany
Cpl	Grimmond	George	14 Bn	15 Apr 1917	Wounds	Hem-Lenglet Communal Cemetery, France

Rank	Surname	First name	Battalion	Date	Cause	Cemetery/Memorial
Pte	Stevens	Timothy	13 Bn	15 Apr 1917	Wounds	Ontario Cemtery, France
Pte	Rapp	Henry	47 Bn	15 Apr 1917	Wounds	Valenciennes (St Roch) Communal Cemetery, France
Pte	Croft	Arthur	4 Bn	15 Apr 1917	Wounds	Anneux British Cemtery, France
Pte	Watkins	Errol	17 Bn	15 Apr 1917	Wounds	Vis-en-Artois British Cemetery, France
Pte	Turner	Henry	48 Bn	16 Apr 1917	Wounds	Hamburg Cemetery, Germany
LCpl	Cunningham	Phillip	11 Bn	16 Apr 1917	Wounds	Cabaret-Rouge British Cemetery, France
Pte	Martin	Lionel	16 Bn	17 Apr 1917	Wounds	Hamburg Cemetery, Germany
LCpl	MacKenzie	Alexander	13 Bn	18 Apr 1917	Wounds	Hamburg Cemetery, Germany
Pte	Williams	Thomas	46 Bn	18 Apr 1917	Wounds	Hamburg Cemetery, Germany
Pte	Moore	Albert	16 Bn	18 Apr 1917	Wounds	Valencienres (St Roch) Communal Cemetery, France
Lieut	Smith	Stanley	16 Bn	18 Apr 1917	Wounds	Valencienres (St Roch) Communal Cemetery, France
LCpl	McArthur	Alexander	14 Bn	20 Apr 1917	Wounds	Hamburg Cemetery, Germany
Pte	Riley	John	8 Bn	20 Apr 1917	Wounds	Australian National Memorial, Villers-Bretonneux, France
Pte	Jolly	Albert	15 Bn	21 Apr 1917	Wounds	Hamburg Cemetery, Germany

(cont.)

Rank	Surname	First name	Unit	Date of death	Cause	Buried/commemorated
Pte	Calder	James	46 Bn	22 Apr 1917	Wounds	Ontario Cemetery, France
Pte	Harvey	Charles	14 Bn	24 Apr 1917	Wounds	Cabaret-Rouge British Cemetery, France
Pte	Hill	Robert	13 Bn	25 Apr 1917	Wounds	Hamburg Cemetery, Germany
Pte	Cox	Rupert	16 Bn	26 Apr 1917	Wounds	Hamburg Cemetery, Germany
Pte	Elford	Francis	15 Bn	29 Apr 1917	Wounds	Mons (Bergen) Communal Cemetery, Belgium
Pte	Weedon	Thomas	4 MGC	1 May 1917	Killed	Corbehem Communal Cemetery, France
LCpl	Goddard	Owen	4 MGC	1 May 1917	Killed	Corbehem Communal Cemetery, France
Cpl	McEntee	Charles	4 MGC	1 May 1917	Killed	Corbehem Communal Cemetery, France
Pte	Toll	Thorold	4 MGC	1 May 1917	Killed	Corbehem Communal Cemetery, France
Pte	Webb	Charles	4 MGC	1 May 1917	Killed	Corbehem Communal Cemetery, France
Pte	Fraser	George	48 Bn	1 May 1917	Killed	Corbehem Communal Cemetery, France
LCpl	Rawlings	Charles	4 MGC	1 May 1917	Wounds	Hamburg Cemetery, Germany
Pte	McGregor	Herbert	14 Bn	2 May 1917	Wounds	Hamburg Cemetery, Germany

Rank	Surname	Given name	Unit	Date	Cause	Cemetery
Capt	Leane	Allan	48 Bn	2 May 1917	Wounds	Australian National Memorial, Villers-Bretonneux, France
Pte	Cameron	James	15 Bn	3 May 1917	Wounds	Hamburg Cemetery, Germany
Pte	Hindley	John	4 MGC	6 May 1917	Wounds	Cologne Southern Cemetery, Germany
Pte	O'Neil	Daniel	48 Bn	6 May 1917	Wounds	Hamburg Cemetery, Germany
Pte	Hodgetts	Mervyn	15 Bn	6 May 1917	Wounds	Hem-Lenglet Communal Cemetery, France
Pte	Burns	Robert	19 Bn	8 May 1917	Wounds	Flesquieres Hill British Cemetery, France
Pte	Law	Edward	14 Bn	10 May 1917	Illness	Cologne Southern Cemetery, Germany
Pte	Harrington	William	16 Bn	10 May 1917	Wounds	Hamburg Cemetery, Germany
Pte	Grange	Samuel	17 Bn	10 May 1917	Wounds	Australian National Memorial, Villers-Bretonneux, France
Pte	Meredith	Luton	11 Bn	13 May 1917	Wounds	Y Farm Military Cemetery, France
Pte	Clark	Archie	13 Bn	14 May 1917	Wounds	Hamburg Cemetery, Germany
Pte	Holt	Richard	13 Bn	16 May 1917	Illness	Mons (Bergen) Communal Cemetery, Belgium
Pte	Weaver	Charles	16 Bn	16 May 1917	Illness	Ontario Cemetery, France

Rank	Surname	First name	Unit	Date of death	Cause	Buried/commemorated
Sgt	Drew	Frederick	16 Bn	21 May 1917	Wounds	Hamburg Cemetery, Germany
Pte	Terry	Guy	13 Bn	22 May 1917	Wounds	Hamburg Cemetery, Germany
Pte	Fraser	Findley	48 Bn	23 May 1917	Wounds	Cologne Southern Cemetery, Germany
Pte	Grover	Percy	16 Bn	23 May 1917	Wounds	Hamburg Cemetery, Germany
Pte	Lucas	Leonard	16 Bn	24 May 1917	Wounds	Valenciennes (St Roch) Communal Cemetery, France
Lieut	Killingsworth	Harry	38 Bn	28 May 1917	Wounds	Australian National Memorial, Villers-Bretonneux, France
Pte	McClelland	Samuel	18 Bn	31 May 1917	Wounds	Cologne Southern Cemetery, Germany
Pte	Muller	Alfred	14 Bn	2 Jun 1917	Wounds	Valenciennes (St Roch) Communal Cemetery, France
Pte	McKernan	Edward	16 Bn	13 Jun 1917	Wounds	Valenciennes (St Roch) Communal Cemetery, France
Pte	Tudor	Daniel	15 Bn	14 Jun 1917	Illness	Cologne Southern Cemetery, Germany
Pte	Jenkins	Joseph	11 Bn	18 Jun 1917	Illness	Maubeyge-Centre Cemetery, France
Pte	Perry	John	15 Bn	19 Jun 1917	Wounds	Hamburg Cemetery, Germany

Rank	Surname	Forename	Bn	Date	Cause	Cemetery
Pte	Croston	William	16 Bn	20 Jun 1917	Wounds	Cologne Southern Cemetery, Germany
Pte	Johannesen	Peter	16 Bn	23 Jun 1917	Wounds	Valenciennes (St Roch) Communal Cemetery, France
Pte	McNamee	James	16 Bn	27 Jun 1917	Wounds	Cologne Southern Cemetery, Germany
Pte	Wallace	Alexander	16 Bn	28 Jun 1917	Wounds	Hamburg Cemetery, Germany
Pte	Mills	John	16 Bn	3 Jul 1917	Illness	Cologne Southern Cemetery, Germany
Pte	Miller	Joseph	16 Bn	7 Jul 1917	Killed	Valencienres (St Roch) Communal Cemetery, France
Pte	Nicholas	Clarence	48 Bn	8 Jul 1917	Wounds	Hamburg Cemetery, Germany
Pte	Bee	Stephen	14 Bn	10 Jul 1917	Wounds	Ypres (Menin Gate) Memorial, Belgium
Pte	Freeman	Herbert	57 Bn	14 Jul 1917	Illness	Maubeyge-Centre Cemetery, France
Pte	Carey	James	15 Bn	14 Jul 1917	Illness	Mortagne-du-Nord Communal Cemetery, France
Pte	Henderson	William	18 Bn	16 Jul 1917	Illness	Berlin South-Western Cemetery, Germany
Pte	Hemsley	Cecil	48 Bn	21 Jul 1917	Wounds	Hamburg Cemetery, Germany

(*cont.*)

Rank	Surname	First name	Unit	Date of death	Cause	Buried/commemorated
Lieut	Holmes	Kenneth	AFC	11 Aug 1917	Wounds	Noyelles-Codault Communal Cemetery, France
LCpl	Hocking	Joseph	15 Bn	13 Aug 1917	Wounds	Hamburg Cemetery, Germany
Pte	McWhinney	Stanley	16 Bn	16 Aug 1917	Illness	Sauchy-Lestree Communal Cemetery, France
Pte	Giddins	Walter	13 Bn	17 Aug 1917	Illness	Tornai Communal Cemetery Allied Extension, Belgium
Pte	Blanchard	Alfonso	16 Bn	20 Aug 1917	Illness	Cabaret-Rouge British Cemetery, France
Pte	Scott	Joseph	16 Bn	20 Aug 1917	Wounds	Hamburg Cemetery, Germany
Pte	Harrison	Frederick	15 Bn	21 Aug 1917	Illness	Cologne Southern Cemetery, Germany
Pte	Cronk	Edwin	15 Bn	28 Aug 1917	Illness	Cabaret-Rouge British Cemetery, France
Pte	Bell	Frederick	16 Bn	8 Sep 1917	Illness	Demain Communal Cemetery, France
Pte	Pritchard	Charles	16 Bn	9 Sep 1917	Illness	Niederzwehren Cemetery, Germany
Spr	Renshall	Arthur	1 Tun Coy	17 Sep 1917	Wounds	Hamburg Cemetery, Germany
Pte	Hall	Harold	16 Bn	17 Sep 1917	Illness	Cabaret-Rouge British Cemetery, France
Pte	Demasson	Hubert	16 Bn	19 Sep 1917	Illness	Niederzwehren Cemetery, Germany

Pte	Sherriff	William	20 Bn	9 Oct 1917	Illness	Niederzwehren Cemetery, Germany
Pte	Smith	Arthur	16 Bn	14 Oct 1917	Illness	Tornai Communal Cemetery Allied Extension, Belgium
Pte	Hillyard	Reginald	47 Bn	15 Oct 1917	Wounds	Harlebeke New British Cemetery, Belgium
Pte	Wright	John	48 Bn	15 Oct 1917	Wounds	Harlebeke New British Cemetery, Belgium
Pte	Rigney	Rufus	48 Bn	15 Oct 1917	Wounds	Harlebeke New British Cemetery, Belgium
Pte	Howe	William	28 Bn	17 Oct 1917	Wounds	Niederzwehren Cemetery, Germany
Pte	Kerr	William	47 Bn	17 Oct 1917	Wounds	Harlebeke New British Cemetery, Belgium
Cpl	Spang	Harold	16 Bn	18 Oct 1917	Accident	Valenciennes (St Roch) Communal Cemetery, France
Pte	Walker	Alvin	15 Bn	21 Oct 1917	Illness	Cologne Southern Cemetery, Germany
Pte	Thompson	Arthur	16 Bn	2 Nov 1917	Illness	Mons (Bergen) Communal Cemetery, Belgium
Pte	McGregor	Roy	16 Bn	2 Nov 1917	Accident	Cabaret-Rouge British Cemetery, France

(cont.)

Rank	Surname	First name	Unit	Date of death	Cause	Buried/commemorated
Pte	Bond	Alexander	16 Bn	5 Nov 1917	Wounds	Cologne Southern Cemetery, Germany
Pte	Gordon	Norman	15 Bn	17 Nov 1917	Accident	Berlin South-Western Cemetery, Germany
Spr	Young	Walter	2 Tun Coy	18 Nov 1917	Illness	Cologne Southern Cemetery, Germany
Pte	Hoole	Harold	32 Bn	9 Dec 1917	Illness	Tornai Communal Cemetery Allied Extension, Belgium
Pte	Hurrell	William	11 Bn	18 Dec 1917	Illness	Niederzwehren Cemetery, Germany
Pte	White	Horace	10 Bn	19 Dec 1917	Illness	Pont-du-Hem Military Cemetery, France
Pte	Pittman	Samuel	34 Bn	11 Jan 1918	Wounds	Cologne Southern Cemetery, Germany
Pte	Mawby	Fred	50 Bn	18 Jan 1918	Illness	Niederzwehren Cemetery, Germany
Pte	Colgrave	Roy	12 Bn	19 Jan 1918	Illness	Hamburg Cemetery, Germany
Pte	Cousins	Vernel	48 Bn	9 Feb 1918	Suicide	Hamburg Cemetery, Germany
Pte	Grimson	Charles	36 Bn	6 Mar 1918	Wounds	Laventine Military Cemetery, France
Pte	Cook	Alfred	32 Bn	30 Mar 1918	Wounds	Australian National Memorial, Villers-Bretonneux, France

Rank	Surname	First Name	Battalion	Date	Cause	Cemetery
Pte	Cooke	William	35 Bn	5 Apr 1918	Wounds	Australian National Memorial, Villers-Bretonneux, France
Pte	Curtis	Frank	47 Bn	5 Apr 1918	Killed	Australian National Memorial, Villers-Bretonneux, France
Pte	Murphy	Frank	47 Bn	6 Apr 1918	Wounds	Australian National Memorial, Villers-Bretonneux, France
Pte	Bergin	Arthur	52 Bn	9 Apr 1918	Wounds	Tincourt New British Cemetery, France
Sgt	Clifton	Max	20 Bn	9 Apr 1918	Wounds	Tincourt New British Cemetery, France
Pte	Nickolas	Phillip	34 Bn	15 Apr 1918	Wounds	Heath Cemetery, France
Pte	Springer	Simon	35 Bn	16 Apr 1918	Wounds	Heath Cemetery, France
Cpl	Ravaillion	William	35 Bn	16 Apr 1918	Wounds	Heath Cemetery, France
Pte	Howarth	Percy	20 Bn	23 Apr 1918	Wounds	La Chapelette British and Indian Cemetery, France
Pte	Hoskins	Walter	48 Bn	23 Apr 1918	Wounds	Le Quesnoy Communal Cemetery, France
Pte	Henney	William	47 Bn	23 Apr 1918	Wounds	Péronne Communal Cemetery Extension, France
Pte	Rose	Andrew	18 Bn	25 Apr 1918	Wounds	Valenciennes (St Roch) Communal Cemetery, France

(cont.)

Rank	Surname	First name	Unit	Date of death	Cause	Buried/commemorated
Pte	Whitby	William	35 Bn	26 Apr 1918	Wounds	Tincourt New British Cemetery, France
LCpl	Pearce	William	4 MGC	27 Apr 1918	Wounds	Péronne Communal Cemetery Extension, France
Pte	Wood	Sydney	52 Bn	28 Apr 1918	Wounds	Péronne Communal Cemetery Extension, France
Sgt	Lake	Halbert	13 Bn	1 May 1918	Wounds	Brookwood Military Cemetery, England
Pte	Williams	Stanley	36 Bn	1 May 1918	Illness	Noyers-Pont-Maugis French National Cemetery, France
Lieut	Coolahan	John	5 MGC	3 May 1918	Wounds	Valenciennes (St Roch) Communal Cemetery, France
Pte	Fordham	George	47 Bn	4 May 1918	Illness	Berlin South-Western Cemetery, Germany
Cpl	Myles	John	45 Bn	11 May 1918	Wounds	Valenciennes (St Roch) Communal Cemetery, France
Pte	Sharman	John	3 Bn	13 May 1918	Wounds	Audenarde Communal Cemetery, Belgium

Rank	Surname	First name	Unit	Date	Cause	Cemetery
Pte	Kennett	James	46 Bn	17 May 1918	Wounds	Valenciennes (St Roch) Communal Cemetery, France
Sgt	Murray	William	52 Bn	19 May 1919	Wounds	Valenciennes (St Roch) Communal Cemetery, France
Pte	Avery	Harry	45 Bn	25 May 1918	Wounds	Péronne Communal Cemetery Extension, France
Pte	Ballinger	Ernest	29 Bn	15 Jun 1918	Illness	Cologne Southern Cemetery, Germany
QMS	Russell	Selby	47 Bn	15 Jun 1918	Wounds	Berlin South-Western Cemetery, Germany
Pte	Hann	Thomas	15 Bn	11 Jul 1918	Wounds	Cologne Southern Cemetery, Germany
Spr	Westwood	James	2 Tun Coy	21 Jul 1918	Illness	Niederzwehren Cemetery, Germany
Pte	Crossland	Edward	47 Bn	22 Jul 1918	Illness	Valenciennres (St Roch) Communal Cemetery, France
Pte	Evans	John	20 Bn	24 Jul 1918	Suicide	Berlin South-Western Cemetery, Germany
Lieut	Doig	Allan	17 Bn	27 Jul 1918	Wounds	Le Quesnoy Communal Cemetery, France
LCpl	Bolton	Reginald	39 Bn	3 Aug 1918	Wounds	Le Chateau Military Cemetery, France

(*cont.*)

Rank	Surname	First name	Unit	Date of death	Cause	Buried/commemorated
Pte	Annett	Ernest	35 Bn	4 Aug 1918	Illness	Le Chateau Military Cemetery, France
Pte	MacGowan	Melville	43 Bn	9 Aug 1918	Unknown	Niederzwehren Cemetery, Germany
Pte	Pedgrift	Albert	25 Bn	15 Aug 1918	Illness	Cologne Southern Cemetery, Germany
LCpl	Carr	William	48 Bn	20 Aug 1918	Illness	Alexandria (Hadra) War Memorial Cemetery, Egypt
Pte	Oliver	Henry	35 Bn	20 Aug 1918	Illness	Cologne Southern Cemetery, Germany
Pte	Laycock	Frederick	48 Bn	23 Aug 1918	Wounds	Berlin South-Western Cemetery, Germany
Pte	Simmons	Albert	6 Bn	31 Aug 1918	Unknown	Cologne Southern Cemetery, Germany
Pte	Rusconi	William	47 Bn	1 Sep 1918	Illness	Etreaupont Communal Cemetery, France
Pte	Harris	Harold	4 MGC	9 Sep 1918	Illness	Valenciennes (St Roch) Communal Cemetery, France
Gnr	McNeill	Roy	2 Fld Bde	13 Sep 1918	Illness	Niederzwehren Cemetery, Germany
Pte	Gaylard	Henry	17 Bn	17 Sep 1918	Illness	Niederzwehren Cemetery, Germany

Rank	Surname	Forename	Unit	Date	Cause	Cemetery
Pte	Bisset	David	57 Bn	19 Sep 1918	Illness	Le Cateau Military Cemetery, France
Pte	McMillan	James	14 Bn	25 Sep 1918	Illness	Berlin South-Western Cemetery, Germany
Pte	Peisley	Lindon	19 Bn	1 Oct 1918	Wounds	Le Cateau Military Cemetery, France
Pte	Phister	Clifford	47 Bn	9 Oct 1919	Killed	Landrecies Communal Cemetery, France
Cpl	Scott	Norman	45 Bn	10 Oct 1918	Illness	Valenciennes (St Roch) Communal Cemetery, France
Pte	McKenzie	Alexander	16 Bn	12 Oct 1918	Illness	Cologne Southern Cemetery, Germany
Pte	Troyle	Konrat	16 Bn	13 Oct 1918	Illness	Berlin South-Western Cemetery, Germany
Pte	Badmington	Richard	53 Bn	14 Oct 1918	Illness	Cologne Southern Cemetery, Germany
Pte	Munn	George	54 Bn	15 Oct 1918	Illness	Berlin South-Western Cemetery, Germany
Pte	Lupton	Alexander	15 Bn	15 Oct 1918	Illness	Berlin South-Western Cemetery, Germany
Pte	Baird	Frederick	17 Bn	15 Oct 1918	Illness	Cologne Southern Cemetery, Germany
Pte	Richardson	George	5 MGC	17 Oct 1918	Illness	Hamburg Cemetery, Germany
Pte	Meredith	Henry	19 Bn	17 Oct 1918	Illness	Hamburg Cemetery, Germany

(*cont.*)

Rank	Surname	First name	Unit	Date of death	Cause	Buried/commemorated
Pte	Siefken	Otto	21 MGC	21 Oct 1918	Illness	Berlin South-Western Cemetery, Germany
Pte	Calvert	Hughie	21 MGC	21 Oct 1918	Illness	Niederzwehren Cemetery, Germany
Gnr	Hurman	Ernest	2 FAB	24 Oct 1918	Illness	Hamburg Cemetery, Germany
Pte	Allen	Frederick	53 Bn	25 Oct 1918	Illness	Torquay Cemetery and Extension, England
Pte	Henson	Thomas	10 Bn	25 Oct 1918	Illness	Cologne Southern Cemetery, Germany
Pte	Sweeney	Terrance	25 Bn	28 Oct 1918	Illness	Cologne Southern Cemetery, Germany
Pte	Summerton	Walter	46 Bn	28 Oct 1918	Illness	Niederzwehren Cemetery, Germany
Pte	Kelly	Patrick	53 Bn	29 Oct 1918	Illness	Posen Old Garrison Cemetery, Poland
Pte	Mason	Clarence	13 Bn	30 Oct 1918	Illness	Berlin South-Western Cemetery, Germany
Spr	Clingin	George	3 Tun Coy	31 Oct 1918	Illness	Berlin South-Western Cemetery, Germany
Pte	Petersen	Hans	26 Bn	31 Oct 1918	Illness	Niederzwehren Cemetery, Germany

Rank	Surname	Given Name	Unit	Date	Cause	Cemetery
Pte	Moir	Percival	48 Bn	31 Oct 1918	Illness	Hamburg Cemetery, Germany
Pte	McMahen	Herbert	51 Bn	2 Nov 1918	Illness	Cologne Southern Cemetery, Germany
Pte	Greenwood	Albert	46 Bn	4 Nov 1918	Illness	Vevey (St Martin's) Cemetery, Switzerland
Pte	Gannaway	Benjamin	11 Bn	4 Nov 1918	Illness	Berlin South-Western Cemetery, Germany
Pte	Crebert	Walter	55 Bn	5 Nov 1918	Unknown	Niederzwehren Cemetery, Germany
LCpl	Bromfield	Charles	14 Bn	7 Nov 1918	Illness	Vevey (St Martin's) Cemetery, Switzerland
Pte	Elliott	Albert	4 Pnr Bn	8 Nov 1918	Illness	Berlin South-Western Cemetery, Germany
LCpl	Smith	Percival	22 Bn	10 Nov 1918	Illness	Australian National Memorial, Villers-Bretonneux, France
Pte	Derrick	Harry	37 Bn	12 Nov 1918	Wounds	Niederzwehren Cemetery, Germany
Spr	Nielsen	Clair	2 Tun Coy	16 Nov 1918	Illness	Niederzwehren Cemetery, Germany
LCpl	Stewart	John	4 MGC	18 Nov 1918	Illness	Belgrade Cemetery, Belgium
Pte	McMahon	John	16 Bn	19 Nov 1918	Illness	Berlin South-Western Cemetery, Germany

(cont.)

Rank	Surname	First name	Unit	Date of death	Cause	Buried/commemorated
Pte	Lomesney	Michael	13 Bn	20 Nov 1918	Illness	Posen Old Garrison Cemetery, Poland
Pte	Challenor	Gordon	4 Pnr Bn	20 Nov 1918	Illness	Perreuse Château Franco-British National Cemetery, France
Pte	Yde	Ernest	4 MGC	21 Nov 1918	Unknown	Cologne Southern Cemetery, Germany
Pte	McNeil	Donald	22 Bn	28 Nov 1918	Illness	Berlin South-Western Cemetery, Germany
Pte	O'Neill	John	55 Bn	30 Nov 1918	Illness	Berlin South-Western Cemetery, Germany
Pte	Pell	John	14 Bn	3 Dec 1918	Illness	Berlin South-Western Cemetery, Germany
Spr	Lewis	George	2 Tun Coy	5 Dec 1918	Illness	Niederzwehren Cemetery, Germany
Pte	Martin	Alfred	48 Bn	11 Dec 1918	Illness	Terlincthun British Cemetery, England
Pte	Slight	John	16 Bn	12 Dec 1918	Illness	Berlin South-Western Cemetery, Germany
Pte	Andrews	Alfred	15 Bn	16 Dec 1918	Illness	Berlin South-Western Cemetery, Germany

Rank	Surname	First name	Unit	Date	Cause	Location
Spr	Dunn	Edward	2 Tun Coy	29 Dec 1918	Illness	Djon (Le Pejoces) Cemetery, France
Pte	Francis	John	14 Bn	30 Dec 1918	Illness	Brookwood Military Cemetery, England
Pte	Moody	Ernest	12 Bn	7 Jan 1919	Illness	Copenhagen Western Cemetery, Denmark
Pte	McGarry	Albert	33 Bn	8 Jan 1919	Illness	Australian National Memorial, Villers-Bretonneux, France
Pte	Savage	Elvin	13 Bn	8 Feb 1919	Illness	Brookwood Military Cemetery, England
Pte	Arney	Richard	15 Bn	3 Mar 1919	Illness	Bournemouth East Cemetery, England
Pte	Marsh	Thomas	51 Bn	26 May 1919	Suicide	Fremantle Cemetery, Western Australia
Pte	Barnes	Clifford	15 Bn	14 Jun 1919	Illness	Springvale Necropolis, Melbourne
Pte	Walsh	Joseph	15 Bn	19 Jun 1919	Unknown	Towong Cemetery, Brisbane
Pte	Burrows	Marshall	4 Pnr Bn	24 Aug 1919	Illness	Rookwood Necropolis, Sydney
Pte	Hodges	William	48 Bn	26 Sep 1919	Cancer	West Terrace Cemetery, Adelaide
Pte	Barrett	John	48 Bn	13 Jan 1919	Suicide	Lilydale Civil Cemetery, Lilydale
LCpl	Tubby	Robert	51 Bn	14 Mar 1920	Unknown	Fremantle Cemetery, Fremantle
Pte	Elliott	Charles	47 Bn	10 May 1920	Acute Alcoholism	Brisbane General Cemetery, Brisbane

(cont.)

Rank	Surname	First name	Unit	Date of death	Cause	Buried/commemorated
Pte	Hansen	Peter	47 Bn	8 Jun 1920	Wounds	Yangan General Cemetery, Yangan
Pte	Sully	Reginald	50 Bn	21 Jul 1920	Unknown	West Terrace Cemetery, Adelaide
Pte	Cleaver	Arthur	15 Bn	24 Dec 1920	Unknown	Cora Villa, Tasmania
Pte	O'Neill	John	47 Bn	11 Jan 1921	Unknown	Mount Morgan Cemetery, Queensland
LCpl	Davis	Adolphus	47 Bn	9 Mar 1921	Infection	Toowong Cemetery, Brisbane
Pte	Geddes*	Jack	13 Bn	14 Jun 1921	Illness	Waverley Cemetery, Sydney
Pte	Farley*	Jack	1 Bn	21 Jun 1921	Suicide	Unknown

* Died after 31 March 1921. These men are not included on the AWM Roll of Honour, but seem to have been included in official figures of Australians who died in or as a consequence of German captivity during the First World War.

AWARDS AND ESCAPES FROM GERMAN CAPTIVITY, 1916-18

Australians who made successful escapes from German captivity did not always receive bravery awards. In May 1917, the War Office issued instructions that precluded prisoners from being considered for an award if the act for which they were recommended was in any way associated with their capture. Recommendations also had to be accompanied by a statement signed by an officer who had first-hand knowledge.[1] This requirement did not favour prisoners of war, most of whom were other ranks who spent their captivity detained separately from officers. The situation changed in May 1919, when the War Office issued new instructions that welcomed recommendations for men who had displayed meritorious service in captivity by caring for the sick and wounded or had displayed courage in attempts at escape. Recommendations were to be 'substantiated by at least two witnesses who had first-hand knowledge of the services under consideration, *one of whom must be an officer* [emphasis in original]'.[2]

This recommendation process similarly favoured officers, three of whom were recognised for their unsuccessful escapes from German captivity: Lieut Henry Fitzgerald, 19 Bn (Military Cross), Capt Joseph Honeysett, 48 Bn (Military Cross) and Lieut Peter Lyons, 11 Bn (Mentioned in Despatches). For tending to sick and wounded prisoners, WOII John Bannigan, 2nd FAB, LCpl Christopher Hanckel, 13 Bn and Pte Alfred Rawlings, 2 Bn were awarded the Meritorious Service Medal. Pte Richard Cash, 19 Bn, was awarded the Meritorious Service Medal for his role in the Holzminden escape.

The following made successful escapes from German captivity:

- LCpl Hamilton Parsons, 16 Bn, captured at Bullecourt on 11 April 1917. Awarded Military Medal for successful escape from behind German lines on 20 May 1917 with Private George Stewart
- Pte George Stewart, 16 Bn, captured at Bullecourt on 11 April 1917. Awarded Military Medal for successful escape from behind German lines on 20 May 1917 with LCpl Hamilton Parsons
- Pte Hugh West, 51 Bn, captured at Mouquet Farm, 3 September 1916. Awarded the Military Medal for successful escape from Walsum, Germany, to Holland on 9 September 1917
- Capt John Mott, 48 Bn, captured at Bullecourt on 11 April 1917. Awarded Military Cross for successful escape from Ströhen Moor to Holland on 26 September 1917
- Pte Alec Waterhouse, 12 Bn, wounded and taken prisoner at Mouquet Farm on 22 August 1916. Awarded the Military Medal for successful escape from Dülmen to Holland in October 1917
- LCpl Norman Collings, 10 Bn, captured at Mouquet Farm on 22 August 1916. Awarded Military Medal for successful escape from Soest to Holland on 7 October 1917
- Pte Henry Thomas, 30 Bn, captured at Fromelles on 20 July 1916. Awarded Military Medal for successful escape with Pte Hector Holmes, 56th Bn, from Duisburg Meidrich to Holland on 27 October 1917
- Pte Hector Holmes, 56 Bn, captured at Fromelles on 20 July 1916. Awarded Military Medal for successful escape from Duisberg to Holland with Pte Henry Thomas, 30th Bn, on 27 October 1917
- Pte John McIntosh, 47 Bn, captured at Passchendaele on 12 October 1917. Awarded Military Medal for escape from Termonde, Belgium, to Holland with Ptes Alexander Falconer and Ashburton Thompson on 24 October 1917
- Pte Alexander Falconer, 47 Bn, captured at Passchendaele on 12 October 1917. Awarded Military Medal for successful escape from Termonde, Beligum, to Holland with Ptes John McIntosh and Ashburton Thompson on 24 October 1917
- Pte Ashburton Thompson, 48 Bn, captured at Passchendaele, 12 October 1917. Awarded the Military Medal for successful escape from Termonde, Beligum, to Holland with Ptes Alexander Falconer and John McIntosh on 24 October 1917
- Sgt Frederick Peachey, 15 Bn, captured at Bullecourt on 11 April 1917. Awarded Military Medal for successful escape from Tournai to Holland with Pte John Lee on 5 November 1917

- Pte John Lee, 14 Bn, captured at Bullecourt on 11 April 1917. Awarded Military Medal for successful escape from Tournai to Holland on 5 November 1917 with Sgt Frederick Peachey
- Lieut Herbert Johnston, 21 MGC, captured at Lagnicourt on 15 April 1917. Awarded Military Cross for successful escape from Ströhen Moor to Holland on 30 November 1917
- Pte William Pitts, 50 Bn, captured at Mouquet Farm on 16 August 1916. Awarded the Military Medal for successful escape to Holland in December 1917
- Pte Wesley Choat, 32 Bn, captured at Fromelles on 20 July 1916. Awarded Military Medal for successful escape from Düsseldorf to Holland on 28 December 1917
- Pte Edward Gardiner, 10 Bn, captured at Mouquet Farm on 22 August 1916. Awarded Military Medal for successful escape from Friedrichsfeld to Holland, February 1918
- Dvr Leslie Barry, 1 FCE, captured at Flers on 4 November 1916. Awarded Military Medal for successful escape from Germany to Holland, February 1918
- CSM Sydney Edwards, 51 Bn, captured at Mouquet Farm on 3 September 1916. Awarded Military Medal for successful escape from Lechfeld to Switzerland on 9 May 1918
- Pte Percy Cooke MM, 15 Bn, captured at Mouquet Farm on 12 August 1916. Awarded bar to Military Medal for escape from Ossenberg to Holland, on 5 April 1918
- Pte George Reed, 54 Bn, captured at Fromelles on 20 July 1916. Awarded Military Medal for successful escape to Holland in April 1918
- Pte Robert Saunders, 50 Bn, captured at Villers-Bretonneux on 25 April 1918. Escaped from behind German lines in April 1918
- Cpl Charles Lane, 4th MGC, captured at Dernancourt on 5 April 1918. Escaped from behind German lines with Pte Reinhardt Ruschpler on 13 April 1918
- Pte Reinhardt Ruschpler, 4 MGC, captured at Dernancourt on 5 April 1918. Escaped from behind German lines with Cpl Charles Lane on 13 April 1918
- Pte Kenneth Farley, 35 Bn, captured at Villers-Bretonneux on 4 April 1918. Awarded Military Medal for escape from behind German lines in June 1918
- Pte Joseph Newman, 17 Bn, captured at Lagnicourt on 15 April 1917. Awarded Military Medal for successful escape from Germany to Petrograd, Russia, in June 1918

- Pte Russel Badcock, 26 Bn, captured at Pozières on 29 July 1916. Awarded Military Medal for successful escape to Holland in June 1918
- Cpl Thomas Olsen, 19 Bn, captured at Hangard Wood on 7 April 1918, escaped from behind German lines on 10 August 1918
- Sgt Edward Facer, 21 MGC, captured at Lagincourt on 15 April 1917. Awarded Military Medal for escape from Dülmen to Holland in September 1918
- Pte Albert Keating, 7 Bn, captured near Harbonnières 9 August 1918. Awarded Military Medal for escape from behind German lines in September 1918
- Pte Frederick Allen, 53 Bn, captured at Fromelles on 20 July 1916. Successfully escaped from Münster to Holland in September 1918. Died of disease in England, October 1918
- Pte Percy Fleming, 15 Bn, captured at Bullecourt on 11 April 1917. Awarded Military Medal for successful escape from Friedrichsfeld to Holland, October 1918
- Cpl George Hemming, 45 Bn, captured at Messines on 9 June 1917. Awarded Military Medal for successful escape from Friedrichsfeld to Holland, October 1918
- Pte John Johnston, 13 Bn, captured at Bullecourt on 11 April 1917. Awarded Military Medal for successful escape to Holland in October 1918
- Pte Dennis Ferry, 25 Bn, captured at Pozières on 29 July 1916. Escaped from Kalzwinkel to Holland on 18 October 1918
- LCpl Claude Benson, 13 Bn, captured at Bullecourt on 11 April 1917. Mentioned in Despatches for successful escape from Güstrow to Holland in October 1918
- Pte James Bayes, 32 Bn, captured at Fromelles on 20 July 1916. Escaped from Berge-Borbeck to Holland on 3 November 1918 with Pte Edward Amy, 29th Battalion
- Pte Edward Amy, 29 Bn, captured at Fromelles on 20 July 1916. Escaped from Berge-Borbeck to Holland with Pte James Bayes, 32 Bn, on 3 November 1918
- Pte Christopher Davidson, 16 Bn. Captured at Bullecourt on 11 April 1917. Successfully escaped from Friedrichsfeld to Belgium, 5 November 1918
- Pte Thomas Taylor, 14 Bn, captured at Bullecourt on 11 April 1917. Successfully escaped from Heilsburg to Russia in November 1918. Arrived in London in April 1919

- Pte Hay Hansen, 4 MGC, captured at Bullecourt on 11 April 1917. Escaped to Russia on 3 November 1918, arrived London on 5 December 1918
- Pte Aubury Whittington, 16 Bn, captured at Bullecourt on 11 April 1917. Awarded Military Medal for successful escape from Dülmen to Holland on 12 November 1918
- Pte Ronald MacKay, 56 Bn, captured at Hollebeke on 18 November 1917. Awarded Military Medal for successful escape from Dülmen to Switzerland on 14 November 1918

NOTES

Introduction

1 Lynch, *Somme Mud*, p. 314.
2 Butler, *Special Problems and Services*, vol. 3, *Official History of the Australian Army Medical Services* [hereafter Butler, *Special Problems and Services*], pp. 896–7.
3 Bean, diary entry, 3 October 1916, Charles Bean papers, 3DRL606/60, AWM38.
4 Gammage, *The Broken Years*, p. 260.
5 Pte Otto Nielsen, 25 Bn, reflections, *Mutiny on the Western Front* (video), Mingara Films Productions, 1979. 'Blighty', in this instance, refers to a wound serious enough for treatment and a period of recuperation in either England or (in extreme cases) Australia.
6 Blair, *No Quarter*; Cook, 'The politics of surrender', pp. 637–65; Kramer, *Dynamic of Destruction*, pp. 62–4.
7 Bean, *The Australian Imperial Force in France, 1916*, pp. 514–15.
8 Doegen, *Kriegsgefangene Völker*, pp. 28–9.
9 Wilkinson, *British Prisoners of War in First World War Germany*, p. 88.
10 Gammage, *The Broken Years*, p. 283; Butler, *Special Problems and Services*, p. 892.
11 Butler, *Special Problems and Services*, pp. 896, 900–1. This differs from the figures presented in the mortality study in chapter 2, which purports that 327 Australians died in German captivity, of whom 200 died of wounds received in combat.
12 Jones, 'A missing paradigm?', pp. 19–48.
13 Butler, *Special Problems and Services*, pp. 896–97. A similar point with reference to British prisoners of the Germans is made in Wilkinson, 'A fate worse than death?', pp. 24–40.
14 Eby, *The Road to Armageddon*, pp. 4–8.
15 Beaumont, 'Australia's global memory footprint', pp. 45–63.
16 Halpin cited in Gerster, *Big-noting*, p. 20.
17 Captain Victor Veness, 13 Bn, diary entry, 11 April 1917, PR01059, AWM.
18 Cull, *At All Costs*, p. 87.
19 Beaumont, Grant and Pegram, 'Remembering and rethinking captivity', pp. 1–8. See also Beaumont, 'Prisoners of war in Australian national memory', pp. 185–94; Garton, 'Changi as television', pp. 84–5.
20 Beaumont, Grant and Pegram, 'Remembering and rethinking captivity', pp. 4–5.

21 Holbrook, *Anzac*; Beaumont, 'Officers and men', p. 174.
22 Twomey, 'Trauma and the reinvigoration of Anzac', pp. 85–105; Twomey, 'POWs of the Japanese', pp. 191–205.
23 Stephen Smith cited in Beaumont, 'Officers and men', p. 174.
24 Bowden, 'Fall of Singapore'.
25 Keegan, *The First World War*, p. 8. For later works suggesting otherwise, see McPhail, *The Long Silence*; Horne and Kramer, *German Atrocities*; Zuckerman, *The Rape of Belgium*; Hull, *Absolute Destruction*; Akçam, *The Young Turks' Crime Against Humanity*; Pickles, *Transnational Outrage*; Babkenian and Stanley, *Armenia, Australia and Great War*.
26 Long, *The Final Campaigns*, pp. 633–64.
27 Among significant works are Nelson, *Prisoners of War*; Beaumont, *Gull Force*; Ramsay Silver, *Sandakan*; Forbes, *Hellfire*; Hearder, *Keep the Men Alive*; Grant, *The Changi Book*; Braithwaite, *Fighting Monsters*.
28 Lawless, 'Starvation, cruelty and neglect?', pp. 40–56; see also Lawless, *Kismet*.
29 Ariotti, 'Coping with captivity'. For the mortality rate, see Butler, *Special Problems and Services*, pp. 35–6.
30 Coombes, *Crossing the Wire*.
31 Smart, '"An ignoble end to all our brilliant aspirations"', pp. 84–100; Regan, 'Neglected Australians'; Noble, 'Raising the white flag', pp. 48–79.
32 Bowden, *The Changi Camera*, p. 73; John Howard cited in Grant, 'Monument and ceremony', pp. 43–4. See also Dawes, *Prisoners of the Japanese*, p. 268.
33 See Moynihan, *Black Bread and Barbed Wire*, pp. 57–78; Jackson, *The Prisoners 1914–18*, pp. 83–102; Clarke and Burgess, *Barbed Wire and Bamboo*, pp. 8–12; Adam-Smith, *Prisoners of War*, pp. 49–54; Morton, *Silent Battle*, pp. 95–117; Hanson, *Escape from Germany*; Cook, *The Real Great Escape*; Lewis-Stempel, *The War Behind the Wire*; Hardy, *The Great Escapes of World War I*.
34 Garton, *The Cost of War*, p. 210.
35 Millard, *Hero of the Empire*.
36 Isherwood, 'Writing the "ill-managed nursery"', pp. 267–86.
37 MacKenzie, 'The ethics of escape', pp. 1–16.
38 Cull, 'Great escapes', pp. 282–95.
39 Cook, *The Real Great Escape*, p. 2.
40 MacKenzie, *The Colditz Myth*, p. 2.
41 Monteath, 'Behind the Colditz myth', p. 117.
42 Kent, '*The Anzac Book* and the Anzac Legend', pp. 376–90.
43 Thomson, '"Steadfast until death?"', p. 477.
44 Cutlack, *The Australian Flying Corps*, pp. 25–8; Jones, 'Imperial captivities', pp. 177–8.
45 Bean, *The Australian Imperial Force in France, 1916*, pp. 205–6, 442; Bean, *The Australian Imperial Force in France During the Main German Offensive, 1918*, pp. 395–7.
46 Garton, *The Cost of War*, p. 209; Maughan, *Tobruk and El Alamein*, pp. 755–822; Wigmore, *The Japanese Thrust*, pp. 511–642, 679–83; Herington, *Air Power over Europe, 1944–1945*, pp. 466–98; Walker, *Middle East and*

Far East, pp. 523–674, 400–18; Walker, *Medical Services of the Royal Australian Navy and Royal Australian Air Force*, pp. 79–91.

47 'Transfer note', archival series dossier, AWM30.

48 Bean, *The Australian Imperial Force in France, 1916*, pp. 404, 422, 432, 436.

49 Bean, *The Australian Imperial Force in France, 1917*, pp. 332–4, 342–3; Bean, *The Australian Imperial Force in France During the Main German Offensive, 1918*, pp. 390, 396.

50 Bean, *The Australian Imperial Force in France, 1916*, pp. 249, 254, 514; Bean, *The Australian Imperial Force in France, 1917*, p. 766.

51 Bean, *Australian Imperial Force in France during the Allied Offensive, 1918*, pp. 147, 906.

52 Bean, *The Australian Imperial Force in France, 1916*, p. 717.

53 Bean, 'Albert Jacka', pp. 2–3.

54 Lieut L. Carter, letter to Lieut Col R. Leane, 8 August 1916, Charles Bean papers, 3DRL606/244/1, AWM38.

55 Capt Lionel Carter, 48 Bn, 'Record of Service', service dossier, B2455, NAA.

56 Gammage, *The Broken Years*, p. xi.

57 These include Becker, *Oubliés de la Grande Guerre*; Abbal, *Soldats oubliés*; Rachamimov, *POWs and the Great War*; Oltmer, *Kriegsgefangene im Europa des Ersten Weltkrieg*; Jones, 'The final logic of sacrifice?', pp. 770–91; Jones, *Violence Against Prisoners of War in the First World War*; Panayi, *Prisoners of Britain*.

58 Speed, *Prisoners, Diplomats and the Great War*, pp. 63–80; Hinz, *Gefangen im Großen Krieg*.

59 Hinz, *Gefangen im Großen Krieg*, p. 362.

60 Jones, *Violence Against Prisoners of War*, pp. 127–66.

61 Thomson, *Anzac Memories*, p. 9.

62 ABC Radio National marked the 75th anniversary of the Fall of Singapore by making the radio series *Australians Under Nippon* available via its website and podcast channel. See www.abc.net.au/radionational/programs/australians-under-nippon/ (retrieved 23 February 2017).

63 Chalk, 'Talks with old *Gefangeners*', pp. 11–23.

64 Stone, 'Prosopography', p. 46.

65 Butler, *Special Problems and Services*, pp. 896–7.

66 The names of these men are commemorated on the Australian National Memorial at Villers-Bretonneux alongside 10 737 Australians who died in France and have no known grave. One man is listed on the Ypres (Menin Gate) Memorial in Ieper among the 6187 Australians who died in Belgium and have no known grave. Having died in German hands as prisoners of war, they are commemorated no differently from Australian soldiers who died in the fighting.

67 Heather Jones defines violence in terms of a prisoner's right to seek medical attention when sick. This assumes front-line soldiers were granted this right, but in many cases were not. See Butler, *The Western Front*, pp. 86–92; Jones, 'The final logic of sacrifice?', p. 773.

68 Sheldon, *The German Army on the Somme*, p. 40.

69 '5th Annual Report, 1918–19', NO13, Publications, ARCS NO.

70 For recent scholarship on these captured Australians, see Smith, *Australasians Captured by the Raider Wolf*; Stibbe, *British Civilian Internees in Germany*; Ludewig, 'For King or Kaiser?', pp. 249–68; Guilliatt and Hohnen, *The Wolf*.
71 No seamen of the Royal Australian Navy were captured by German forces during the First World War.

Chapter 1 Raising the white flag

1 Cpl David Austin, 20 Bn, POW statement, AWM30 B6.14 (1); Bean, *The Australian Imperial Force in France, 1916*, p. 203.
2 Jones, *Violence Against Prisoners of War*, pp. 29–33; Hinz, *Gefangen im Großen Krieg*, pp. 9–33. An exception is Feltman, *The Stigma of Surrender*, pp. 43–72.
3 Noble, 'Raising the white flag', pp. 78–9.
4 Ferguson, *The Pity of War 1914–1918*, p. 339.
5 Shils and Janowitz, 'Cohesion and disintegration in the Wehrmacht in World War II', pp. 280–315; Marshall, *Men Against Fire*, pp. 123–37; Grossman, *On Killing*, p. 147; Holmes, *Acts of War*, pp. 316–20; Ferguson, 'Dynamics of defeat', pp. 34–78; Watson, *Enduring the Great War*.
6 War Office, *Statistics of the Military Effort of the British Empire During the Great War, 1914–1920* [hereafter *Statistics of the Military Effort*], p. 237.
7 Butler, *Special Problems and Services*, pp. 896–7.
8 Bean, *The Australian Imperial Force in France, 1916*, p. 940.
9 Bourke, 'Swinging the lead', pp. 10–18; Wahlert, *The Other Enemy?*, pp. 58–9; Stanley, *Bad Characters*, pp. 66–8.
10 Bean, *The Australian Imperial Force in France, 1916*, p. 940.
11 Glenister, 'Desertion without execution', p. 25.
12 Groves, 'Captivity', 31 March 1932, p. 44.
13 Butler, *The Western Front*, p. 864.
14 Ashworth, *Trench Warfare 1914–1918*, pp. 191–2.
15 Cpl David Austin, 20 Bn, POW statement, AWM30 B6.14 (1).
16 Pte Edward Jones, 1 Pnr Bn, POW statement, AWM30 B5.54; Bean, *The Australian Imperial Force in France, 1916*, p. 217.
17 Bean, *The Australian Imperial Force in France, 1916*, p. 201.
18 Pegram, '"Nightly suicide operations"', pp. 190–203.
19 Bean, *The Australian Imperial Force in France, 1916*, p. 273.
20 *Aussagen eines Gefangenen vom IX. Batl, 3. Brig., 1. Austr. Division, gefangen genommen am 2.7.16 nordwestl. Fromelles*, 2 July 1916; Ibid., *Aussagen eines gefangenen Australiers von der b-Komp. des IX Inf. Batl. (Queensland). 3. austral. Inf. Brig. 1. austr. J.D.*, 4.7.16 6, BRD, Bd. 23, Abt.IV/BayHStA.
21 War Office, *German Methods of Trench Warfare*; War Office, 'Manual of positional warfare for all arms'; War Office, 'Army order regarding the execution of counter-attacks'.
22 Gudmundsson, *Stormtroop Tactics*, pp. 34–5.
23 Pte Lancelot Davies, 13 Bn, untitled manuscript, p. 2, PR00140, AWM.
24 Butler, *The Western Front*, p. 48.
25 LCpl John Aldham, 54 Bn, POW statement, AWM30 B14.5.
26 Pte Patrick Gill, 53 Bn, POW statement, AWM30 B14.1.

27 Pte William Gillingham, 30 Bn, POW statement, AWM30 B16.4.
28 Butler, *The Western Front*, p. 73.
29 Bean, *The Australian Imperial Force in France, 1916*, p. 593.
30 Sgt Ernest Fitch, 5 Bn, POW statement, AWM30 B5.13.
31 Pte Frank Derne, 5 Bn, POW statement, AWM30 B5.13.
32 Bean, *The Australian Imperial Force in France, 1916*, p. 642.
33 Pte Bertram Hoult, 26 Bn, POW statement, AWM30 B6.3.
34 Sgt Lewis Marshall, 28 Bn, POW statement, AWM30 B6.9 (2).
35 Cpl Francis Brennan, 15 Bn, POW statement, AWM30 B13.15.
36 Capt Arthur Fox, 13 Bn, POW statement, AWM30 B13.2.
37 Pte Edward Gardiner, 10 Bn, POW statement, AWM30 B5.33.
38 Pte Percival Deadman and Pte Samuel Greenhill, 16 Bn, POW statement, AWM30 B13.12.
39 CQMS Sydney Edwards, 51 Bn, POW statement, AWM30 B11.3.
40 Butler, *The Western Front*, pp. 48, 73.
41 Ibid., p. 211.
42 The figure of eighty-five is based on the number of men from 4th Division registered with the Red Cross as being captured on 2 April 1917. German sources claim 'around 300' had been captured but were cut down by Australian machine-gun fire. Bean acknowledges that a friendly fire incident did occur, killing about twenty, but says the number of Australians captured in the Noreuil action was more like sixty (Bean, *The Australian Imperial Force in France, 1917*, pp. 219–20).
43 Capt Leslie Todd and Capt Maxwell Gore, 50 Bn, POW statement, AWM30 B11.1.
44 Bean, *The Australian Imperial Force in France, 1917*, p. 284.
45 Ibid., p. 342.
46 Groves, 'Things I remember', 29 February 1932, p. 24.
47 Ibid., 31 March 1932, p. 44.
48 Bean, *The Australian Imperial Force in France, 1917*, p. 342.
49 This figure is based on the number of 1st and 2nd Australian Division men registered by the Red Cross as being captured on 15 April 1917. Bean gives the estimated number of Australians captured at Lagnicourt to be 'around 300' (Bean, *The Australian Imperial Force in France, 1917*, p. 399).
50 Lieut John Stuart, 11 Bn, POW statement, AWM30 B5.44.
51 WO John Bannigan, 2 FAB, manuscript, 'Two years in German prison camps', p. 2, A1336/10246, NAA [hereafter Bannigan, 'Two years in German prison camps'].
52 Horner, *Reason or Revolution? An Australian Prisoner in the Hands of the Hun* [hereafter *An Australian Prisoner*], p. 47.
53 Butler, *The Western Front*, pp. 864–5.
54 Ibid., p. 156.
55 Lieut Walter Mortensen, 2 Aust Tunn Coy, POW statement, AWM30 B6.13. See also Bean, *The Australian Imperial Force in France, 1917*, pp. 960–4.
56 Butler, *The Western Front*, p. 243.
57 Bean, *The Australian Imperial Force in France, 1917*, p. 947.

58 Pte Frank Warrener and Pte Edward Fisher, 31 Bn, POW statement, AWM30 B16.10.
59 Pte Thomas Gillespie, 47 Bn, POW statement, AWM30 B10.7.
60 Pte Alexander Falconer, 47 Bn, POW statement, AWM30 B10.7.
61 Stevenson, *To Win the Battle*, pp. 177–8; Stevenson, 'The battalion', pp. 46–57; Griffith, *Battle Tactics of the Western Front*, pp. 76, 78–9; Pedersen, *Monash as Military Commander*, pp. 146–8.
62 Bean, *The Australian Imperial Force in France, 1917*, p. 761.
63 Lee, *No Parachute*, pp. 219–25. See also Molkentin, *Fire in the Sky*, pp. 44–5; Clark, *Aces High*, p. 77.
64 AIF Records Section, *Statistics of Casualties, Etc*, p. 10.
65 Lieut Leslie Ward, Sqn AFC, diary entry for 21 November 1917, PR83/230, AWM; Lieut Frank Willmott, 4 Sqn AFC, POW statement, AWM30 B3.17; 2nd Lieut William Nicholls, 4 Sqn AFC, POW statement, AWM30 B3.9; 2nd Lieut Oscar Flight, 2 Sqn AFC, POW statement, AWM30 B3.6; 2nd Lieut Archie Rackett, 2 Sqn AFC, POW statement, AWM30 B3.11.
66 Lieut Victor Norvill, 2 Sqn AFC, POW statement, AWM30 B3.10.
67 Lieut Arthur Wearne, 2 Sqn AFC, POW statement, AWM30 B3.16.
68 Pte Hugo Blomquist, 45 Bn, POW statement, AWM30 B10.2; Pte Leslie Farrington, 54 Bn, POW statement, AWM30 B16.5; Pte Peter Kettle, 5th Div Salv Coy, POW statement, AWM30 B15.1; Pte Charles Hughes, 9 Bn, AWM30 B5.29.
69 Glenister, 'Desertion without execution', p. 25.
70 Edmonds, *March–April: Continuation of the German Offensive*, p. 489.
71 Cpl Charles Lane and Pte Reinhold Ruschpler, 4 MG Coy, POW statement, AWM30 B10.5.
72 Lieut Joshua Allen, 45 Bn, POW statement, AWM30 B10.5.
73 The official history does not give any figures for men lost as prisoners in these actions. This figure and those for Dernancourt are based on the number of Australians registered with the Red Cross as being captured in these actions.
74 Bean, *The Australian Imperial Force in France During the Main German Offensive, 1918*, p. 673.
75 Sgt Cyril Higgs and LCpl Stanley Lane, 33 Bn, POW statement, AWM30 B7.2.
76 Pte Harold Fuller, 58 Bn, POW statement, AWM30 B15.8.
77 LCpl Stanley Vardon, 37 Bn, POW statement, AWM30 B8.3. See also Pte William Evans, 23 Bn, POW statement, AWM30 B6.5 (2); Pte Jack Columbine, 4 MG Bn, POW statement, AWM30 B10.17; Pte Warwick Walker, 5 Bn, POW statement, AWM30 B5.11; Pte Edward Cox, 37 Bn, POW statement, AWM30 B8.2.
78 For rescues, see Bean, notebook 193, p. 16, 3DRL606, AWM38; Bean, notebook 187, p. 85, 3DRL606, AWM38; Bean, notebook 189, p. 10, 3DRL606, AWM38. Bean, *The Australian Imperial Force in France During the Allied Offensive*, p. 1024.
79 Bean, *The Australian Imperial Force in France During the Allied Offensive*, p. 1043.
80 2nd Lieut John Peacock, 2nd Pnr Bn, POW statement, AWM30 B17.16.
81 Cutlack, *The Australian Flying Corps on the Western Front*, p. 379.

Chapter 2 The reciprocity principle

1 Sgt George Bruce-Drayton, report, 9 January 1919, re Pte Noel Sainsbury, 28 Bn, ARCS WMB, 1DRL/0428, AWM.
2 Cook, 'The politics of surrender', pp. 637–65.
3 War Office, *Statistics of the Military Effort*, p. 237.
4 Ferguson, *The Pity of War*, p. 369.
5 Bean, *The Australian Imperial Force in France, 1916*, p. 514.
6 Pte David Williams, report, 11 February 1919, re Pte Roy Fox, 21 Bn, ARCS WMB, 1DRL/0428, AWM.
7 Pte John Findlow, report, 6 October 16, re Pte Charles Baker, 14 Bn, ARCS WMB, 1DRL/0428, AWM. For an example at Dernancourt, see Pte James O'Rourke, report, 13 November 1918, re Pte Frank Curtis, 17 Bn, ARCS WMB, 1DRL/0428, AWM. See also Bean, *The Australian Imperial Force in France During the Main German Offensive, 1918*, pp. 396–7.
8 Kramer, *Dynamic of Destruction*, pp. 63–4.
9 LCpl John Cooke, 5 Bn, letter, 14 March 1917, ARCS WMB, 1DRL/0428, AWM.
10 Horner, *An Australian Prisoner*, p. 48. See also Pte William Gillingham, 30 Bn, POW statement, AWM30 B16.4.
11 Jones, 'International or transnational?', p. 700.
12 Dennett, *Prisoners of the Great War*, p. 38.
13 War Office, *Statistics of the Military Effort*, p. 632; Doegen, *Kriegsgefangene Völker*, p. 28.
14 Davies, 'Prisoners of war in twentieth-century war economies', p. 629.
15 Gerard, *My Four Years in Germany*, p. 111.
16 Yarnall, *Barbed Wire Disease*, pp. 66–7.
17 Doegen, *Kriegsgefangene Völker*, p. 29.
18 McCarthy, *The Prisoner of War in Germany*, p. 21.
19 Jones, 'A missing paradigm?', p. 28.
20 Berghahn, *Imperial Germany, 1871–1918*, pp. 289–90.
21 Doegen, *Kriegsgefangene Völker*, pp. 28–9.
22 Beckett, *The Great War*, p. 319; Nagornaja and Mankoff, 'United by barbed wire', p. 489.
23 Pte David Storey, 13 Bn, POW statement, AWM30 B16.4.
24 Dent, *Fourteen Months a Prisoner of War*, p. 15.
25 Cpl David Austin, 20 Bn, POW statement, AWM30 B6.14 (1). Winter, *Death's Men*, pp. 213–14. For Australian troops 'ratting' German prisoners, see Bean, *The Australian Imperial Force in France, 1916*, pp. 549–50.
26 Cull, *At All Costs*, p. 88.
27 Pte John Cotter, 51 Bn, POW statement, AWM30 B11.2; LCpl Charles Stewart, 13 Bn, POW statement, AWM30 B13.5; Pte John Murphy, 50 Bn, POW statement, AWM30 B11.1.
28 This figure is based on the analysis of the mortality study statistics presented in Appendix 1 of this book. Official statistics say 267. See Butler, *Special Problems and Services*, p. 896.

29 Untitled medical document, 20 July 1916, 6. BRD, Bd. 141, Abt.IV/BayHStA; *Gefechtsbericht ü.d Gefechte bei Fromelles, 19./20.7 1916*, 6. BRD, Bd. 8, Abt.IV/BayHStA.

30 Pte William Barry, 29 Bn, untitled manuscript, p. 147, PR00814, AWM.

31 Dent, *Fourteen Months a Prisoner of War*, p. 6.

32 General Staff, *The German Army Handbook of 1918*, pp. 139–41; Butler, *The Western Front*, pp. 921–5.

33 General Staff, *German Army Handbook*, pp. 139–41; Butler, *The Western Front*, pp. 921–5.

34 Pte William Gillingham, 30 Bn, POW statement, AWM30 B16.4; Butler, *The Western Front*, p. 983.

35 'Report on Operations 22–27 July 1916', 6 Bde, 23–27 August 1916, AWM26 58/3.

36 Pte Walter Birch, 23 Bn, POW statement, AWM30 B17.12.

37 Sgt Fred Peachey, POW statement, 15 Bn, AWM30 B13.18; Pte John Lee, 14 Bn, POW statement, AWM30 B13.11.

38 German troops also shot the wounded at Fromelles after a senior Australian commander put an end to an informal truce to clear the wounded from No Man's Land. See Pte Adrian Nelligan, 32 Bn, POW statement, AWM30 B16.11, 32 Bn; War diary, 15 Bde, entry for 23 July 1916, AWM4 23/15/5; Pte Michael Ryan, report, 9 March 1917, re Pte Norman Taylor, 59 Bn, ARCS WMB, AWM 1DRL/0428.

39 Pte William Barry, 29 Bn, untitled manuscript, PR00814, AWM, pp. 150–1.

40 Pte Adrian Nelligan, 32 Bn, POW statement, AWM30 B16.11; Pte James Morton, 51 Bn, POW statement, AWM30 B11.3; Sgt William Littlewood, 47 Bn, POW statement, AWM30 B10.10.

41 Butler, *The Western Front*, p. 48.

42 Bean questioned whether the German troops encountered at Dernancourt bore a grudge against the Australians. See Bean, *The Australian Imperial Force in France During the Main German Offensive, 1918*, p. 396–7.

43 Cull, *At All Costs*, p. 101.

44 Pte George Bell, 16 Bn, diary entry, 16 April 1917, MLMSS893, SLNSW. See also Pte Colin Kennedy, 5 Bn, POW statement, AWM30 B5.15.

45 Jünger, *Storm of Steel*, p. 116.

46 Pte Frederick Klingner, 4 Pnr Bn, diary entry, 5–9 April 1918, PR91/099, AWM.

47 Pte Leopold Gillan, 21 Bn, POW statement, AWM30 B6.16 (1); Pte James O'Rourke, 47 Bn, POW statement, AWM30 B10.5; LCpl Peter Freirat, 53 Bn, POW statement, AWM30 B14.1; Capt Donald Wells, 13 Bn, POW statement, AWM30 B13.5; Pte James Benson, 13 Bn, POW statement, AWM30 B13.5; Lieut Arthur McQuiggan, 14 Bn, POW statement, AWM30 B13.11.

48 Pte Basil Hardy, 51 Bn, POW statement, AWM30 B11.3.

49 Pte George Bell, 16 Bn, diary entry, 16 April 1917, MLMSS893, SLNSW.

50 Cull, *At All Costs*, p. 98.

51 Capt Charles Mills, report, 23 September 1919, Pte Edward Waters, 15 Bn, ARCS WMB, 1DRL/0428, AWM; Pte Frederick Symes, report, 31 January 1919, Pte Aldred Muller, 14 Bn, ARCS WMB, 1DRL/0428, AWM; Capt Charles Mills, report, 25 April 1919, Pte William Whitby, 35 Bn, ARCS WMB, 1DRL/0428, AWM.

52 Pte George Bell, 16 Bn, diary entry, 16 April 1917, ML MSS893, SLNSW.

53 Jones, 'The final logic of sacrifice?', p. 772.

54 Cull, *At All Costs*, p. 119.

55 Cpl Harry Still, 31 Bn, untitled memoir, p. 8, PR00753, AWM.

56 This figure is based on numbers provided by captured Australians. See CSM Albert Compton, 13 Bn, POW statement, AWM30 B13.5; Pte Charles Emerson, 15 Bn, POW statement, AWM30 B13.8; Pte John Murphy, 50 Bn, POW statement, AWM30 B11.1.

57 Speed, *Prisoners, Diplomats and the Great War*, p. 77; Yarnall, *Barbed Wire Disease*, pp. 96–8; Bean, *The Australian Imperial Force in France, 1917*, p. 91.

58 Jones, *Violence Against Prisoners of War*, p. 145; Ludendorff, *My War Memories, 1914–1918*, pp. 329, 336.

59 Jones, *Violence Against Prisoners*, p. 153.

60 Ibid., p. 134. See also Jones, 'The German Spring reprisals of 1917', pp. 335–56.

61 Jones, *Violence Against Prisoners*, pp. 150–2.

62 Ibid., pp. 144–9, 152.

63 Speed, *Prisoners, Diplomats and the Great War*, pp. 101–2.

64 Jones, *Violence Against Prisoners*, p. 155.

65 Cpl Lancelot Davies, 13 Bn, untitled manuscript, p. 5, PR00140, AWM. See also Pte Raymond Ayres, 13 Bn, untitled manuscript, p. 3, PR89/126, AWM [hereafter Ayres, untitled manuscript].

66 Pte John Collins, 14 Bn, POW statement, AWM30 B13.11; Cpl Hamilton Parsons and Pte George Stewart, 16 Bn, POW statement, AWM30 B13.22.

67 Cpl Lancelot Davies, 13 Bn, untitled manuscript, p. 5, PR00140, AWM.

68 Pte Joseph Newman, 17 Bn, POW statement, AWM30 B6.3 (2).

69 Jones, 'A missing paradigm?', p. 28.

70 Groves, 'Captivity', 1 September 1932, p. 28; Cpl Hamilton Parsons and Pte George Stewart, 16 Bn, POW statement, WO161/98, NA UK; Horner, *An Australian Prisoner* , p. 55; Ayres, untitled manuscript, p. 3; Pte John Murphy, 50 Bn, POW statement, AWM30 B11.1; Pte Joseph Newman, 17 Bn, POW statement, AWM30 B6.3 (2). Some Australian prisoners captured at Fromelles reported similar treatment at Lille (see Pte Sidney McGarvey, 30 Bn, POW statement, AWM30 B16.4).

71 Jones, *Violence Against Prisoners*, p. 189.

72 Sgt Roy Stephens, 14 Bn, untitled poem, papers, 3DRL/7153 (A), AWM.

73 Groves, 'Captivity', 1 December 1932, p. 26.

74 Ibid., p. 26.

75 Ibid., 1 November 1932, p. 30.

76 Horner, *An Australian Prisoner*, p. 58; Cpl Lancelot Davies, 13 Bn, untitled manuscript, pp. 14–16, PR00140, AWM; Pte John Murphy, 50 Bn, POW statement, AWM30 B11.1.

77 Since the German Army was willing to mistreat prisoners deliberately in such a way, one would assume that the Australians at Fort MacDonald were prisoners *without* respite. The confusion could be due to a mistranslation of the German term for 'reprisal prisoner' (*Vergeltungsgefangenen*).

78 Groves, 'Captivity', 1 December 1932, p. 56.

79 Pte William Lucas, 50 Bn, POW statement, AWM30 B11.1; Pte Alfred Grey, 14 Bn, 'In the hands of the Hun: Experiences of Private Alfred Grey, of Kyneton', manuscript, p. 4, MSS1690, AWM [hereafter Grey, 'In the hands of the Hun']; Groves, 'Captivity', 1 December 1932, p. 56; Pte John Murphy, 50 Bn, POW statement, AWM30 B11.1.

80 Pte Joseph Webb, 14 Bn, letter to Fisher, 24 May 1917, 'Prisoners of war: Employment and treatment of British prisoners', WO32/5381, NA UK. See also Bowen, letter to Young, 24 May 1917, 'Employment of prisoners in France and Russia near the front line', FO383/291, NA UK.

81 Pte Haddon Bowen, 50 Bn, letter to Young, 24 May 1917, FO/383/291, NA UK.

82 Pte William Rowe, 14 Bn, letter to Fisher, 8 June 1917, WO23/5381, NA UK; Pte William Wheeler, 50 Bn, POW statement, AWM30 B11.1.

83 Ayres, untitled manuscript, p. 10.

84 Sgt Roy Stephens, 14 Bn, diary entry, 1–6 June 1917, 3DRL/7153 (A).

85 Pte Jack Hines, 4 Bn, reprisal declaration, 29 April 1917, privately held by Alan Hind, Newtown, NSW.

86 Pte Ernest Chalk, 15 Bn, untitled manuscript, privately held by Ian Chalk, Burnie, Tas.

87 Cpl Hamilton Parsons and Pte George Stewart, 16 Bn, POW statement, WO161/98, NA UK; Pte John Murphy, 50 Bn, POW statement, AWM30 B11.1.

88 Pte Victor Perrie, 11 Bn, POW statement, AWM30 B5.44.

89 Pte John Murphy, 50 Bn, POW statement, AWM30 B11.1.

90 Ayres, untitled manuscript, p. 10.

91 Pte Claude Benson, 13 Bn, untitled manuscript, p. 7, ML MSS885, SLNSW; Groves, 'Captivity', 1 January 1932, p. 19.

92 Pte Herbert Loechel, report, 13 January 1919, re Pte Harold Hall, 16 Bn, ARCS WMB, 1DRL/0428, AWM.

93 Pte Thomas Leiper and Pte Norman Byron, report, 30 December 1918, re Pte Joseph Miller, 16 Bn, ARCS WMB, 1DRL/0428, AWM.

94 Pte Thomas McCabe, Pte Theodore McCarthy et al., POW statement, AWM30 B5.44.

95 Groves, 'Captivity', 1 January 1933, p. 29.

96 Pte Victor Perrie, 11 Bn, POW statement, AWM30 B5.44.

97 Pte Claude Benson, 13 Bn, POW statement, AWM30 B13.5; Pte Thomas Rampton, 50 Bn, POW statement, AWM30 B11.1; Pte John Murphy, 50 Bn, POW statement, AWM30 B11.1.

98 Pte John Murphy, 50 Bn, POW statement, AWM30 B11.1.

99 Pte Thomas McCabe, Pte Theodore McCarthy et al., joint POW statement, AWM30 B5.44.

100 Pte Sydney Carter, report, 20 April 1918, re Pte Herbert Freeman, 57 Bn, ARCS WMB, 1DRL/0428, AWM; Pte Victor Perrie, 11 Bn, POW statement, AWM30 B5.44.

101 Ayres, untitled manuscript, p. 11.

102 Sgt Fred Peachey, 15 Bn, POW statement, AWM30 B13.18; Pte John Murphy, 50 Bn, POW statement, AWM30 B11.1.

103 Pte Matthew Holder, report, 31 January 1919, re Pte George Fraser, 48 Bn, ARCS WMB, 1DRL/0428, AWM; Pte John Murphy, 50 Bn, POW statement, AWM30 B11.1.

104 Sgt Fred Peachey, 15 Bn, POW statement, AWM30 B13.18; Pte Ernest Gatley, 15 Bn, POW statement, AWM30 B13.18; Pte John Murphy, 50 Bn, POW statement, AWM30 B11.1.

105 Spoerer, 'The mortality of Allied prisoners of war', pp. 121–36.

106 Jones, 'The final logic of sacrifice?', p. 786.

107 Ibid., p. 772.

108 The Royal Flying Corps and Royal Naval Air Service merged in April 1918 to form the Royal Air Force.

109 Pte Benjamin Peachey, Pte Edward Zimmerlie, Pte Ernest Connors and Pte William Caley, 47 Bn, POW statements, AWM30 B10.5; Pte John Turner, Pte John Baker, Pte Albert Beal and Pte Cecil Anderson, 47 Bn, POW statements, AWM30 B10.5; Pte Severin Jappe, Pte David McGimpsey and Pte Jack Martin, 15 Bn, POW statements, AWM30 B13.18; Horner, *An Australian Prisoner*, p. 68.

110 Spoerer, 'The mortality of Allied prisoners of war', p. 129.

111 LCpl Frank Caught and Pte John McGaghan, 47 Bn, POW statement, AWM30 B10.5.

Chapter 3 Giving the game away

1 Capt Charles Mills, 31 Bn, POW statement, AWM30 B16.7; Solleder, *Vier Jahre Westfront*, pp. 229–31; *Ergebnis der Unterhaltung mit den gefangenen australischen Offizieren*, 22 July 1916, RIR21, Bü 7, Abt.IV/BayHStA. Bean refers to the incident in the official history but makes no mention of Mills (see Bean, *The Australian Imperial Force in France, 1916*, p. 442). For an excerpt from Mills' captured diary, see *Auszüge aus Briefen an Angehörige der 5. austral. Division*, 5 August 1916, Bü 23, 6BRD, Abt.IV/BayHStA.

2 Pöhlmann, 'German intelligence at war, 1914–1918', p. 35. See also Jones, 'A process of modernization?', pp. 18–35; Larsen, 'Intelligence in the First World War', pp. 282–302.

3 Nicolai, *The German Secret Service*, p. 182.

4 One of the few works on the subject during the First World War is that of Heather Jones, who maintains that violence was sometimes used during interrogations when all other avenues of intelligence-gathering had been exhausted. Her findings differ significantly from those in this study. See Jones, 'A process of modernization?', pp. 18–35.

5 Bean, *The Australian Imperial Force in France, 1916*, p. 206.

6 'Example set by an officer and man of our forces after capture (March 1918)', AWM27 312/12.

7 War diary, 13 Bn, entry for 27–28 September 1916, AWM4 23/30/21. See Also 'Appendix B4' and 'Appendix 19', war diary, 13 Bn, Sept 16, AWM4 23/30/21.

8 Pte Donald Muir, 13 Bn, Military Medal recommendation, AWM28.

9 *Aussagen des am 28. 9. morgens im Diependaal Grund am Taleck vom J.R. 127 gemachten Gefangenen*, 28 September 1916, XIIIAK, Bü 578, M33/2, B-WürHStA; untitled handwritten intelligence document, 30 September 1916, XIIIAK, Bü 588, M33/2, B-WürHStA.

10 *Aussagen des am 28. 9. morgens im Diependaal Grund am Taleck vom J.R. 127 gemachten Gefangenen*, 28 September 1916, XIIIAK, Bü 578, M33/2, B-WürHStA; untitled handwritten intelligence document, 30 September 1916, XIIIAK, Bü 588, M33/2, B-WürHStA.

11 Pte Donald Muir, 13 Bn, POW statement, AWM30 B13.1; *Aussagen des am 28. 9. morgens im Diependaal Grund am Taleck vom J.R. 127 gemachten Gefangenen*, 28 September 1916, XIIIAK, Bü 578, M33/2, B-WürHStA; untitled handwritten intelligence document, 30 September 1916, XIIIAK, Bü 588, M33/2, B-WürHSta.

12 War Office, *Field Service Regulations 1909*, Part 2, pp. 148–55.

13 War Office, *Notes for Infantry Officers in Trench Warfare*, p. 51.

14 'Instructions for intelligence duties, Second Army, revised 23 March and 10 June 1916', AWM25 423/4; 'Notes on the prevention of espionage and leakage of information, 21 October 1915', AWM27 491/4.

15 'Operation Order No. 14', war diary, 7 Bde, June 1916, AWM4 23/7/10.

16 'Memorandum No. 27', war diary, 5 Div, September 1916, AWM4 1/50/7, Part 2.

17 Ibid.

18 Butler, *Special Problems and Services*, p. 140.

19 'The soldier's DONT'S of international law', AWM2 474/7.

20 'Notes on the prevention of espionage and leakage of information', AWM27 491/1.

21 Royal Air Force, *Instructions Regarding Precautions to be Taken in the Event of Falling into the Hands of the Enemy*.

22 Untitled extract, *Newsletter of the Society of Australian World War 1 Aero Historians*, April 1971.

23 *Nachrichtengewinnung durch Gefangenenvernehmungen*, 29 July 1916, Bü 23, 6BRD, Abt.IV/BayHStA.

24 Ibid.; *Eintreffen von Gefangenen*, c. 1917, Bü 588, XIIIAK, M33/2, B-WürHStA.

25 *Auszug aus Armeebefehl Nr. 3*, 30 July 1916, Bü 588, XIIIAK, M33/2, B-WürHStA.

26 Ibid.

27 LCpl Ernest Gaunt, 13 Fld Amb, POW statement, AWM30 B11.10.

28 LCpl Claude Benson, 13 Bn, 'Benson war diary kept while a prisoner of war in Germany, 1917–1918', manuscript, p. 2, MLMSS885, SLNSW.

29 Cpl Lancelot Davies, 13 Bn, untitled manuscript, p. 6, PR00140, AWM.

30 Capt Joseph Honeysett, 47 Bn, 'Aussies in exile', manuscript, p. 17, AWM 3DRL/4043 [hereafter Honeysett, 'Aussies in exile'].

31 Duffy, *Through German Eyes*, p. 41.
32 *Vernehmung von 4. Gef. vom 22. austr. Batl. 6. austr. Brig. 2. austr. Div. gef. gen. am Morgen des 26. II. im Warlencourtriegel (Abschnitt E) auf Höhe 124,* 26 February 1917, Bü 581, XIIIAK, M33/2, B-WürHStA.
33 Ibid.
34 Pte Alexander Falconer, 47 Bn, POW statement, AWM30 B10.7, 47 Bn.
35 Pte Luke Ramshaw, 51 Bn, POW statement, AWM30 B11.3. See also Pte Frederick Glynn, 14 Bn, POW statement, AWM30 B13.10; Capt Charles Mills, 31 Bn, POW statement, AWM30 B16; Lieut Albert Bowman, 53 Bn, POW statement, AWM30 B14.1, 53 Bn.
36 Sig Frederick Flynn, 14 Bn, POW statement, AWM30 B13.10.
37 Cutlack, *The Australian Flying Corps*, p. 178.
38 2nd Lieut Ivo Agnew, 2 Sqn AFC, diary entry, 2 October 1917, PR0112, AWM. Agnew is most likely describing the *Jastaschule* at Famars, south of Valenciennes, where a number of captured British and French aircraft were flown against trainee German pilots.
39 *Vernehmung eines am 2.10. mittags südöstlich Valenciennes notgelandeten englischen Fliegeroffizieres,* 5 October 1917, Bü 582, XIIIAK, M33/2, B-WürHStA; Lieut Frederick Shepperd, report, 26 November 1917, re 2nd Lieut Ivo Agnew, 2 Sqn AFC, ARCS WMB, AWM 1DRL/0428.
40 Lieut Wentworth Randell, 4 Sqn AFC, POW statement, AWM30 B3.12.
41 Lieut Archie Rackett, 2 Sqn AFC, untitled manuscript held privately by Allison Rackett, Howrah, Tas, pp. 35–6.
42 Cull, *At All Costs*, p. 143.
43 Pte Percy Cook, 51 Bn, POW statement, AWM30 B13.14. The New Zealander referred to could be Pte William Nimot, 1st Bn Wellington Regiment NZEF, who deserted to German troops at Houplines in June 1916. See Pugsley, *On the Fringe of Hell*, pp. 77–90.
44 Cpl Thomas Grosvenor, 30 Bn, POW statement, AWM30 B6.7. Official memoranda after the Somme warned of such practices. See 'Memorandum prevention of espionage and leakage of information', AWM27 491/1.
45 Bean, *The Australian Imperial Force in France, 1917*, p. 343.
46 *Vernehmung von 26 Australiern vom X/austral. Batl., 3. Brig., 1. Div. und 1 Mann vom XI/austral. Batl., 3 Brig., 1. Div., gefangen genomen südöstl. Der Fme. Du Mouquet in der Nacht vom 21/22 August 1916,* 23 August 1916, Bü 579, XIIIAK, M33, B-WürHStA; Bean, *The Australian Imperial Force in France, 1916*, p. 858.
47 Pte Hugh West, 51 Bn, POW statement, AWM30 B11.3.
48 Pte Percy Cook, 51 Bn, POW statement, AWM30 B13.14.
49 'Interpretation of a captured German document', war diary, 13 Bde, August 1918, AWM4 23/13/31.
50 *Aussagen von 1 Offizier und 10 Mann vom XX/Bat New South Wales 'B' und 'C' Comp, 5. Brig., 2nd austral. Div. (Australian Imperial Exp. Force),* 6 May 1916, Bü 23, 6BRD, Abt.IV/BayHStA.
51 Lieut Norman Blanchard, 20 Bn, POW statement, AWM30 B6.14(1); *Aussagen von 1 Offizier und 10 Mann vom XX/Bat New South Wales 'B' und*

'C' Comp, 5. Brig., 2nd austral. Div. (Australian Imperial Exp. Force), 6 May 1916, Bü 23, 6BRD, Abt.IV/BayHStA.

52 Aussagen von 1 Offizier und 10 Mann vom XX/Bat New South Wales 'B' und 'C' Comp, 5. Brig., 2nd austral. Div. (Australian Imperial Exp. Force), 6 May 1916, Bü 23, 6BRD, Abt.IV/BayHStA. Haupt. For a visual aid relating to the 3rd Australian Division, see Aussagen von 2 Mann vom 33. Jnf. Batl. (a-Komp.) 9. austr. Brig., 3. austr. Div. gefangen genommenen am 12.12. abends hart nördlich der Strasse Armentières-Lomme, 14.12.16, Bü 35, 6BRD, Abt.IV/ BayHStA.

53 Bericht ueber Dienst im Gefangenen-Lager der 1. Armee getrennt nach Vernehmungs-und Lager-Dienst, no date. Bü 588, XIIIAK, M33/2, B-WürHStA.

54 Vernehmung eines Sergeanten des V. Jnf Batl. (2 austr. Brig. 1. Austr. J.D.), gefangenen genommen 26.7.16 früh nördlich Pozières, 27 July 1916, Bü 579, XIIIAK, M33/2, B-WürHStA.

55 Duffy, Through German Eyes, p. 55.

56 Vernehmung eines Sergeanten des V. Jnf Batl. (2 austr. Brig. 1. Austr. J.D.), gefangenen genommen 26.7. 3 früh nördlich Pozières, 27 July 1916, Bü 579, XIIIAK, M33/2, B-WürHStA.

57 Nachrichten über den Gegner vor der Front der Armeegruppe Böhn (25–28.7.16), 29 July 1916, Bü 579, XIIIAK, M33/2, B-WürHStA.

58 Vernehmung von in der Nacht vom 14. zum 15. VIII. 16. gef. gen. Offizieren und Mannschaften des XIII. Batl., 4.Brig., 4. austr. Div., 21 August 1916, Bü 579, XIIIAK, M33/2, B-WürHStA.

59 Der Angriff auf die 6. bayer. Res-Div. in der Gegend nordwestlich von Fromelles am 19.7. wie von Gefangenen beschrieben (hauptsäschlich Offizieren), 30 July 1916, Bü 23, 6BRD, Abt.IV/BayHStA.

60 Auszüge aus dem Tagebuch eines Unteroffiziers vom XXV. austr. Batl. (2. austr. Div.), 10 August 1916, Bü 579, XIIIAK, M33/2, B-WürHStA.

61 Aus australischen Papieren, 30 March 1917, Bü 581, XIIIAK, M33/2, B-WürHStA; 'Abstracts from German broadcasts relating to Australian POWs', AWM38 3DRL 8042/86.

62 Lieut Harold Ferguson, 7 MGC, 'Court of Enquiry Proceedings', service dossier, B2455 NAA; Lieut Harold Ferguson, 7 MGC, 'Service and Casualty Form', service dossier, B2455 NAA.

63 Lieut Harold Ferguson, 7 MGC, POW statement, AWM30 B6.11 (2).

64 The orders were those issued to 7 Bde on 17 September 1917. 'Order No. 127', war diary, 7 Bde, Sept 17, AWM4 23/7/25.

65 Bean, The Australian Imperial Force in France, 1916, p. 951.

66 Ibid., pp. 951–2.

67 In all fairness, the other man was Pte Frederick Glynn, 14 Bn. See Pte Frederick Glynn, 14 Bn, POW statement, AWM30 B13.10.

68 Bean, The Australian Imperial Force in France, 1916, pp. 951–2.

69 'Order No. 94', war diary, 4 Bde, Nov 16, AWM4 23/4/14.

70 2nd Lieut Thomas Loughhead, report, 5 April 1917, re Pte Allan Yeo, 14 Bn, ARCS WMB, 1DRL/0428, AWM. The incident is also described in Edgar

Rule's unedited manuscript of *Jacka's Mob* (1933) held in Bean's papers at AWM. See 'Diary of Lieut. E. J. Rule, 14th Battalion', Folder 245, pp. 115–16, C.E.W. Bean papers, AWM38, 3DRL/606/245/1.

71 Entry for 1 December 1916, war diary, 4 Div, Dec 16, AWM4 1/48/9; Charles Bean, notebook 245, p. 115, 3DRL606/245, AWM38.

72 'Intelligence Summary No. 126' and 'Information Obtained From Prisoner (Wounded) Belonging to the Ist Co., I Bn, 101 RIR. Captured in N.20.I. on 1st December 1916', war diary, I Anzac Corps Intelligence Headquarters, December 1916, AWM4 1/20/11; Bean, *The Australian Imperial Force in France, 1916*, pp. 951–2.

73 Peter Christian Christiansen Petersen, 'Certificate of naturalisation', 1914/2454, A1, NAA.

74 Pte Charles Christiansen, 44 Bn, 'Court of enquiry', 21 March 1917, service dossier, B2455, NAA.

75 *Aussagen eines Überläufers der A – Komp. des XXXXIV. Btl., der 11. Brig. der 3. austr. Div.*, 18 March 1917, Bü 9, 23. Inf. Regt, Abt.IV/BayHStA.

76 War diary, 11 Bde, March 1917, AWM4 23/61/6.

77 *Aussagen eines Überläufers der A – Komp. des XXXXIV. Btl., der 11. Brig. der 3. austr. Div.*, 18 March 1917, Bü 9, 23. Inf. Regt, Abt.IV/BayHStA.

78 Duffy, *Through German Eyes*, p. 38.

79 Nicolai, *The German Secret Service*, p. 184.

80 Pte Charles Christiansen, 44 Bn, 'Re: 161 Pte C. Christiansen, 44 Bn', memo, 22 January 1919 and 'Casualty Form – Active Service', service dossier, B2455, NAA; Pte Allan Yeo, 14 Bn, 'Casualty Form – Active Service', service dossier, B2455, NAA.

81 '7th Australian Infantry Brigade Circular – Extracts from German Intelligence Summary Indicating Information Passed by Captured Men (May 1918)', AWM27 312/12. See also Bean, *The Australian Imperial Force in France during the Allied Offensive, 1918*, pp. 90–1; officers and men of 33 and 34 Bns captured between 6 and 10 May 1918, POW statements, AWM30 B7.2.

82 C.E.W. Bean, diary entry for 31 May 1918, notebook 113, AWM38, 3DRL606.

83 Bean, *The Australian Imperial Force in France during the Allied Offensive, 1918*, p. 109.

84 Bean, *The Australian Imperial Force in France, 1916*, pp. 443–4.

Chapter 4 Saving lives

1 Davies, 'Prisoners of war in twentieth-century war economies', p. 626.

2 Cull, *At All Costs*, pp. 158–9, 164.

3 Becker, *Oubliés de la Grande Guerre*; Hinz, 'Humanität im Krieg?', pp. 216–38; Djurović, *L'Agence Centrale de Recherches du Comité International de la Croix-Rouge*.

4 Jones, 'International or transnational?', p. 699.

5 Moorehead, *Dunant's Dream*, p. 202.

6 Hutchinson, *Champions of Charity*.

7 Doegen, *Kriegsgefangene Völker*, pp. 56–7.

8 Australian Red Cross Society (ARCS), 5th Annual Report, 1918–1919, Box 13, ARCS NO.

9 'Monthly Report of Red Cross Work', March 1918, Box 11, ARCS NO.

10 Ibid., February 1918, Box 11, ARCS NO.

11 Hallihan, *In the Hands of the Enemy*, p. 13.

12 Oppenheimer, '"The best PM for the Empire in war"', p. 110.

13 Scott, *Australia During the War*, p. 712.

14 Winter, *Sites of Memory, Sites of Mourning*, p. 30.

15 ARCS 5th Annual Report, 1918–1919, Box 13, ARCS NO

16 Beaumont, 'Whatever happened to patriotic women, 1914–1918?', p. 282.

17 'Reporting the casualties', *Argus*, 20 May 1915, p. 4; 'Notification of casualties', *Sunday Times*, 3 October 1915, p. 6.

18 Oppenheimer, '"The best PM for the Empire"', p. 110; Beaumont, 'Whatever happened to patriotic women, 1914–1918?', p. 282.

19 Rickard, 'White, Vera Deakin (1891–1978)', ADB.

20 'History of the Enquiry Bureau', March 1919, ARCS, Box 40, AWM 1DRL/0428.

21 'Monthly report of Red Cross work', June 1917, Box 11, NO13, ARCS NO; Stanley, *Lost Boys of Anzac*, pp. 191–203.

22 Rita Wilson, letter to ARCS, 3 September 1916, re Pte Herbert Wilson, 32 Bn, SARC EB, SRG76/1, SLSA.

23 Lieut Geoffrey Leslie, 3 Bn, letter to Harvey, 10 March 1917, re Pte Richard Harvey, 3 Bn, ARCS WMB, AWM 1DRL/0428.

24 E.A. Tait, letter to ARCS, 29 September 1918 and 28 October 1918, re Pte David Tait, 22 Bn, ARCS WMB, AWM 1DRL/0428; 'Son mourned dead found alive', *Barrier Miner*, 26 September 1918, p. 4. See also Langer Owen, letter to Vera Deakin, 17 October 1918, re Pte Errol Watkins, 17 Bn, ARCS WMB, 1DRL/0428, AWM; A. Dyke, letter to ARCS, 13 October 1916, re Pte Thomas Dyke, 32 Bn, SARC EB, SRG76/1, SLSA.

25 Schneider, 'The British Red Cross Wounded and Missing Enquiry Bureau', p. 298.

26 Deakin, letter to SARC EB, 29 May 1917, 'Correspondence with ARCS Commissioners in London', SARC EB, SRG76/17, SLSA.

27 Pte Ernest Meskell, report, 19 April 1917; Pte John Simpson, report, 3 April 1917; Pte William Billingham, report, 12 April 1917, re Pte Reginald Hawkins, 42 Bn, ARCS WMB, 1DRL/0428, AWM.

28 Pte Phillip Rubie, report, 3 October 1917, re Pte Errol Watkins, 17 Bn, ARCS WMB, 1DRL/0428, AWM.

29 Pte Errol Watkins, 17 Bn, 'Casualty Form', service dossier, B2455, NAA.

30 Deakin, letter to Melbourne, 18 January 1918, re Pte George Abbott, 14 Bn, ARCS WMB, 1DRL/0428, AWM.

31 'Report on the Prisoners of War Department of the Australian Red Cross Society', c. 1918, Box 33, ARCS NO.

32 Anderson, postcard to Harris, 22 July 1917, Pte Thomas Anderson, 23 Bn, service dossier, B2455, NAA.

33 Pte Francis Wright, 14 Bn, letter to Lilian Ryan-Smith, 8 August 1918, Pte Francis Wright, 14 Bn, ARCS WMB, 1DRL/0428, AWM.

34 ICRC, cable to C. Cahill, 17 November 1917, re Pte William Cahill, 59 Bn, service dossier, B2455, NAA.

35 Base Records, letter to C. Cahill, 6 July 1918, re Pte William Cahill, 59 Bn, service dossier, B2455, NAA.

36 'Monthly report of Red Cross work', September 1917, Box 11, NO13, ARCS NO.

37 Unattributed letter cited in report from Murdoch to Munro Ferguson, 27 July 1917, SARC EB, SRG76/22, SLSA.

38 'Death of noted war worker', *Age*, 25 June 1960, p. 5; Gibbney and Smith, *A Biographical Register 1788–1939*, vol. 1, p. 124.

39 'The Ladies Letter', *Punch*, 17 February 1916, p. 32. The caption on a photo of Mary Chomley at Princess Christian's Hospital describes her as 'house keeper'. See SLVIC, H2013.231/53.

40 Anderson, 'Dear Miss Chomley', pp. 44–6; Kildea, 'Bridging the divide', pp. 50–1.

41 Ariotti, *Captive Anzacs*, p. 78.

42 Forster, 'Ryan, Sir Charles Snodgrass (1853–1926)', ADB.

43 'Report of Geneva Mission', 15 July 1916, Box 196, NO33, ARCS NO.

44 Central POW Committee, 'Canadian Red Cross', p. 57; ARCS, *Final Report of the Prisoner of War Department*, p. 13.

45 'Miss Kathleen O'Connor's concert', *Sydney Morning Herald*, 10 May 1913, p. 22.

46 'Australia Day', *Werribee Shire Banner*, 15 July 1915, p. 3.

47 Hardie, 'Oliver, Alexander (1832–1904)', ADB; Maguire, *Who's Who in the World of Women*, p. 48.

48 ARCS, *Final Report of the Prisoner of War Department*, p. 12.

49 'Death of Mr F. Fairbairn', *Argus*, 23 February 1925, p. 10.

50 'Red Cross: Work of society abroad', *Sydney Morning Herald*, 9 November 1916, p. 6.

51 'Monthly Report of Red Cross Work', December 1916, NO13, ARCS NO.

52 ARCS, *Final Report of the Prisoner of War Department*, pp. 1–2.

53 POW Department Report, October 1916, Box 196, NO33, ARCS NO.

54 ARCS, *Final Report of the Prisoner of War Department*, pp. 1–6. The wounded received infant formula because it was known that some were arriving in Germany severely malnourished. It helped prevent refeeding syndrome, which could be fatal if malnourished men gorged themselves on solids.

55 Yarnall, *Barbed Wire Disease*, p. 108.

56 ARCS, *Final Report of the Prisoner of War Department*, p. 4.

57 Ibid., p. 4; Bremner, letter to Chomley, 17 July 1918, Mary Chomley papers, 1DRL/0615, AWM.

58 Chomley, letter to Smith, 11 December 1916, 'Correspondence by 11th Battalion POW Committee Regarding POW in German hands', AWM25 937/4; 'Australian prisoners in Germany', *Singleton Argus*, p. 8 February 1917: 1; Chomley, letter to Robertson, 28 September 1917, NO33, ARCS NO.

59 'Report of the Committee on Clothing for British Prisoners of War in Germany', WO33/3081, NA UK.

60 Wilkinson, *British Prisoners of War in First World War Germany*, p. 116.

61 Horner, *An Australian Prisoner*, p. 78.
62 Cpl Harry Still, 31 Bn, untitled manuscript, p. 9, PR00753, AWM.
63 Horner, *An Australian Prisoner*, p. 78.
64 Pte Alfred Grey, 14 Bn, untitled manuscript, p. 9, MSS1690, AWM.
65 Adam-Smith, *Prisoner of War*, p. 38.
66 Bannigan, 'Two years in German prison camps', p. 22.
67 'Recommendations of meritorious service of POW, January–February 1918', 9982/1/21, AWM18. See LSgt Joseph Whitbread, 13 Bn, POW statement, AWM30 B13.5; LSgt William Ferguson, 46 Bn, POW statement, AWM30 B10.4.
68 ARCS, *Final Report of the Prisoner of War Department*, p. 4; Yarnall, *Barbed Wire Disease*, pp. 116–18. For examples of pilfering, see Pte Patrick O'Donnell, 8 Bn, POW statement, AWM30 B5.27; Pte Stephen Noell, 51 Bn, POW statement, AWM30 B11.3; Sgt Patrick Donovan, 29 Bn, POW statement, AWM30 B16.1; Pte William Lucas, 50 Bn, POW statement, AWM30 B11.1; Pte Frank Hallihan, 21 Bn, POW statement, AWM30 B6.16 (1).
69 Pte Jeremiah Casey, 48 Bn, POW statement, AWM30 B10.13. See also Pte George Hilton, 21 Bn, POW statement, AWM 30 B6.16 (1); LCpl Rupert Wallach, 13 Bn, POW statement, AWM30 B13.3.
70 Wilkinson, *British Prisoners of War in First World War Germany*, p. 116.
71 'War prisoner's letter', *Kyneton Guardian*, 10 January 1918, p. 2.
72 Horner, *An Australian Prisoner*, p. 90.
73 Wilkinson, *British Prisoners of War in First World War Germany*, pp. 112–17. This was also a feature of the Second World War. See Makepeace, *Captives of War*, pp. 63–4.
74 Pte Daniel Greenlees, 16 Bn, letter to Chomley, 27 August 1917, Mary Chomley papers, 1DRL/0615, AWM.
75 Winter, *Sites of Memory, Sites of Mourning*, p. 40.
76 Pte Edwin Burgess, 32 Bn, letter to Chomley, 23 December 1917, Mary Chomley papers, 1DRL/0615, AWM.
77 Pte Frederick Bell, 16 Bn, postcard to ARCS, 6 June 1917, service dossier, B2455, NAA.
78 Pte Albert Clare, 51 Bn, letter to Chomley, 28 March 1917, Mary Chomley papers, AWM 1DRL/0615.
79 Chomley, letter to AIF HQ Registry, 28 August 1918, 'Requests for clothing by POW in Germany', 9982/2/10, AWM18; 'Book scheme for Australian POW August 1918–1919', 9982/1/6, AWM18. For more on the reading practices of prisoners, see King, '"Books are more to me than food"', pp. 246–71; Laugeson, *Boredom is the Enemy*, pp. 105–33.
80 LCpl Patrick Durham, 10 Bn, letter to Chomley, 5 June 1917, NO33, ARCS NO; Chomley, letter to Munro-Ferguson, 8 June 1917, NO33, ARCS NO.
81 Chomley, letter to Beckett, 23 May 1917, ARCS POW Dept; Pte Charles Christiansen, 44 Bn, ARCS POW Dept, 1DRL/0428, AWM.
82 Chomley, letter to Griffiths, 17 May 1918, 'POW AAMC', AWM10, 4432/18/29.
83 'Australians who were prisoners', *Argus*, 23 April 1919, p. 5.
84 'War prisoners' friend', *Argus*, 6 September 1919, p. 19.

Chapter 5 Challenging the Holzminden illusion

1 'Wartime escape', *West Australian*, 4 May 1938, p. 15.
2 Garton, *The Cost of War*, p. 210.
3 Cook, *The Real Great Escape*, p. 2.
4 Jones, *Violence Against Prisoners of War*, p. 321.
5 Honeysett, 'Aussies in exile', p. 62.
6 Keegan, *The First World War*, p. 8.
7 War Office, *Field Service Regulations 1909*, pp. 148–55.
8 War Office, *Manual of Military Law*, pp. 268–9, 299.
9 McCarthy, *The Prisoner of War in Germany*, pp. 21, 53.
10 Doegen, *Kriegsgefangene Völker*, p. 176.
11 Jones and Hinz, 'Prisoners of war (Germany)'.
12 Jones, 'Imperial captivities', pp. 175–93.
13 Yarnall, *Barbed Wire Disease*, pp. 129–30.
14 McCarthy, *The Prisoner of War in Germany*, p. 107.
15 Beaumont, 'Rank, privilege, and prisoners of war', pp. 67–94.
16 War Office, *Statistics of the Military Effort*, p. 329.
17 Ibid., p. 329. Only one Australian, Capt Thomas White of the Australian Half Flight, succeeded in escaping Ottoman captivity. See White, *Guests of the Unspeakable*.
18 War Office, *Statistics of the Military Effort*, p. 329.
19 McPhail, *The Long Silence*, pp. 27, 137–44.
20 MacKenzie, *The Story of the Seventeenth Battalion*, p. 239.
21 Blanch and Pegram, *For Valour*, p. 312.
22 'Narrative of escaped Australian prisoner of war', war diary, 5th Division, April 1918, AWM4 1/50/26, Part 15.
23 Lunden, 'Captivity psychosis among prisoners of war', p. 726.
24 Hallihan, *In the Hands of the Enemy*, p. 2.
25 Ayres, untitled manuscript, p. 19.
26 Pte Francis Neal, 14 Bn, POW statement, AWM30 B13.11.
27 Lieut Herbert Johnson, 21 MGC, escape report, service dossier, B2455, NAA.
28 LCpl Hamilton Parsons and Pte George Stewart, 16 Bn, POW statement, AWM30 B13.22.
29 Bean, 'Punishing Australians', pp. 2809–11.
30 'Recruiting', *West Australian*, 20 October 17, p. 4.
31 Bean, *The Australian Imperial Force in France, 1917*, p. 579.
32 Pte Wilfred Gallwey, 47 Bn, letter, 2 August 1917, 2DRL/0785, AWM.
33 LCpl Rupert Wallach, 13 Bn, POW statement, AWM30 B13.5.
34 Pte Richard Nock, 13 Fld Amb, POW statement, AWM30 B11.4.
35 Honeysett, 'Aussies in exile', p. 40.
36 Ibid.
37 Lieut Herbert Johnson, 21 MGC, POW statement, NA UK, WO161/96.
38 'Sport in German prison camps', *Referee*, 19 June 1919, p. 1.
39 Capt Albert Bowman, 53 Bn, POW statement, AWM30 B14.1.
40 Capt John Mott, 48 Bn, POW statement, AWM30 B10.13; Capt John Mott, 48 Bn, POW statement, WO161/96, NA UK.

41 'An Apollo Bay soldier escapes from Germany', *Colac Herald*, 22 October 1917, p. 2; 'Escaped from Germany', *Bendigonian*, 25 October 1917, p. 3.

42 'Escape from Germany', *Daily Standard*, 8 December 1917, p. 9.

43 Lieut Herbert Johnson, 21 MGC, citation for MC, service dossier, B2455, NAA.

44 Lieut Henry Baker, 2nd Bn, Lancashire Fusiliers, letter, 17 December 1919, MLDOC 1285, SLNSW.

45 Capt Joseph Honeysett, 47 Bn, 'Extract', 8 November 1918, service dossier, B2455, NAA.

46 Cpl Thomas Gray, 34 Bn, POW statement, AWM30 B7.2; Pte Theophilus Richards, 47 Bn, POW statement, AWM30 B10.5.

47 Lieut John Edwards, 50 Bn, POW statement, AWM30 B11.1.

48 Lieut Herbert Johnson, 21 MGC, escape report, service dossier, B2455, NAA.

49 Capt John Mott, 48 Bn, letter, 29 August 1917, EXDOC004, AWM.

50 MacKenzie, *The Colditz Myth*, p. 330.

51 Chomley, letter to Robertson, 28 September 1917, NO33 Box 196, ARCS NO; 'Australian war prisoners', *West Australian*, 31 January 1917, p. 7.

52 Pte William Johnston, 55 Bn, POW statement, AWM30 B14.6; Pte Archibald Fleming, 15 Bn, POW statement, AWM30 B13.18; Pte William Collins, 11 Bn, POW statement, AWM30 B5.44; Pte William Collins, 11 Bn, POW statement, AWM30 B5.44.

53 Durnford, *The Tunnellers of Holzminden*, p. 86.

54 Bannigan, 'Two years in German prison camps', p. 12.

55 'Experiences of Private R. Badcock', unpublished manuscript held privately by Neville Badcock, Moriarty, Tas.

56 Pte Russel Badcock, 26 Bn, POW statement, AWM30 B6.3 (1).

57 Ibid.

58 Ibid.; 'Evaded the Germans', *Examiner*, 2 October 1918, p. 7.

59 'Australian prisoners of war', *Mercury*, 14 September 1918, p. 14.

60 'Hero of escape from Germany', *Journal*, 26 January 1918, p. 2.

61 Pte Wesley Choat, 32 Bn, POW statement, AWM30 B16.11. See also Pte Wesley Choat, 32 Bn, 'A bold bid for Blighty', manuscript, MLMSS 1504, SLNSW.

62 See Horner, *An Australian Prisoner*, pp. 97–9.

63 Pte Joseph Newman, 17 Bn, POW statement, AWM30 B6.3 (2).

64 Pte Thomas Taylor, 14 Bn, 'Casualty Form – Active Service', service dossier, B2455, NAA; Pte Thomas Taylor, 14 Bn, POW statement, AWM30 B13.11.

65 Ziemann, *War Experiences in Rural Germany*, pp. 156–7.

66 Pte Harry Lenihan, 15 Bn, letter to Chomley, 7 November 1918, Mary Chomley papers, 1DRL/0615, AWM.

67 Pte John Withnell, 28 Bn, letter to Chomley, 15 September 1918, Mary Chomley papers, 1DRL/0615, AWM. See also Pte Alfred Leathard, 51 Bn, letter to Chomley, 16 December 1917, Mary Chomley papers, 1DRL/0615, AWM.

68 Williams, *German Anzacs and the Great War*, p. 272; Ziemann, *War Experiences*, p. 164. See Pte Harry Corish, 13 Bn, 'Venereal Disease Case

Card', service dossier, B2455, NAA; Pte Herbert Loechel, 50 Bn, 'Venereal Disease Case Card', service dossier, B2455, NAA.

69 McCarthy, *The Prisoner of War in Germany*, pp. 322–3; Pte James Robertson, 51 Bn, POW statement, AWM30 B11.3; Cpl Edwin Maxwell, 51 Bn, POW statement, AWM30 B11.5; LCpl Peter Freirat, 53 Bn, POW statement, AWM30 B14.1; Capt Donald Wells, 13 Bn, POW statement, AWM30 B13.5. See also See Picot, *The British Interned in Switzerland*.

70 Cull, *At All Costs*, p. 186.

71 Yarnall, *Barbed Wire Disease*, p. 163.

72 Vischer, *Barbed Wire Disease*, pp. 25–7; War Office, *Statistics of the Military Effort*, p. 343.

73 Cull, *At All Costs*, p. 192.

74 Ibid., p. 197.

75 Pte Arthur Warren, 13 Bn, POW statement, AWM30 B13.5.

76 Yarnall, *Barbed Wire Disease*, p. 157.

77 Captain Charles Mills, 31 Bn, report to British Officer in Charge of Interned in Switzerland, 21 June 1918, AWM18, 9982/5/1.

78 Yarnall, *Barbed Wire Disease*, p. 157.

79 Pte George Hilton, 21 Bn, POW statement, AWM30 B6.16 (1); Pte Raymond Membrey, 21 Bn, POW statement, AWM30 B6.16 (1); Sgt Francis Pulford, 14 Bn, POW statement, AWM30 B13.13.

80 Captain Charles Mills, 31 Bn, letter to Major Neale, 10 June 1918, AWM18, 9982/5/1.

81 'Roll of Members of the Australian Imperial Force interned in Holland showing Employment, Study, etc', 9 October 1918, AWM 18, 9982/4/4, Part 1.

82 Major John Hughes, 32 Bn, report to AIF records, 11 November 1918, AWM18, 9982/4/4, Part 2.

83 Memo to OC records, 20 September 1918, AWM18, 9982/4/4, Part 1; Major John Hughes, 32 Bn, report, 26 October 1918, AWM18, 9982/4/4, Part 2.

84 Honeysett, 'Aussies in exile', p. 98.

85 'Wartime escape', *West Australian*, 4 May 1938, p. 15.

86 MacKenzie, *The Colditz Myth*, p. 2.

87 Pte Henry Thomas, 30 Bn, 'Statement of service', service dossier, B2455, NAA. After repatriation to England, Thomas transferred to the artillery and returned to France as a gunner attached to the 2nd Field Artillery Brigade. His battery fired in support of the 2nd Australian Division's attack at Montbrehain on 5 October 1918, the final Australian infantry action of the First World War.

Chapter 6 Well fed and plenty of freedom

1 Capt Charles Mills, 31 Bn, letter to Maj James Coglin, 31 Bn, 5 January 1917, Mary Chomley papers, 1DRL/0615, AWM.

2 Pte George Anderson, 48 Bn, letter to Chomley, 15 April 1917, Mary Chomley papers, 1DRL/0615, AWM.

3 Chickering, *Imperial Germany and the Great War*, pp. 118–19.

4 Nagornaja and Mankoff, 'United by barbed wire', pp. 477–84.

5 McCarthy, *The Prisoner of War in Germany*, p. 19.

6 Beatrice Burke, letter to Aaron Pegram, 6 February 2009, author's notes.

7 Pte John Cotter, 51 Bn, POW statement, AWM30 B11.3.

8 Halpin cited in Gerster, *Big-noting*, p. 20.

9 Lawless, 'The forgotten Anzacs', p. 29; Ariotti, 'Coping with captivity', p. 56.

10 Dent, *Fourteen Months a Prisoner of War*, p. 28.

11 Ibid., p. 28.

12 Roper, *The Secret Battle*, pp. 50, 63.

13 Feltman, 'Letters from captivity', pp. 87–110.

14 LCpl George Gale, 48 Bn, POW statement, AWM30 B10.16; LCpl Rupert Wallach, 13 Bn, POW statement, AWM30 B13.5; Lieut Arthur McQuiggan, 14 Bn, POW statement, AWM30 B13.11.

15 Capt Victor Veness, 13 Bn, diary entry, 24 June 1917, PR01059, AWM.

16 Capt William Cull, 22 Bn, letter to family, 23 October 17, ML MSS 1165, SLNSW.

17 LCpl Herbert Eastaugh, 52 Bn, letter, 3 February 1918, Mary Chomley papers, 1DRL/0615, AWM.

18 Pte Sydney Whitbourne, 23 Bn, letter to Chomley, 16 May 1918, Mary Chomley papers, 1DRL/0615, AWM.

19 Pte Sydney Whitbourne, 23 Bn, letter to Chomley, 2 August 1918, Mary Chomley papers, 1DRL/0615, AWM.

20 Vischer, *Barbed Wire Disease*.

21 Havers, *Reassessing the Japanese Prisoner of War Experience*, pp. 5–6; Wilkinson, 'Captivity in print', pp. 227–43; Grant, *The Changi Book*, pp. 27–8; Ariotti and Crotty, 'The role of sport for Australian POWs of the Turks in the First World War', pp. 2362–74.

22 King, '"Books are more to me than food"', pp. 246–71. See also Laugesen, *Boredom is the Enemy*, pp. 43–78, 105–36.

23 Honeysett, 'Aussies in exile', p. 53.

24 Radford, 'The economic organisation of a POW camp', p. 196.

25 Stephens, *In All Respects Ready*, p. 349.

26 Pte Ernest Chalk, 15 Bn, untitled manuscript, privately held by Ian Chalk, Burnie, Tas.

27 Pte Malcolm Brown, 50 Bn, POW statement, AWM30 B11.1.

28 Pte Colin Mitchell, 53 Bn, POW statement, AWM30 B14.1.

29 Yarnall, *Barbed Wire Disease*, p. 124.

30 McCarthy, *The Prisoner of War in Germany*, pp. 170–1.

31 For examples, see Pte Leslie Morrall, 55 Bn, POW statement, AWM30 B14.6; Pte Alexander Hurt, 16 Bn, POW statement, AWM30 B13.22; Pte Roland Webb, 26 Bn, POW statement, AWM30 B6.5 (1); Pte Luke Ramshaw, 51 Bn, POW statement, AWM30 B11.3.

32 Dvr Leslie Barry, 1 FCE, 'Memoirs of my experiences in Germany, November 1916–January 1918', p. 15, ML MSS695, SLNSW [hereafter Barry, 'Memoirs of my experiences in Germany'].

33 Pte Frank Hallihan, 21 Bn, POW statement, report, AWM30 B6.16 (1).

34 Pte Arthur Bullock, 21 Bn, POW statement, AWM30 B6.17; Pte Hugh West, 51 Bn, POW statement, AWM30 B11.3.

35 Barry, 'Memoirs of my experiences in Germany', p. 15.
36 LCpl John Gribben, 43 Bn, letter to Chomley, 12 March 1918, Mary Chomley papers, 1DRL/0615, AWM.
37 For an example where an Australian prisoner lost a leg in an accident in the iron mine at Biersdorf, see Pte Bertram Hoult, 26 Bn, POW statement, AWM30 B6.3 (1).
38 Pte Norman Gordon, 15 Bn, Miller letter, 4 December 1917, service dossier, B2455, NAA.
39 Pte Leslie Cole, 4 January 1919, report re Pte Norman Gordon, 15 Bn, ARCS WMB, 1DRL/0428, AWM.
40 Pte James Steele, 53 Bn, POW statement, AWM30 B14.1.
41 Pte Edmund Sadler, 16 Bn, POW statement, AWM30 B13.22.
42 Pte John Cotter, 51 Bn, POW statement, AWM30 B11.3.
43 Spr John Wiedmer, 2nd Aust Tunn Coy, letter to Chomley, no date, Mary Chomley papers, 1DRL/0615, AWM.
44 Grey, 'In the hands of the Hun', p. 4.
45 Wise, 'The lost labour force', pp. 166–7.
46 Cpl Harry Still, 31 Bn, 'Some experiences as a member of the Australian Imperial Forces', p. 13, PR00753, AWM.
47 Bannigan, 'Two years in German prison camps', p. 2.
48 Wilkinson, *British Prisoners of War in First World War Germany*, pp. 112–18; Feltman, *The Stigma of Surrender*, pp. 108–9.
49 MacKenzie, *The Colditz Myth*, pp. 204–9.
50 Capt Maxwell Gore, 50 Bn, diary entries for 6 and 7 June 1917, held privately by Maxine Taylor of Wembley Downs, WA.
51 Honeysett, 'Aussies in exile', p. 56.
52 Capt Maxwell Gore, 50 Bn, diary entry for 11 June 1917, held privately by Maxine Taylor of Wembley Downs, WA.
53 Yarnall, *Barbed Wire Disease*, p. 125.
54 'Tales of ill-treatment at Torrens Island', *Barrier Miner*, 26 November 1918, p. 4.
55 Pte Fred MacKenzie, 48 Bn, POW statement, AWM30 B10.15; Pte William MacKenzie, 10 Bn, POW statement, AWM30 B6.1(1); Pte Patrick O'Donnell, 8 Bn, POW statement, AWM30 B5.27; Pte Edmund Linton, 13 Bn, POW statement, AWM30 B12.1.
56 CSM Albert Compton, 13 Bn, POW statement, AWM30 B13.5.
57 Pte Horace Collier, 13 Bn, POW statement, AWM30 B13.5.
58 CSM Sydney Edwards, 51 Bn, POW statement, AWM30 B11.3.
59 Bannigan, 'Two years in German prison camps', p. 13.
60 Pte Hamilton Warrell, 13 Bn, untitled manuscript, p. 26, PR00416, AWM [hereafter Warrell, untitled manuscript].
61 Pte William Pearce, 50 Bn, POW statement, AWM30 B10.20; Sgt George Bruce-Drayton, 28 Bn, POW statement, AWM30 B6.9 (2); Pte Alexander Stevenson, 13 Bn, POW statement, AWM30 B13.5; Pte Matthew Finn, 16 Bn, POW statement, AWM30 B13.22; Pte Patrick Coleman, 12 LTMB, POW statement, AWM30 B10.3; Pte Victor Arthur, 13 Bn, POW statement, service

dossier, B2455, NAA; Pte Frank Hanckel, 13 Bn, POW statement, service dossier, B2455, NAA.

62 *London Gazette*, 30 January 1920, p. 1225.

63 Pte Ernest Chalk, 15 Bn, untitled manuscript, privately held by Ian Chalk of Burnie, Tas.

64 Pte Justin Dawson, 15 Bn, letter to home, 14 December 1918, 'POW survives horrendous conditions', Australians at War.

65 Pte Vernal Cousins, 48 Bn, '*Note verbale*', 1 March 1918, ARCS WMB, 1DRL/0428, AWM. See also J. Allen, letter to ARCS, 26 July 1918, Pte John Evans, 20 Bn, ARCS WMB, 1DRL/0428, AWM.

66 Murray and Howes, 'Douglas Grant and Rudolf Marcuse'. The author acknowledges the assistance of Michael Bell and Garth O'Connell at the Australian War Memorial for their efforts in identifying Indigenous members of the AIF who endured captivity on the Western Front.

67 Pte Douglas Grant, 13 Bn, letter to Mary Chomley, 5 May 1918, Mary Chomley papers, 1DRL/0615, AWM.

68 Jones, 'Imperial captivities', pp. 175–83.

69 Kartinyeri, *Ngarrindjeri Anzacs*, p. 21.

70 Evans, *Anthropology at War*, p. 131.

71 Ibid., p. 135.

72 Pte William Grigsby, 51 Bn, recording, 20 March 1917, 'Englisch (Australien), *Der Verlorene Sohn*, PK740', Lautarchiv, Humboldt-Universität zu Berlin.

73 'The black Scotsman: The story of Douglas Grant', ABC radio script, SP1297/2, NAA.

74 Ibid. See also Osborn, 'Rudolf Marcuses Völkertypen aus dem Weltkrieg', pp. 281–6.

75 Murray and Howes, 'How we tracked down the only known sculpture of a WWI Indigenous soldier'.

76 Pte Roland Carter, 50 Bn, letters to ARCS, 19 March and 14 August 1918, ARCS WMB, 1DRL/0428, AWM.

77 Pte Roland Carter, 50 Bn, letter to home, 19 March 1918, ARCS WMB, 1DRL/0428, AWM.

78 'The black Scotsman: The story of Douglas Grant', ABC radio script, SP1297/2, NAA.

79 Pte Douglas Grant, 13 Bn, letters and receipts, items 1–4, ML MSS2766, SLNSW.

80 Pegram, 'Under the Kaiser's crescent moon', pp. 32–7.

81 Pte Douglas Grant, 13 Bn, letter to Chomley, 5 May 1918, Mary Chomley papers, 1DRL/0615, AWM.

82 Horner, *An Australian Prisoner*, pp. 122–7.

83 'My prisoner', *Northern Star*, 17 June 1918, p. 6.

84 Ziemann, *War Experiences*, pp. 156–7.

85 Ayres, untitled manuscript, p. 147.

86 Grey, 'In the hands of the Hun', p. 4.

87 Roper, *The Secret Battle*, pp. 50, 63.

88 Warrell, untitled manuscript, p. 16.
89 Ibid., p. 17.
90 Horner, *An Australian Prisoner*, pp. 80, 86–7.
91 Diary entry for 14 March 1918, Pte Frank Sturrock, 16 Bn, PR00122, AWM.
92 Horner, *An Australian Prisoner*, pp. 86–7.
93 Ayres, untitled manuscript, p. 147.
94 Ibid., p. 147; Barry, 'Memoirs of my experiences in Germany', pp. 19–21.
95 Adolf Vischer cited in Jones, 'Prisoners of war', in *1914–1918 Online*, ed. Daniel et al.
96 Durnford, *The Tunnellers of Holzminden*, p. 83.
97 Vischer, *Barbed Wire Disease*, p. 42. For one such platonic friendship, see Cull, *At All Costs*, p. 153.
98 Rachamimov, 'The disruptive comforts of drag', pp. 362–82. For a suggestion of homosexual relationships among British officers interned in Switzerland, see Ackerley, *The Prisoners of War*; Feltman, *The Stigma of Surrender*, pp. 130, 132.
99 Cpl Roy Bauer, 26 Bn, letter to Walster, 30 May 1918, PUB00071, AWM.
100 Todd, '"The soldier's wife who ran away with the Russian"', pp. 257–78. See also Sauertig, 'Sex, medicine and morality during the First World War', pp. 167–88.
101 Pte Frank Sturrock, 16 Bn, diary entries, May–June 1918, PR00122, AWM.

Chapter 7 Hun haunted?

1 Lieut Les Ward, 2 Sqn AFC, diary entry, 10 November 1918, PR83/230, AWM.
2 Ibid., 12 November 1918.
3 Ayres, untitled manuscript, p. 3.
4 Jones, 'The Danish scheme'.
5 Knowles, 'Out of the shadows', p. 21.
6 Yarnall, *Barbed Wire Disease*, p. 177.
7 War Office, *Statistics of the Military Effort*, p. 343.
8 Yarnall, *Barbed Wire Disease*, p. 178.
9 Pte William Leslie and Pte Ashleigh Young, both 13 Bn, 'Medical report on an invalid', service dossiers, B2455, NAA.
10 War Office, *Manual of Military Law*, pp. 521–2. For enquiries into the conduct of Australian officers, see memo, 7 February 1920, 'Statements of POW October 1918–February 1920', AWM18, 9982/1/2. For the rehabilitation of prisoners returning from Europe in the Second World War, see Abraham, 'Bringing them all back home'.
11 Memo, 6 November 1918, Miscellaneous POW statements, AWM30 B18.2.
12 Pte Sidney McGarvey, 30 Bn, POW statement, AWM30 B16.4.
13 Pte Leslie Farrington, 54 Bn, POW statement, AWM30 B16.5.
14 Capt Donald Wells, 13 Bn, POW statement, AWM30 B13.5.
15 Pte Henry Neale, 14 Bn, POW statement, AWM30 B13.11.
16 Pte Benjamin Ross, 29 Bn, POW statement, AWM30 B16.1.
17 AIF Headquarters London to Dept of Defence, Melbourne, 5 November 1918, Repatriation, AWM27, 424/28.

18 Challinger, *Anzacs in Arkhangel*, pp. 232–53.
19 Sgt Andrew Gove DCM and Pte Leslie Adams, both 13 Bn, 'Record of Non-Military Employment', service dossiers, B2455, NAA.
20 'German brutality', *Mercury*, 10 February 1919, p. 6; Defence Department, *How the Germans Treated Australian Prisoners of War*, p. i.
21 Beaumont, *Broken Nation*, p. 538.
22 Yarnall, *Barbed Wire Disease*, pp. 184–5.
23 Mott, *Experiences and Narrow Escapes of Capt. J.E. Mott*; Dent, *Fourteen Months a Prisoner of War*; Hallihan, *In the Hands of the Enemy*; Gray, *In the Hands of the Hun*; Horner, *An Australian Prisoner*; Taylor, *Peregrinations of an Australian Prisoner of War*.
24 Cull, *At All Costs*, p. 114.
25 Groves, 'Things I remember', 31 January 1932, p. 13.
26 Pte Findlay Fraser, 48 Bn, 'German Death Certificate', 24 September 1919, ARCS WMB, 1DRL/0428, AWM.
27 Wilkinson, 'A fate worse than death?', pp. 24–40.
28 E. Fraser, letter to Base Records office, 28 February 1923, service dossier, Pte Findley Fraser, 48 Bn, B2455, NAA.
29 Beaumont, *Broken Nation*, p. 538. Yarnall, *Barbed Wire Disease*, pp. 184–5.
30 Fussell, *The Great War and Modern Memory*, p. 327.
31 Lawless, 'The forgotten Anzacs', p. 28. See also Gerster, 'Hors de combat', p. 273.
32 Gray, *In the Hands of the Hun*, p. 3.
33 Cull, *At All Costs*, p. 158.
34 Gerster, *Big-noting*, p. 52.
35 'The Leipzig trials', *Advertiser*, 13 July 1921, p. 10.
36 'Suicide at Fremantle', *Daily News*, 26 May 1919, p. 6; entries for 26–31 May 1919, Occurrence Book, East Fremantle Police Station, Book 8, S4833, SROWA.
37 Pte Alfred Holton, 33 Bn, untitled manuscript, p. 98, PR05317, AWM.
38 Newman, 'The prisoner of war mentality', pp. 8–10; Whiles, 'A study of neurosis among repatriated prisoners of war', pp. 697–8; Cochrane, 'Notes on the psychology of prisoners of war', pp. 282–4; Lunden, 'Captivity psychoses among prisoners of war', pp. 721–33. See also Jones and Wessely, 'British prisoners of war', pp. 163–83.
39 Scates, Wheatley and James, *World War One*; Crotty and Larsson, *Anzac Legacies*; Larsson, *Shattered Anzacs*; Ziino, *A Distant Grief*; McKernan, *This War Never Ends*; Damousi, *Living with the Aftermath*.
40 Warrell, untitled manuscript, p. 65.
41 For more on the Soldier Settlement Scheme, see Scates and Oppenheimer, *The Last Battle*.
42 Thomson, *Anzac Memories*, p. 284.
43 Scott, *Australia During the War*, p. 888.
44 Ibid., fn., pp. 817–88; 'Statisticians Report', *Census of the Commonwealth of Australia*, 30 June 1933, p. 398.
45 For examples, see Garton, *The Cost of War*, p. 87.

46 LCpl Donald Muir MM, 13 Bn, 'Medical report on an invalid', 26 April 1919, service dossier, B2455, NAA.

47 Donald Muir, 'Search for particulars of death', 14 January 1957, Repatriation Commission file, C138/2, R50281, NAA.

48 Garton, *The Cost of War*, p. 86.

49 Pte Ashleigh Young, 13 Bn, 'Medical report on an invalid', service dossier, B2455, NAA.

50 Ariotti, *Captive Anzacs*, p. 137.

51 Alfred MacNab, 'Summary of Particulars for Application', 3 April 1928, Repatriation Commission file, C138, M109484 Part 2, NAA.

52 Ibid., 16 January 1935.

53 Ibid., 10 December 1954.

54 Twomey, 'Compensating prisoners of war of Japan in post-war Australia', pp. 260–1.

55 In 2001, the Australian Government provided former prisoners of the Japanese and their dependants a one-off payment of $25 000. Six years later, Australian prisoners of the Germans and Italians received an ex-gratia payment of $25 000.

56 'Personal', *Nowra Leader*, 12 December 1930, p. 4; 'Organising at Cambewarra and Kangaroo Valley', *Nowra Leader*, 15 September 1939, p. 7.

57 Notes compiled from conversations with Mary Newing of Nowra, NSW, re Pte Oswald McClelland, 13 Bn; Oswald McClelland, 'Record of Evidence', 21 June 1956, Repatriation Commission file, C138/2, M188784, NAA.

58 Oswald McClelland, 'Record of Evidence', 21 June 1956, Repatriation Commission file, C138/2, M188784, NAA.

59 Oswald McClelland, death notification, 20 September 1965, Repatriation Commission file, C138, M188784, NAA.

60 Scates, Wheatley and James, *World War One*, pp. 11–13.

61 'Quarter Sessions', *Sydney Morning Herald*, 23 June 1923, p. 9. For other examples, see 'Four persons charged', *Sydney Morning Herald*, 29 July 1922, p. 11; 'Thefts in company', *Argus*, 8 December 1922, p. 18; 'The war changed him', *Daily News*, 13 March 1924, p. 7; 'Abuses barmaids', *Morning Bulletin*, 5 November 1935, p. 11; 'Imprisoned for forgery', *Argus*, 6 April 1937, p. 11.

62 See Australian Institute of Health and Welfare, 'Table S6.1: Life expectancy (expected age at death in years) at different ages by sex, 1881–1890 to 2014–2016'.

63 'Fighting 13th', *Sun*, 10 September 1929, p. 12.

64 'Prisoners of war', *Sun*, 3 July 1938, p. 4; 'Ex-POW to Unite', *Sydney Morning Herald*, 8 July 1939, p. 9.

65 'Ex-Prisoners of War Club', *Smiths Weekly*, 28 December 1935, p. 16.

66 'Private Don Fraser', *Western Herald*, 28 May 1919, p. 2.

67 Donald Fraser, Returned Soldier Settlement Loan file, 12/6908, NSW State Archives and Records.

68 'Public welcome to returned soldiers', *Western Herald*, 26 October 1945, p. 6.

69 Notes compiled from conversations with Wendy Wakeham, Winston Hills, NSW, and Ella Herbert, Dubbo, NSW, re Pte Donald Fraser, 13 Bn.

70 For more on Fraser's wartime experience, including his time in German captivity, see oral history interview between Donald Fraser and David Chalk, 11 December 1985, S01182, AWM.

Conclusion

1 Hinz, *Gefangen im Großen Krieg*, p. 362.
2 See Monteath, *POW*, pp. 128–30; Vance, 'Shackling incident', p. 270; Kochavi, *Confronting Captivity*, pp. 47–51.
3 Lynch, *Somme Mud*, p. 314.

Appendix 2

1 War Office memo, 3 May 1917, 'Regulations for the War Office Concerning Awards to Prisoners of War', AWM27, 268/16.
2 War Office, *Army Orders*, 5 May 1919, pp. 6–7.

BIBLIOGRAPHY

PRIMARY SOURCES
Archival material
Australian Red Cross Society National Office, Heritage Collection, Melbourne
NO11, Publications (Red Cross Reports)
NO13, Annual Reports, 1916–19
NO33, Executive Correspondence

Australian War Memorial, Canberra
Official records
AWM4, AIF Unit War Diaries, 1914–18 war
AWM8, Unit Embarkation Nominal Roll, 1914–18 war
AWM10, AIF Administrative Headquarters Registry, 'A' files
AWM18, AIF Administrative Headquarters Registry 'Records Registry' files
AWM27, Records Arranged According to AWM Library Subject Classification
AWM28, Recommendation Files for Honours and Awards, AIF, 1914–18 war
AWM30, Prisoner of War Statements, 1914–18 war
AWM38, Official History, 1914–18 war, records of C.E.W. Bean, Official Historian
AWM46, Captured German Documents, 1914–18 war
AWM47, German Records Collected by Captain J.J.W. Herbertson
AWM133, AIF Nominal Roll
AWM131, Roll of Honour Circulars, 1914–18 war
AWM145, Roll of Honour Cards, 1914–18 war

Private records
PR86/243, Australian Red Cross Prisoner of War Department Account Book, Germany
1DRL/0428, Australian Red Cross Society, Prisoner of War Department Files, 1914–18 war
1DRL/0428, Australian Red Cross Society, Wounded and Missing Enquiry Bureau Files, 1914–18 war
PR0112, 2nd Lieut Ivo Agnew, 2 Squadron Australian Flying Corps
1DRL/0028, Pte Frederick Allen, 53rd Battalion
PR89/126, Pte Raymond Ayres, 13th Battalion
PR00814, Pte William Barry, 29th Battalion
3DRL/7481, Cpl Arthur Bowen, 54th Battalion

1DRL/0615, Mary Chomley, Prisoner of War Department
PR00140, Cpl Lancelot Davies, 13th Battalion
PR00857, Lieut Cecil Feez, 4 Squadron, Australian Flying Corps
3DRL/6608, Lieut Alfred Fell, 34th Battalion
2DRL/0785, Pte Wilfred Gallwey, 47th Battalion
2DRL/0268, Sgt William Groves, 14th Battalion
3DRL/4043, Capt Joseph Honeysett, 47th Battalion
PR91/099, Pte Frederick Kligner, 4th Pioneer Battalion
PR04253, Lieut Peter Lyon, 11th Battalion
PR01877, LCpl Arnold Mason, 14th Field Company Engineers
PR02022, Pte Raymond Membrey, 21st Battalion
1DRL/0498, Lieut Cyril Meyer, 13th Battalion
2DRL/0122, Lieut George McLean, 16th Battalion
2DRL/0012, Capt John Mott, 48th Battalion
PR01602, Pte Charles Neander, 46th Battalion
3DRL/7153 (A), Sgt Roy Stephens, 14th Battalion
PR00753, Cpl Harry Still, 31st Battalion
PR00122, Pte Frank Sturrock, 16th Battalion
PR01059, Capt Victor Veness, 13th Battalion
PR00416, Pte Hamilton Warrell, 13th Battalion
PR86/249, Sgt Stuart Webb, 28th Battalion
PR03237, Pte Hugh West, 51st Battalion
1DRL/0605, Pte Walter Wilson, 15th Battalion

Baden-Württemberg Hauptstaatsarchiv, Stuttgart, Germany
Generalkommando XIII. Armeekorps, M33/2

Bayerisches Hauptstaatsarchiv, Abt. IV, Kriegsarchiv, Munich, Germany
6. *Bayerisches Reserve Division*, Bund 23 and 35
23. *Infanterie Regiment*, Bund 9
21. *Reserve Infanterie Regiment*, Bund 7

Lautarchiv, Humboldt-Universität zu Berlin, Germany
Recording of Pte William Grigsby, 51 Bn, 20 March 1917, 'Englisch (Australien),
   Der Verlorene Sohn', PK740

National Archives of Australia, Canberra
A1, Certificate of Naturalisation, Peter Christian Christiansen Petersen
A1336/10246, manuscript, Warrant Officer John Bannigan, 2nd Field Artillery
   Brigade, 'Two years in German prison camps'
B2455, AIF Service Dossiers, 1914–18 war
C138, Department of Repatriation, Personal Case Files, Single Number Series
   (Australian, 1914–18 war)
C139, Department of Repatriation, Personal Case Files, Single Number Series
   with 'X' Prefix
SP1297/2, ABC radio script, 'The black Scotsman: The story of Douglas Grant'

National Archives, Kew, United Kingdom
FO383/291, 'Germany: Prisoners, Including Employment of Prisoners in France and Russia near the Front Line'
WO32/5381, 'Prisoners of War: Employment and Treatment of British Prisoners of War by Germans behind Firing Line'
WO33/3081, 'Report of the Committee on Clothing for British Prisoners of War in Germany'
WO161, Repatriated Prisoner Statements Collected by the Committee on the Treatment of British Prisoners of War

National Library of Australia, Canberra
Argus (Melbourne, Vic)
Barrier Miner (Broken Hill, NSW)
Brisbane Courier (Brisbane, Qld)
Colac Herald (Colac, Vic)
Cumberland and Argus Fruitgrowers Advocate (Parramatta, NSW)
Daily News (Perth, WA)
Daily Standard (Brisbane, Qld)
Geraldton Guardian (Geraldton, WA)
Goulburn Evening Penny Post (Goulburn, NSW)
Journal (Adelaide, SA)
Kalgoorlie Miner (Kalgoorlie, WA)
Kyneton Guardian, (Kyneton, Vic)
Mercury (Hobart, Tas)
Northern Star (Lismore, NSW)
Nowra Leader (Nowra, NSW)
Referee (Sydney, NSW)
Singleton Argus (Singleton, NSW)
South Coast Times and Wollongong Argus (Wollongong, NSW)
Sunday Times (Perth, WA)
Sydney Morning Herald (Sydney, NSW)
West Australian (Perth, WA)

State Archives and Records Authority New South Wales, Sydney
NRS2467, Photographic Description Book, Long Bay Gaol

State Library of New South Wales, Sydney
MLDOC, Lieut Henry Baker, 2nd Battalion, Lancashire Fusiliers
MSS695, Dvr Leslie Barry, 1st Field Company Engineers
MSS893, Pte George Bell, 16th Battalion
MSS885, Pte Claude Benson, 13th Battalion
MSS1504, Pte Wesley Choat, 32nd Battalion
MSS1165, Capt William Cull, 22nd Battalion
MSS2766, Pte Douglas Grant, 13th Battalion
CY4885, Pte Edwin Phelps, 45th Battalion
MSS2743, Capt Donald Wells, 13th Battalion

State Library of South Australia, Adelaide
SRG76/1, South Australian Red Cross Enquiry Files

State Library of Victoria, Melbourne
MS9571, Pte George Hicks, 5th Battalion
MS10989, Pte Allan Hislop, 25th Battalion
MS12756, Sgt Harold Morris, 14th Battalion

State Record Office Western Australia, Perth
S4833, Occurrence Book, East Fremantle Police Station

SECONDARY SOURCES
Published accounts

Cull, W., *At All Costs*, Australasian Authors Agency, Melbourne, 1919
Dent, A., *Fourteen Months a Prisoner of War*, North Western Courier Print, Narrabri, 1919
Durnford, H., *The Tunnellers of Holzminden*, Cambridge University Press, Cambridge, 1920
Gray, A., *In the Hands of the Hun*, Guardian Office, Kyneton, 1920
Groves, W., 'Captivity: A prisoner of war looks back', *Reveille*, 1 January 1932, p. 19
——'Things I remember: A prisoner of war looks back', *Reveille*, 31 January 1932, pp. 13, 31
——'Things I remember: A prisoner of war looks back', *Reveille*, 29 February 1932, pp. 4, 23
——'Captivity: A prisoner of war looks back', *Reveille*, 31 March 1932, pp. 44, 60
——'Captivity: A prisoner of war looks back', *Reveille*, 1 September 1932, p. 28
——'Captivity: A prisoner of war looks back', *Reveille*, 1 November 1932, pp. 17, 30
——'Captivity: A prisoner of war looks back', *Reveille*, 1 December 1932, pp. 26, 56
——'Captivity: A prisoner of war looks back', *Reveille*, 1 January 1933, p. 29
Hallihan, F., *In the Hands of the Enemy: A Record of the Experiences of Frank Hallihan, 21st Battalion, in German Prison Camps*, Baxter & Stubbs, Ballarat, 1920
Horner, H., *Reason or Revolution? An Australian Prisoner in the Hands of the Hun*, V.K. Jones & Co., Perth, 1920
Knowles, H., 'Out of the shadows: War prisoners come home', *Reveille*, 1 September 1932, p. 21
Lee, A., *No Parachute*, Harrods, London, 1968
Ludendorff, E., *My War Memories, 1914–1918*, vol. 1, Naval and Military Press, Uckfield, 2005
Lynch, E., *Somme Mud: The Experiences of An Australian Infantryman in France, 1916–19*, ed. W. Davies, Random House Australia, Milsons Point, 2006
Mott, J., *Experiences and Narrow Escapes of Capt. J.E. Mott*, Chiswick Press, London, 1917

Taylor, T., *Peregrinations of an Australian Prisoner of War: The Experiences of an Australian Soldier in Germany and Bolshevik Russia*, E.W. Cole, Melbourne, 1920

White, T., *Guests of the Unspeakable*, Angus & Robertson, Sydney, 1935

Articles

Anderson, N., 'Dear Miss Chomley', *Wartime*, iss. 21, 2003, pp. 44–6

Ariotti, K., and Crotty, M., 'The role of sport for Australian POWs of the Turks in the First World War', *International Journal of the History of Sport*, vol. 31, iss. 18, 2014, pp. 2362–74

Bean, C., 'Albert Jacka', *Reveille*, 31 January 1931, pp. 2–3

——'Punishing Australians', *Commonwealth Gazette*, No. 184, 1917, pp. 2809–11.

Beaumont, J., 'Rank, privilege, and prisoners of war', *War and Society*, vol. 1, no. 1, 1983, pp. 67–94

——'Whatever happened to patriotic women, 1914–1918?', *Australian Historical Studies*, vol. 31, iss. 115, 2000, pp. 273–86

——'Australia's global memory footprint: Memorial Building on the Western Front, 1916–2015', *Australian Historical Studies*, vol. 46, iss. 1, 2015, pp. 45–63

Bourke, J., 'Swinging the lead: Malingering, Australian soldiers and the Great War', *Journal of the Australian War Memorial*, iss. 26, 1995, pp. 10–18

Central POW Committee, 'Canadian Red Cross', *British Prisoner of War*, vol. 1, iss. 5, 1918, p. 56

Chalk, D., 'Talks with old *Gefangeners*', *Journal of the Australian War Memorial*, no. 14, 1989, pp. 11–23

Cochrane, A.L., 'Notes on the psychology of prisoners of war', *British Medical Journal*, 23 February 1946, pp. 282–4

Cook, T., 'The politics of surrender: Canadian soldiers and the killing of prisoners in the Great War', *Journal of Military History*, vol. 70, iss. 3, 2006, pp. 637–65

Cull, N., 'Great escapes: "Englishness" and the prisoner of war genre', *Film History*, vol. 14, 2002, pp. 282–95

Davies, G., 'Prisoners of war in twentieth-century war economies', *Journal of Contemporary History*, vol. 12, iss. 4, 1977

Ferguson, N., 'Dynamics of defeat: Prisoner taking and prisoner killing in the age of total war', *War in History*, no. 11, 2004, pp. 34–78

Garton, S., 'Changi as television: Myth, memory, narrative and history', *Journal of Australian Studies*, iss. 73, 2002, pp. 79–88

Gerster, R., 'Hors de combat: The problems and postures of Australian prisoner-of-war literature', *Meanjin Quarterly*, vol. 42, no. 2, 1982, pp. 221–9

Isherwood, I., 'Writing the "ill-managed nursery": British POW memoirs of the First World War', *First World War Studies*, vol. 5, iss. 3, 2014, pp. 267–86

Jones, E., and Wessely, S., 'British prisoners of war: From resilience to psychological vulnerability: Reality or perception', *Twentieth-Century British History*, vol. 21, no. 2, 2010, pp. 163–83

Jones, H., 'The final logic of sacrifice? Violence in German prisoner of war labor companies in 1918', *Historian*, vol. 68, iss. 4, 2006, pp. 770–91

———'A missing paradigm? Military captivity and the prisoner of war, 1914–18', *Immigrants and Minorities*, vol. 26, iss. 1–2, 2008, pp. 19–48

———'The German Spring reprisals of 1917: Prisoners of war and the violence of the Western Front', *German History*, vol. 23, iss. 3, 2008, pp. 335–56

———'International or transnational? Humanitarian action in the First World War', *Revue Européenne d'Histoire*, vol. 16, no. 5, 2009, pp. 697–713

Kent, D., '*The Anzac Book* and the Anzac Legend: C.E.W. Bean as editor and image-maker', *Historical Studies*, vol. 21, no. 84, 1985, pp. 376–90

Kildea, J., 'Bridging the divide', *Wartime*, iss. 41, 2008, pp. 50–1

King, E., '"Books are more to me than food": British prisoners of war as readers, 1914–1918', *Book History*, vol. 16, 2013, pp. 246–71

Larsen, D., 'Intelligence in the First World War: The state of the field', *Intelligence and National Security*, vol. 29, no. 2, 2014, pp. 282–302

Lawless, J., 'The forgotten Anzacs: Captives of the Turks', *Southerly*, vol. 65, no. 2, 2006, pp. 26–41

Ludewig, A., 'For King or Kaiser? Competing loyalties among Australian civilian internees in Ruhleben during World War I', *Journal of the Royal Australian Historical Society*, vol. 98, iss. 2, 2012, pp. 249–68

Lunden, W., 'Captivity psychosis among prisoners of war', *Journal of Criminal Law and Criminology*, vol. 9, iss. 6, 1949, pp. 721–33

MacKenzie, S.P., 'The ethics of escape: British officer POWs in the First World War', *War in History*, vol. 15, no. 1, 2008, pp. 1–16

Murray, T., and Howes, H., 'Douglas Grant and Rudolf Marcuse: Wartime encounters at the edge of art', *History and Anthropology*, 13 May 2019, https://doi.org/10.1080/02757206.2019.1607730

———'How we tracked down the only known sculpture of a WW1 Indigenous soldier', *The Conversation*, 5 June 2019, http://theconversation.com/how-we-tracked-down-the-only-known-sculpture-of-a-wwi-indigenous-soldier-117246 (retrieved 12 June 2019)

Nagornaja, O., and Mankoff, J., 'United by barbed wire: Russian POWs in Germany, national stereotypes, and international relations, 1914–1922', *Kritika: Explorations in Russian and Eurasian History*, vol. 10, no. 3, 2009, pp. 475–98

Newman, P.H., 'The prisoner of war mentality: Its effect after repatriation', *British Medical Journal*, 1 January 1944, pp. 8–10

Noble, R., 'Raising the white flag: The surrender of Australian soldiers on the Western Front', *Revue Internationale d'Histoire Militaire*, no. 72, 1990, pp. 48–79

Oppenheimer, M., '"The best PM For the Empire in war": Lady Helen Munro Ferguson and the Australian Red Cross Society, 1914–1920', *Australian Historical Studies*, vol. 33, iss. 119, 2002, pp. 108–24

Osborn, M., 'Rudolf Marcuses Völkertypen aus dem Weltkrieg', *Ost und West: Illustrierte Monatsschrift für das gesamte Jusendtum*, iss. 11–12, 1919, pp. 281–6

Pegram, A., 'Under the Kaiser's crescent moon', *Wartime*, iss. 76, 2016, pp. 32–7

Pöhlmann, M., 'German intelligence at war, 1914–1918', *Journal of Intelligence History*, vol. 5, no. 2, 2005, pp. 25–54

Rachamimov, A., 'The disruptive comforts of drag: (Trans)gender performances among prisoners of war in Russia, 1914–1920', *American Historical Review*, vol. 111, no. 2, 2006, pp. 362–82

Radford, R.A., 'The economic organisation of a POW camp', *Economica*, vol. 12, no. 48, 1945, pp. 189–201

Schneider, E., 'The British Red Cross Wounded and Missing Enquiry Bureau: A case of truth-telling in the Great War', *War in History*, vol. 4, iss. 3, 1997, pp. 296–315

Shils, E., and Janowitz, M., 'Cohesion and disintegration in the Wehrmacht in World War II', *Public Opinion Quarterly*, no. 12, 1948, pp. 280–315

Smart, J., '"An ignoble end to all our brilliant aspirations": Australian POW memoirs of the First World War and the transition from soldier to captive', *Melbourne Historical Journal*, vol. 43, iss. 1, 2015, pp. 84–100

Spoerer, M., 'The mortality of Allied prisoners of war and Belgian civilian deportees in German custody during the First World War: A reappraisal of the effects of forced labour', *Population Studies*, vol. 60, iss. 2, 2006, pp. 121–36

Stephens, D., *In All Respects Ready: Australia's Navy in World War One*, Oxford University Press, South Melbourne, 2014

Stone, L., 'Prosopography', *Daedalus*, vol. 100, no. 1, *Historical Studies Today*, 1971, pp. 47–79

Thomson, A., '"Steadfast until death?" C.E.W. Bean and the representation of Australian military manhood', *Australian Historical Studies*, vol. 23, 1989, pp. 462–78

Todd, L., '"The soldier's wife who ran away with the Russian": Sexual infidelities in World War I Germany', *Central European History*, vol. 44, no. 2, 2011, pp. 257–78

Twomey, C., 'Trauma and the reinvigoration of Anzac: An argument', *History Australia*, vol. 10, no. 3, 2013, pp. 85–105

——'POWs of the Japanese: Race and trauma in Australia, 1970s–2005', *Journal of War and Culture Studies*, vol. 7, no. 3, 2014, pp. 191–205

Whiles, W.H., 'A study of neurosis among repatriated prisoners of war', *British Medical Journal*, 17 November 1945, pp. 697–8

Wilkinson, O., 'A fate worse than death? Lamenting First World War captivity', *Journal of War and Culture Studies*, vol. 8, no. 1, 2015, pp. 24–40

Wise, N., 'The lost labour force: Working-class approaches to military service during the First World War', *Labour History*, no. 93, 2007, pp. 161–76

Books and book chapters

Abbal, O., *Soldats oubliés: Les Prisonniers de Guerre Français*, Etudes et communication, Bez-et-Esparon, 2001

Ackerley, J., *The Prisoners of War: A Play in Three Acts*, Chatto & Windus, London, 1925

Adam-Smith, P., *Prisoners of War: From Gallipoli to Korea*, Viking, Melbourne, 1992

Akçam, T., *The Young Turks' Crime Against Humanity: The Armenian Genocide and Ethnic Cleansing in the Ottoman Empire*, Princeton University Press, Princeton, 2012

Andrew, C., and Tobia, S. (eds), *Interrogation in War and Conflict: A Comparative and Interdisciplinary Analysis*, Routledge, Abingdon, 2014

Ariotti, K., '"At present everything is making us most anxious": Families of Australian prisoners in Turkey', in *Beyond Surrender*, ed. Beaumont, Grant and Pegram, pp. 57–74

——*Captive Anzacs: Australian POWs of the Ottomans during the First World War*, Cambridge University Press, Melbourne, 2018

Ashworth, T., *Trench Warfare 1914–1918: The 'Live and Let Live' System*, Macmillan, London, 1980

Babkenian, V., and Stanley, P., *Armenia, Australia and the Great War*, UNSW Press, Sydney, 2016

Bean, C., *The Australian Imperial Force in France, 1916*, vol. 3, *Official History of Australia in the War of 1914–1918*, Angus & Robertson, Sydney, 1929

——*The Australian Imperial Force in France, 1917*, vol. 4, *Official History of Australia in the War of 1914–1918*, Angus & Robertson, Sydney, 1933

——*The Australian Imperial Force in France During the Main German Offensive, 1918*, vol. 5, *Official History of Australia in the War of 1914–1918*, Angus & Robertson, Sydney, 1937

——*Australian Imperial Force in France during the Allied Offensive, 1918*, vol. 6, *Official History of Australia in the War of 1914–1918*, Angus & Robertson, Sydney, 1942

Beaumont, J., *Gull Force: Survival and Leadership in Captivity, 1941–1945*, Allen & Unwin, Sydney, 1990

——'Prisoners of war in Australian national memory', in *Prisoners of War: Prisoners of Peace: Captivity, Homecoming and Memory in World War II*, ed. B. Moore and B. Hately-Broad, Berg, Oxford, 2005, pp. 185–94

——*Broken Nation: Australians in the Great War*, Allen & Unwin, Sydney, 2013

——'Officers and men: Rank and survival on the Thai–Burma Railway', in *Beyond Surrender*, ed. Beaumont, Grant and Pegram, pp. 174–95

Beaumont, J., Grant, L., and Pegram, A. (eds), *Beyond Surrender: Australian Prisoners of War in the Twentieth Century*, Melbourne University Press, Carlton, 2015

——'Remembering and rethinking captivity', in *Beyond Surrender*, ed. Beaumont, Grant and Pegram, pp. 1–8

Becker, A., *Oubliés de la Grande Guerre: Humanitaire et culture de guerre, 1914–1918: Populations occupies, déportés civils, prisonniers de guerre*, Noêsis, Paris, 1998

Beckett, I., *The Great War*, Pearson Longman, Harlow, 2007

Berghahn, V., *Imperial Germany, 1871–1918: Economy, Society, Culture and Politics*, Berghahn Books, New York, 2005

Blair, D., *No Quarter: Unlawful Killing and Surrender in the Australian War Experience, 1915–18*, Ginninderra Press, Canberra, 2005

Blanch, C., and Pegram, A., *For Valour: Australians Awarded the Victoria Cross*, NewSouth Publishing, Sydney, 2018

Bou, J. (ed.), *The AIF in Battle: How the Australia Imperial Force Fought, 1914–1918*, Melbourne University Press, Carlton, 2016

Bowden, T., *The Changi Camera: A Unique Record of Changi and Thai–Burma Railway*, Hachette, Sydney, 2012

Braithwaite, R., *Fighting Monsters: An Intimate History of the Sandakan Tragedy*, Australian Scholarly Publishing, Melbourne, 2016

Butler, A., *The Western Front*, vol. 2, *The Official History of the Australian Army Medical Services in the War of 1914–1918*, Australian War Memorial, Canberra, 1940

——*Special Problems and Services*, vol. 3, *The Official History of the Australian Army Medical Services*, Australian War Memorial, Canberra, 1943

Carr, G., and Mytum, H. (ed.), *Cultural Heritage and Prisoners of War: Captivity Behind Barbed Wire*, Routledge, New York, 2012

Challinger, M., *Anzacs in Arkhangel: The Untold Story of Australia and the Invasion of Russia, 1918–19*, Hardie Grant, Melbourne, 2010

Clark, A., *Aces High: The War in the Air Over the Western Front, 1914–1918*, Weidenfeld & Nicolson, London, 1973

Clarke, H., and Burgess, C., *Barbed Wire and Bamboo: Australian POW Stories*, Allen & Unwin, Sydney, 1992

Cook, J., *The Real Great Escape: The Story of the First World War's Most Daring Mass Breakout*, Vintage Books, North Sydney, 2013

Coombes, D., *Crossing the Wire: The Untold Stories of Australian POWs in Battle and Captivity During WWI*, Big Sky Publishing, Sydney, 2011

Crotty, M., and Larsson, M. (eds), *Anzac Legacies: Australians and the Aftermath of War*, Australian Scholarly Publishing, North Melbourne, 2010

Cutlack, F., *The Australian Flying Corps*, vol. 8, *The Official History of Australia in the War of 1914–1918*, Angus & Robertson, Sydney, 1935

Damousi, J., *Living with the Aftermath: Trauma, Nostalgia and Grief in Post-War Australia*, Cambridge University Press, Melbourne, 2001

Dennett, C., *Prisoners of the Great War: Authoritative Statement of Conditions in the Prison Camps of Germany*, Houghton Mifflin, Boston, 1919

Djurović, G., *L'Agence Centrale de Recherches du Comité International de la Croix-Rouge: Activité du CICR en vue du soulagement des souffrances morales des victims de guerre*, Henry Dunant Institute, Geneva, 1981

Doegen, W., *Kriegsgefangene Völker: Der Kriegsgefangenen Haltung und Schicksal in Deutschland*, Verlag Für Politik und Wirtschaft, Berlin, 1921

Duffy, C., *Through German Eyes: The British Army on the Somme 1916*, Weidenfeld & Nicolson, London, 2006

Eby, C., *The Road to Armageddon: The Martial Spirit in English Popular Literature, 1870–1914*, Duke University Press, Durham, NC, 1988

Edmonds, J., *March–April: Continuation of the German Offensive*, vol. 2, *History of the Great War Based on Official Documents, France and Belgium 1918*, Macmillan, London, 1937

Evans, A., *Anthropology at War: World War I and the Science of Race in Germany*, University of Chicago Press, Chicago, 2010

Feltman, B., 'Letters from captivity: The First World War correspondence of the German prisoners of war in the United Kingdom', in *Finding Common Ground: New Directions in First World War Studies*, ed. M. Neiberg and J. Keene, Brill, Boston, 2010, pp. 87–110

———*The Stigma of Surrender: German Prisoners, British Captors, and Manhood in the Great War and Beyond*, University of North Carolina Press, Chapel Hill, 2015

Ferguson, N., *The Pity of War 1914–1918*, Penguin Books, London, 1999

Forbes, C., *Hellfire: The Story of Australia, Japan and the Prisoners of War*, Pan Macmillan, Sydney, 2005

Fussell, P., *The Great War and Modern Memory*, Oxford University Press, Oxford, 1975

Gammage, B., *The Broken Years: Australian Soldiers in the Great War*, 6th edn, Penguin, Ringwood, 1985

Garton, S., *The Cost of War: Australians Return*, Oxford University Press, Melbourne, 1996

Gerard, J., *My Four Years in Germany*, George H. Doran Co., New York, 1917

Gerster, R., *Big-noting: The Heroic Theme in Australian War Writing*, Melbourne University Press, Melbourne, 1992

Gibbney, H., and Smith, A. (eds), *A Biographical Register 1788–1939*, vol. 1, *Australian Dictionary of Biography*, Canberra, 1987

Grant, L. 'Monument and ceremony: The Australian Ex-Prisoners of War Memorial and the Anzac Legend', in *Forgotten Captives in Japanese Occupied Asia*, ed. K. Blackburn and K. Hack, Routledge, London, 2008, pp. 41–56

———(ed.), *The Changi Book*, NewSouth Publishing, Sydney, 2015

Griffith, P., *Battle Tactics of the Western Front: The British Army's Art of Attack 1916–18*, Yale University Press, London, 1994

Grossman, D., *On Killing: The Psychological Cost of Learning to Kill in War and Society*, Little, Brown & Co., New York, 1996

Gudmundsson, B., *Stormtroop Tactics: Innovation in the German Army, 1914–1918*, Praeger, Westport, CT, 1995

Guilliatt, R., and Hohnen, P., *The Wolf: How One German Raider Terrorised Australia and the Southern Oceans in the First World War*, William Heinemann, North Sydney, 2010

Hanson, N., *Escape from Germany: The Greatest POW Break-Out of the First World War*, Doubleday, London, 2011

Hardy, F., *The Great Escapes of World War I: True Escape Stories of Prisoners of War from WWI*, R.W. Press, London, 2014

Havers, R., *Reassessing the Japanese Prisoner of War Experience: The Changi POW Camp, Singapore, 1942–45*, Routledge, London, 2003

Hearder, R., *Keep the Men Alive: Australian POW Doctors in Japanese Captivity*, Allen & Unwin, Sydney, 2009

Herington, J., *Air Power over Europe, 1944–1945*, vol. 4, *Australia in the War of 1930–1945*, Series 3, Australian War Memorial, Canberra, 1963

Hinz, U., *Gefangen im Großen Krieg: Kriegsgefangenschaft in Deutschland, 1914–1921*, Klartext Verlag, Essen, 2006

———'Humanität im Krieg? Internationales Rotes Kreuz und Kriegsgefangenenhilfe im Ersten Weltkrieg', in *Kriegsgefangene im Europa des Ersten Weltkriegs*, ed. J. Oltmer, Ferdinand Schöningh, Munich, 2006, pp. 216–38

Holbrook, C., *Anzac: The Unauthorised Biography*, NewSouth, Sydney, 2014

Holmes, R., *Acts of War: The Behaviour of Men in Battle*, Cassell Military Paperbacks, London, 2004

Horne, J., and Kramer, A., *German Atrocities: A History of Denial*, Yale University Press, London, 2001

Hull, I., *Absolute Destruction: Military Culture and Practices of War in Imperial Germany*, Cornell University Press, New York, 2005

Hutchinson, J., *Champions of Charity: War and the Rise of the Red Cross*, Westview Press, Boulder, 1996

Jackson, R., *The Prisoners 1914–18*, Routledge, London, 1989

Jones, H., *Violence Against Prisoners of War in the First World War: Britain, France and Germany, 1914–1920*, Cambridge University Press, Cambridge, 2008

——'Imperial captivities: Colonial prisoners of war in Germany and the Ottoman Empire, 1914–1918', in *Race, Empire and the First World War*, ed. S. Das, Cambridge University Press, Cambridge, 2011, pp. 177–8

——'A process of modernization? Prisoner of war interrogation and human intelligence gathering in the First World War', in *Interrogation in War and Conflict: A Comparative and Interdisciplinary Analysis*, ed. C. Andrew and S. Tobia, Routledge, Abingdon, 2014, pp. 18–35

Jünger, E., *Storm of Steel* [1920], trans. M. Hofmann, Penguin, London, 2004

Kartinyeri, D., *Ngarrindjeri Anzacs*, Gillingham Printers, Underdale, SA, 1996

Keegan, J., *The First World War*, Pimlico, London, 1999

Kochavi, A., *Confronting Captivity: Britain and the United States and the POWs in Nazi Germany*, University of North Carolina Press, Chapel Hill, 2005

Kramer, A., *Dynamic of Destruction: Culture and Mass Killing in the First World War*, Oxford University Press, New York, 2008

Larsson, M., *Shattered Anzacs: Living with the Scars of War*, UNSW Press, Sydney, 2009

Laugesen, A., *Boredom is the Enemy: The Intellectual and Imaginative Lives of Australian Soldiers in the Great War and Beyond*, Westgate Publishing, Farnham, 2012

Lawless, J., *Kismet: The Story of Gallipoli POWs*, Australian Scholarly Publishing, Melbourne, 2015

——'Starvation, cruelty and neglect? Captivity in the Ottoman Empire, 1915–18', in *Beyond Surrender*, ed. Beaumont, Grant and Pegram, pp. 40–56

Lewis-Stempel, J., *The War Behind the Wire: The Life, Death and Glory of British Prisoners of War 1914–1918*, Weidenfeld & Nicolson, London, 2014

Long, G., *The Final Campaigns*, vol. 7, Series 1, *Australia in the War of 1939–1945*, Australian War Memorial, Canberra, 1963

MacKenzie, K., *The Story of the Seventeenth Battalion, AIF, in the Great War, 1914–1918*, Shipping Newspaper, Sydney, 1946

MacKenzie, S.P., *The Colditz Myth: The Real Story of POW Life in Nazi Germany*, Oxford University Press, Oxford, 2004

McCarthy, D., *The Prisoner of War in Germany*, Moffat, Yard & Co., New York, 1918

McKernan, M., *This War Never Ends: The Pain of Separation and Return*, University of Queensland Press, Brisbane, 2001

McPhail, H., *The Long Silence: Civilian Life under the German Occupation of Northern France, 1914–1918*, I.B. Publishers, London, 1999

Maguire, R. (ed.), *Who's Who in the World of Women*, vol. 2, Reference Press Association, Melbourne, 1934

Makepeace, C., *Captives of War: British Prisoners of War in Europe in the Second World War*, Cambridge University Press, Cambridge, 2017

Marshall, S., *Men Against Fire: The Problem of Battle Command in Future War*, McClelland & Stewart, Toronto, 1949

Maughan, B., *Tobruk and El Alamein*, vol. 3, *Australia in the War of 1939–1945*, Series 1, Australian War Memorial, Canberra, 1966

Millard, C., *Hero of the Empire: The Boer War, A Daring Escape and the Making of Winston Churchill*, Random House, Toronto, 2016

Molkentin, M., *Fire in the Sky: The Australian Flying Corps in the First World War*, Allen & Unwin, Sydney, 2010

Monteath, P., *POW: Australian Prisoners of War in Hitler's Reich*, Pan Macmillan, Sydney, 2011

——'Behind the Colditz myth: Australian experiences of German captivity in World War II', in *Beyond Surrender*, ed. Beaumont, Grant and Pegram, pp. 116–34

Moore, B., and Hately-Broad, B., *Prisoners of War: Prisoners of Peace: Captivity, Homecoming and Memory in World War II*, Berg, Oxford, 2005

Moorehead, C., *Dunant's Dream: War, Switzerland and the History of the Red Cross*, Harper Collins, London, 1998

Morton, D., *Silent Battle: Canadian Prisoners of War in Germany, 1914–1919*, Lester Publishing, Ontario, 1992

Moynihan, M. (ed.), *Black Bread and Barbed Wire*, Leo Cooper, London, 1978

Nelson, H., *Prisoners of War: Australia Under Nippon*, ABC Books, Sydney, 1985

Nicolai, W., *The German Secret Service*, Stanley Paul, London, 1924

Oltmer, J. (ed.), *Kriegsgefangene im Europa des Ersten Weltkrieg*, Schöningh, Paderborn, 2006

Panayi, P., *Prisoners of Britain: German Civilian and Combatant Internees During the First World War*, Manchester University Press, Manchester, 2012

Pedersen, P., *Monash as Military Commander*, Melbourne University Press, Carlton, 1985

Pegram, A., '"Nightly suicide operations": Trench raids and the development of the AIF', in *The AIF in Battle*, ed. Bou, pp. 190–203

Pickles, K., *Transnational Outrage: The Death and Commemoration of Edith Cavell*, Palgrave Macmillan, Basingstoke, 2015

Picot, H., *The British Interned in Switzerland*, Edward Arnold, London, 1919

Pugsley, C., *On the Fringe of Hell: New Zealanders and Military Discipline in the First World War*, Hodder & Stoughton, Auckland, 1991

Rachamimov, A., *POWs and the Great War: Captivity on the Eastern Front*, Berg, Oxford, 2002

Ramsay Silver, L., *Sandakan: A Conspiracy of Silence*, Sally Milner Publishing, Burra Creek, 1998

Roper, M., *The Secret Battle: Emotional Survival in the Great War*, Manchester University Press, Manchester, 2009

Sauertig, L., 'Sex, medicine and morality during the First World War', in *War, Medicine and Modernity*, ed. R. Cooter, M. Harrison and S. Sturdy, Sutton Publishing, Phoenix Mill, Gloucestershire, 1998, pp. 167–88

Scates, B., and Oppenheimer, M., *The Last Battle: Soldier Settlement in Australia, 1916–1939*, Cambridge University Press, Melbourne, 2016

Scates, B., Wheatley, R., and James, L., *World War One: A History in 100 Stories*, Viking, Melbourne, 2015

Scott, E., *Australia During the War*, vol. 11, *Official History of Australia in the War of 1914–1918*, Angus & Robertson, Sydney, 1936

Sheldon, J., *The German Army on the Somme*, Pen and Sword, Barnsley, 2005

Smith, N., *Australasians Captured by the Raider Wolf*, Mostly Unsung Military Publishing, Melbourne, 2006

Solleder, F., *Vier Jahre Westfront: Geschichte des Regiments List R.J.R 16*, M. Schick, Munich, 1932

Speed, R., *Prisoners, Diplomats and the Great War: A Study in the Diplomacy of Captivity*, Greenwood Publishing Group, New York, 1990

Stanley, P., *Bad Characters: Sex, Crime, Murder and Mutiny in the Great War*, Pier 9, Sydney, 2010

——*Lost Boys of Anzac*, NewSouth Publishing, Sydney, 2014

Stevenson, R., *To Win the Battle: The 1st Australian Division in the Great War, 1914–1918*, Cambridge University Press, Port Melbourne, 2013

——'The battalion: The AIF infantry battalion and its evolution', in *The AIF in Battle*, ed. Bou, pp. 46–57

Stibbe, M., *British Civilian Internees in Germany: The Ruhleben Camp, 1914–1918*, Manchester University Press, Manchester, 2008

Thomson, A., *Anzac Memories: Living With the Legend* [1994], Monash University Press, Clayton, 2013

Vance, J., 'Shackling incident', in *Encyclopedia of Prisoners of War and Internment*, ed. J. Vance, p. 270, Grey House Publishing, Toronto, 2000

Vischer, A., *Barbed Wire Disease: A Psychological Study of the Prisoner of War*, John Bale, Sons & Danielsson, London, 1919

Wahlert, G., *The Other Enemy? Australian Soldiers and the Military Police*, Oxford University Press, Melbourne, 1999

Walker, A., *Middle East and Far East*, vol. 2, *Australia in the War of 1939–1945*, Series 5, Australian War Memorial, Canberra, 1953

——*Medical Services of the Royal Australian Navy and Royal Australian Air Force*, vol. 4, *Australia in the War of 1939–1945*, Series 5, Australian War Memorial, Canberra, 1961

Watson, A., *Enduring the Great War: Combat, Morale and Collapse in the German and British Armies, 1914–1918*, Cambridge University Press, Cambridge, 2008

Wigmore, L., *The Japanese Thrust*, vol. 4, *Australia in the War of 1939–1945*, Series 1, Australian War Memorial, Canberra, 1957

——*They Dared Mightily*, Australian War Memorial, Canberra, 1963

Wilkinson, O., 'Captivity in print: The form and function of POW camp magazines', in *Cultural Heritage and Prisoners of War: Captivity Behind Barbed Wire*, ed. G. Carr and H. Mytum, Routledge, New York, 2012, pp. 227–43

——*British Prisoners of War in First World War Germany*, Cambridge University Press, Cambridge, 2017

Williams, J., *German Anzacs and the Great War*, UNSW Press, Sydney, 2004

Winter, D., *Death's Men: Soldiers of the Great War*, Penguin Books, London, 1978

Winter, J., *Sites of Memory, Sites of Mourning: The Great War in European Cultural Memory*, Cambridge University Press, Cambridge, 1995

Yarnall, J., *Barbed Wire Disease: British and German Prisoners of War, 1914–1919*, Spellmount, Stroud, 2011

Ziemann, B., *War Experiences in Rural Germany, 1914–1923*, Berg, Oxford, 2007

Ziino, B., *A Distant Grief: Australians, War Graves and the Great War*, UWA Press, Perth, 2007

Zuckerman, L., *The Rape of Belgium: The Untold Story of World War I*, New York University Press, New York, 2004

Reports

AIF Records Section, *Statistics of Casualties, Etc, Compiled to 30th June 1919*, AIF Records Section, London, 1919

General Staff, *The German Army Handbook of 1918*, War Office, London, 1918

Royal Air Force, *Instructions Regarding Precautions to be Taken in the Event of Falling into the Hands of the Enemy*, F.S. Publications, London, 1918

——'Statisticians Report', *Census of the Commonwealth of Australia*, 30 June 1933, L.F. Johnston, Canberra, 1933

War Office, *Manual of Military Law*, HMSO, London, 1907

——*Field Service Regulations 1909*, Part 2, HMSO, London, 1914

——'Army order regarding the execution of counter-attacks' (translated from German), HMSO, London, 1916

——*German Methods of Trench Warfare*, HMSO, London, 1916

——*Notes for Infantry Officers in Trench Warfare*, HMSO, London, 1916

——'Manual of positional warfare for all arms: Weapons of close combat' (translated from German), HMSO, London, 1917

——*Statistics of the Military Effort During the Great War, 1914–1920* HMSO, London, 1922

Theses

Ariotti, K., 'Coping with captivity: Australian POWs of the Turks and the impact of imprisonment during the First World War', PhD thesis, University of Queensland, 2013

Glenister, R., 'Desertion without execution: Decisions that saved the Australian Imperial Force deserters from the firing squad in World War I', BA (Hons) thesis, La Trobe University, 1984

Jones, M.A., 'The Danish scheme: The repatriation of British prisoners of war through Denmark at the end of the First World War', MA thesis, University of Birmingham, 2009

Noble, R., 'Raising the white flag: The surrender of Australian soldiers in France during the Great War', BA (Hons) thesis, Australian Defence Force Academy, 1988

Regan, P., 'Neglected Australians: Prisoners of war from the Western Front, 1916–1918', MA thesis, Australian Defence Force Academy @ UNSW, 2005

Websites

Abraham, B., 'Bringing them all back home: Prisoners of war contact, recovery and reception units, 1944–45', AWM summer scholarship paper, 2015, www.awm.gov.au/research/grants/summer_scholarship/papers/ (retrieved 11 January 2017)

Australian Institute of Health and Welfare, 'Table S6.1: Life expectancy (expected age at death in years) at different ages by sex, 1881–1890 to 2014–2016', Deaths in Australia, www.aihw.gov.au/reports/life-expectancy-death/deaths-in-australia/data (retrieved 19 February 2019)

Bowden, T., 'Fall of Singapore: Australian POWs' oral history memories of defeat and imprisonment', www.abc.net.au/news/2017-02-15/fall-of-singapore-australian-soldiers-in-their-own-words/8266370 (retrieved 17 February 2017)

Dawson, Pte J., 15 Bn, letter to home, 14 December 1918, 'POW survives horrendous conditions', Australians at War, Department of Veterans' Affairs and Australian War Memorial, www.australiansatwar.gov.au/stories/stories_war=W1_id=243.html (retrieved 5 September 2016)

Forster, F., 'Ryan, Sir Charles Snodgrass (1853–1926)', *Australian Dictionary of Biography*, National Centre of Biography, Australian National University, http://adb.anu.edu.au/biography/ryan-sir-charles-snodgrass-8311/text14575 (retrieved 2 August 2014)

Hardie, M., 'Oliver, Alexander (1832–1904)', *Australian Dictionary of Biography*, National Centre of Biography, Australian National University, http://adb.anu.edu.au/biography/oliver-alexander-4329/text7025, (retrieved 6 August 2014)

Jones, H., 'Prisoners of war', in *1914–1918 Online: International Encyclopedia of the First World War*, ed. U. Daniel, P. Fatrell, O. Janz, H. Jones, J. Keene, A. Kramer and B. Nasson, Freie Universität Berlin, Germany, 2014, http://encyclopedia.1914–1918-online.net/article/prisoners_of_war#cite_note-ftn48–48 (retrieved 14 September 2016)

Jones, H., and Hinz, U., 'Prisoners of war (Germany)', *1914–1918 Online: International Encyclopedia of the First World War*, ed. U. Daniel, P. Gatrell, O. Janz, H. Jones, J. Keene, A. Kramer and B. Nasson, Freie Universität

Berlin, Germany, 2014, http://encyclopedia.1914-1918-online.net/article/pris
oners_of_war_germany#The_German_home_front_and_Etappen_camp_
systems (retrieved 7 January 2016)

Rickard, J., 'White, Vera Deakin (1891–1978)', Australian Dictionary of Biography,   http://adb.anu.edu.au/biography/white-vera-deakin-12014/text21547
(retrieved 20 July 2014)

INDEX

Entries in **bold** indicate figures.